T0381549

TAROT
MYSTERIES OF
THOTH
INITIATION AND INNER ALCHEMY

TAMARA VON FORSLUN

BALBOA.
PRESS
A DIVISION OF HAY HOUSE

Copyright © 2018 Tamara Von Forslun.

Interior Graphics/Art Credit: Tamara Von Forslun, Marco Barboza, Bobooks Art.

All rights reserved. No part of this book may be used or reproduced by any means, graphic, electronic, or mechanical, including photocopying, recording, taping or by any information storage retrieval system without the written permission of the author except in the case of brief quotations embodied in critical articles and reviews.

Balboa Press books may be ordered through booksellers or by contacting:

Balboa Press
A Division of Hay House
1663 Liberty Drive
Bloomington, IN 47403
www.balboapress.com.au
1 (877) 407-4847

Because of the dynamic nature of the Internet, any web addresses or links contained in this book may have changed since publication and may no longer be valid. The views expressed in this work are solely those of the author and do not necessarily reflect the views of the publisher, and the publisher hereby disclaims any responsibility for them.

The author of this book does not dispense medical advice or prescribe the use of any technique as a form of treatment for physical, emotional, or medical problems without the advice of a physician, either directly or indirectly. The intent of the author is only to offer information of a general nature to help you in your quest for emotional and spiritual well-being. In the event you use any of the information in this book for yourself, which is your constitutional right, the author and the publisher assume no responsibility for your actions.

Any people depicted in stock imagery provided by Getty Images are models, and such images are being used for illustrative purposes only.
Certain stock imagery © Getty Images.

Print information available on the last page.

ISBN: 978-1-5043-1516-6 (sc)
ISBN: 978-1-5043-1517-3 (e)

Balboa Press rev. date: 10/17/2018

TABLE OF
CONTENTS

RECOMMENDED
READING

The Complete Book of Witchcraft	Raymond Buckland
Complete Teachings of Wicca Book One –	The Seeker-The Witch of Oz
Complete Teachings of Wicca Book Two –	The Wicce-The Witch of Oz
Crystal Connections	Adam Barralet
An ABC of Witchcraft	Doreen Valiente
The Goddess Path	Patricia Monaghan
Dreaming the Divine	Scott Cunningham
Wicca, Guide for the Solitary Practitioner	Scott Cunningham
Living Wicca, Guide for the Solitary	Scott Cunningham
Encyclopedia of Magical Herbs	Scott Cunningham
Earth Magic	Marion Weinstein
Natural Magic	Doreen Valiente
Principles of Wicca	Vivienne Crowley
Wicca, The Old Religion	Vivienne Crowley
The Witches God	S & J Farrar
The Witches Goddess	S & J Farrar
The Witches Bible 1 & 2	S & J Farrar
The Spell of Making	Blacksun
Never on a Broomstick	Donovan
The Golden Bough	Sir James Fraser
Witchcraft Today	Gerald B. Gardner
Witchcraft, the Sixth Sense and Us	Justine Glass
The Pickingill Papers	WE Liddell & Michael Howard
Pans Daughter	Neville Drury
The God of the Witches	Margaret Murray
The King of the Witches	June Johns
Witchcraft, Ancient and Modern	Raymond Buckland
The White Goddess	Sir Robert Graves
Positive Magic	Marion Weinstein
The Rose-Cross and the Goddess	Gareth Knight
The Master Book of Herbalism	Paul Beyerl
The Mystical Qabalah	Dion Fortune
Magick: An Occult Primer	David Conway

Techniques of High Magic	Francis King
Magick in Theory and Practice	Aleister Crowley
Ceremonial Magick	A E Waite
Practice of Magickal Evocation	Franz Bardon
Drawing Down the Moon	Margot Adler
Witchcraft from the Inside	Raymond Buckland
Hereditary Witchcraft	Raven Grimassi
Creating Magickal Tools	C & S Cicero
Shamanic Guide to Death and Dying	Kristen Madden
Astral Projection For Beginners	Edain Mc Coy
Practical Candle Burning Rituals	Raymond Buckland
Magickal Herbalism	Scott Cunningham
Ariadne's Thread	Mountainwater
Moon Magick	David Conway
Pagan Book of Living and Dying	Starhawk
Way of the Strega	Raven Grimassi
The Dark God	Nicholas Mann
The Underworld Initiation	RJ Stewart
Wicca for Men	A J Drew
The Complete Book of Witchcraft	Israel Regardie
Initiation into Hermetics	Franz Bardon
The Ritual Magick Workbook	Dolores Nowicki
Mastering Witchcraft	Paul Huson
History of Magic	Eliphas Levi

DEEPER MEANING
OF TAROT

This book is *'Book Three'* as part of a complete series in the *"Complete Teachings of Wicca"*, outlining an ancient and esoteric system that uses internal and external Alchemising to create a vibrational healing and reawakening of the many other levels of Conscious Existence and the varied realms within our being from the physical, mental, psychic, astral and the spiritual. By reawakening and being aware, we can improve our deeper communication with our subtler rhythms and create change. We can also move more freely, easily and completely into the Age of Aquarius, with an acknowledgement and acceptance of much higher powers and higher levels to our lives.

These changes of the Dawning Age are inevitable, as part of the micro-macrocosmic tides. But we must be aware that it is up to us, NOT the Goddess and God, but us as individual Wicces and as a species, whether these changes are forward or backward, we the human beings of our planet MUST CHANGE and GROW if we are to survive.

At our level of spiritual existence, we have made the choice to be incarnated into this life and time, and we must now make the choice that we will either decide whether we use the energy to recapture the past, by attributing all that happens to our old external Gods and Goddesses, fix the development of the future by limited or one sided projection, or hopefully learn at last to grow and take our responsible place in the flow of reawakening our greatest potential sensitivities and our divine love. The Magickal System outlined in this book is functionally complete as it is, but at the same time it is an Art. It can and must be developed and shaped by each individual Wicce or Shaman and situation it is used in.

You will find that the results are proportional to the amount of artistic and Magickal involvement you invest. Use your intellect with your Higher Wicce Self to develop rather than inhibit your experiences. Remember the words of the Mighty Ones of the Magick Circle, *"TO KNOW, TO WILL, TO DARE AND TO KEEP SILENT"*. To have complete courage we must be educated and have complete faith in our chosen Path and Ourselves. If you are doing your Craft as a Solo practitioner, or even a small Coven (less than 5) then it must be done away from any major disturbing influences, such as noises and electrical outputs. Have an adventure with your group and search in the country for a space that you can hold your ceremonies in secret and without fear of being observed or interrupted. Maybe you know someone who has a farm and maybe they will let you use a section of it for your workings.

The Tarot Cards and Artwork are done especially for my book, and they are part of my *"Oracles of the Goddesses of the World"*, *card and book set*. As you will notice in this book I use the 21

Major Arcana, (as in the 21 points of the human body; toes, fingers and head, also relating to the 21 Wiccan celebrations of the year, 13 Full Moons (Esbats) and 8 Festivals (Sabbats), as they are the original scribed tablets by Thoth, (Hermes Trismegistos) and they are doorways to different dimensions of thinking and existences. The original sacred tablets of Thoth are called *"The Books of Life"*, and have been in the custody and protection of the Organisation known as the *"Temple of Aset"* of Khnum in Egypt, who are an ancient order of Isarum Priests and Priestesses and the custodians and keepers of the ancient archives of Thoth and the ancient Priesthood of Aset. I have been lucky enough to have been a member of this sacred organisation for over 25 years, and have gained much insight and knowledge into the truth behind the Tarot, its true symbology, origin and Magickal properties.

Each Tarot card is a portal, a doorway, a vibrational key that acts on your psyche and subconscious to a special form of education that will take you on a journey of self-discovery and expression, self-realisation and self-awakening, by using the Tarot cards as Magickal Keys or Portals to sacred teachings from all over the world, they will aid you in reaching hopeful Enlightenment through a series of techniques that will enable you to connect or in some cases reconnect to specific Magickal knowledge and advance your lives into a spiritual Ascension. They are all simple techniques, but you need to be focused, dedicated and prepared to work hard on the journey to your own Truth.

Good luck on your journey may it offer up all that you need on your path to meet with the Ancient Ones.

I wish to acknowledge the help and assistance of every Wiccan, Wicce, Pagan, Magician, Shaman and those of true spirit; past, present and future! Especially my mentors and guides, both physically and spiritually.

Blessed be!

All Ritual and Ceremony is total divine theatre,
For even the environment becomes part of the play.
There are no spectators, only participants,
We are all one with Magick and Nature.

Flags   Flax   Fodder   Frig

Tamara von Forslun
The Wicce of Oz
<u>www.witchofoz.com</u>
<u>www.tamaravonforslun.com</u>

O
THE FOOL

0 The Fool Merlin - Alien or Human Key to Darkness and Nothingness

I will generate the enlightenment thought
So that I attain success for all others and for myself!

For only the Fool searches for everything outside himself, and see's
neither the stars nor the Universe that lies within.

Since the beginning of humankind, we have looked to the stars in wonderment. Human record shows that about fifty thousand years ago, "the Shining Ones," great beings of light, descended to the earth in vehicles of light and Magick. Although many cultures had not the ability to write, they had the ability to form pictographs and rock-art paintings in sacred places such as grottos and caves. The rock-art paintings and etchings in solid rock are about forty thousand to sixty thousand years old, some older. The figures are always depicted as having rays of light surrounding their heads. They are larger beings with elongated eyes and chariots that came from the skies. They are real!

The oldest race on the planet was the first to see these beings and greet the "Sky People." They were the Australian Aboriginals, who have the longest unbroken line of history. These beings were called the Sky People or the Spirits of the Sky, and we of the Western world eventually began to call them the Watchers, the Shining Ones, the Angels and Aliens. These powerful and enlightened beings taught us of Magick and Wiccecraft. They were later adopted by Christian and Judaic systems and called angels, or more correctly, fallen angels.

But these beings had been visiting our earth for a long time prior to this, which shows we are not the first advanced beings to evolve this far on our planet. There have been others before us, and hopefully, there will be many more after us; that is, if we don't screw it up with our ignorance of pollution and the environment. Some of these races have evolved from the stars and out of the solar system entirely, but others haven't.

Before what has been called the "great flood" (about 26,000 years ago), humanity lived in a peaceful matriarchal society (ruled by women) known in many cultures as the Golden Age. We were visited again (not for the first time) by these Sky People from another planet, the Shining Ones - our ancestors who evolved further out in the solar system. These people came here to try to save their dying home world, a world that would not listen to them. They were people who realised and worked with physical beings as well as spiritual life, and who knew both were important. They realised there was a need for the balancing of the physical and the spiritual. They also realised these things developed and elevated each other. But the culture they came from had gone so far past mere physical sensation that they were looked at in much the same way as orthodox medicine looks at natural therapies today in our world.

This society existed on a world that once orbited between Mars and Jupiter. Here, because of the proximity of Jupiter, the Sky People functioned almost entirely in what we would call their etheric and astral forms. This one-sided view led, as our own materialism has led, to the creation of complete imbalance and strain. Pollution occurs when matter is taken forcibly out of a living pattern and the flow between the different levels is interrupted or broken. This results in dead—unanimated—matter that cannot be used, or often even recognised by the living matter around it. It is the same today with ancient herbal lore. They take the herb, break it down, and recreate a chemical alien version of it with no life within it at all. And with dozens of side effects, this medicine becomes so far removed from the natural and original plant. All living matter is characterised by an aura, the result of interaction between the physical and non-physical. This aura is what is used as the point of interaction.

The people who could see the danger of this pollution tried to warn their race but were finally forced to set up colonies on other planets, two of which were on the third planet—our earth. They tried to work from here to save their world. Eventually, the strain became too great, and their planet exploded, forming what we now call the "asteroid belt." This explosion caused a great deal of upheaval throughout the entire solar system. The earth was tumbled end over end through space.

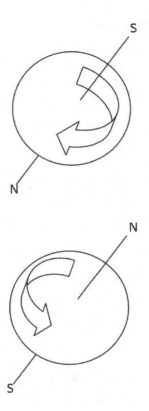

The poles changed places. The sun that use to rise in the west and set in the east began to rise in the east and set in the west. The tumbling also caused a brief speed up of rotation so all the water was pulled into the equator. The great flood buried Atlantis under the Sahara Desert and wiped out Lemuria; it is now under the ocean above and to the west of Australia. Fragments of the exploding planet hit both the moon and the earth, adding to the destruction. Some of the knowledge from these ancient times is supposed to have been preserved by twelve legendary survivors. Of these, four have since chosen to die, and one has been replaced. These are the nine great masters/mistresses or better known by Wicces as the Shining Ones, the Ancient Ones, or Watchers. It is their task to see that this knowledge is not lost. The organisation known as the Star Seeds is very aware of this.

Some of this forbidden knowledge was in the *Legend of the Apocryphal Book of Enoch*. But in the writings of a Shining One, Thoth Tehuti, he writes of the creation of a massive circular disc of solid crystal quartz to be placed between the paws of the Sphinx. This giant crystal was called the "Joppa Hi"—the Stargate—which was a geodetic marker between the solstices and equinoxes and could measure time and space. Sound familiar?

These Shining Ones were adopted by our ancient ancestors as gods and goddesses. Egyptians believed they came from the planet Sirius. In the Great Pyramid of Giza, a window tunnel formed in its side reveals the light of the planet Sirius B when standing in the Kings Chamber and looking up, revealing the place pharaohs, kings and queens longed to go. An ancient Shining One named Senjaza, a female, was the guardian and a Watcher of the skies of Sirius B. She taught Wiccecraft and was Magickally, psychologically and spiritually very deep, creating the first and ancient roots of Wicca.

To those who prefer different names, to each their own. It does not matter at all what name you give your religion or your deity for they are all one in the same; all gods are one God, and all goddesses are one Goddess. Together they dance the eternal rhythms as the One Mother/Father.

Before we gave our religion the name of Wicca, it was called Wiccecraft, Old School, Old Religion, Ways of the Ancients, Shamanism, Knowledge of the Stars, Old Guard, Truth. It is all the same; only the name is different to suit the needs of the changing tides into the twenty-first century.

In his ancient writings, which were written hundreds of years before the birth of Jesus Christ, Noah wrote about the Shining Ones as fallen angels, saying;

> "And thus the Angels, the fallen Children of heaven, saw and lusted after the mortal life, the daughters of men and said to one another: 'Come, let us choose wives and husbands from among the children of man and beget us divine children', and all others took themselves wives and husbands, and each chose for themselves one, and they began to be in amongst them and they defiled themselves with them, and they taught them the Magick of the Earth and the Stars, the Charms and Enchantments, the cutting of roots, and made them acquainted with the Magick and medicines of the plants.

> Azael taught men how to forge metal and make swords, knives, shields and breastplates, and made known to them the sacred metals of the Earth such as iron, copper, bronze, tin, silver and gold, and the Art of working with them. Senjaza taught of Magick and Enchantments and the Magick of root cuttings and plants. Armoros taught the resolve of Enchantments. Baraquiel taught of Astrology. Kokobel taught of the Art of the Celestial Constellations and

Astronomy. Ezequiel taught the Art of the knowledge of Clouds of the Weather, and the Seasons. Araquiel the signs and the Art of the Earth of the animals and husbandry. Shamsiel the signs and Arts of the powers of the Sun. Sariel the signs and Art of the powers of the Moon.

To be of the Earthly realm they had to take on corporeal form and be as humans in physical shape, in doing this they could descend to the Earth Plane for a short time only, but they could not maintain this for very long, so they taught their Divine Children the knowledge of the Stars, and how to connect with the Stars and all Magickal knowledge of Wiccecraft".

We are fast approaching a time when our Star People, the Shining Ones, will visit us again from other worlds, worlds that weren't destroyed by the imbalance. We call them forth at our Magick Circle gatherings when we call the servants of the Goddess and God Azarak and Zomelak (the Shining Ones). These beings have evolved further than our present state of awareness, but they are not superior or inferior. These concepts come from our competitive social structures and have no relevance to an aware state of being.

We need to develop a communication basic enough to realise our essential unity as people, not different races. If we can't do this, we won't survive the cultural shock of meeting extraterrestrial life without trying to destroy it. Once we develop auric sensitivity as a race, we will have a means of communication that is totally honest. You can only disguise parts of your aura and then only to untrained or undeveloped sensitivities. This will enable us to meet our ancestors (they evolved partly on this planet, as we have) and know we are all part of the harmonious whole. I believe they will arrive again on earth around the year 2021. Some are already here!

This may or may not be a Faery-tale, but the lesson is clear. We have a responsibility to the world we live on. SHE ISN'T OURS, She does not belong to us, we belong to Her. Other races that follow ours will need Her. At this point in time (2017) we are still a very great danger to the destruction to the Earth. Lots of good things are happening, but on the other hand, warmongers and power-hungry economical structures will not give up their imaginary powers easily. One man in the wrong place of power could easily set the stage for a nuclear holocaust. The world governments are beginning to see their inability to cope with the rising consciousness of the people and they are frightened. We also have some egotistical leaders in the world that are too busy puffing up their chests, to say that they are bigger and tougher than the next kid in the block, this is just another form of bullying, but at a grander stage where it will not be just one who suffers the consequences, but the entire world.

As Wicces, it is our pleasure to offer or re-offer a different set of standards. Built, not on money or competition, but on the recognition of development of each person's ability to make their life a masterpiece of harmony between the macrocosm and the microcosm, and to truly be One with Nature.

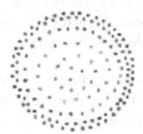

For instance, the metal that is characteristic of the highest sphere of consciousness is Uranium, while the planet's ORGANIC focus of this energy is Ambergris, which comes from whales. If we kill all the whales and mine uranium it will result in this energy becoming entirely depersonalised so that the individual will vanish from our society. On the other hand, if we use our Ocean Sister's gifts we can direct this energy to form a harmonious anarchy where the individual can grow within tribal societies.

This is the commitment of true Magick. Each Wicce makes this commitment by the development of their sensitivity. There is no sacrifice involved in this, except our dedication, it is simply that an aware state of being is much more enjoyable than a diseased state. This applies socially, as well as to the individual. Auric and inner awareness helps you realise the real beauty that every creature, human and otherwise, has, if they take the time to develop it. Once each person 'works' their own divinity, they no longer need to be told what to do. To these people action NEEDS to be harmonious, an art, because this is the most rewarding and pleasant way to live.

Think about this before you start this work. You must decide for yourself!

True Initiation, like true knowledge, can only come from within you. All we, or any group, or Coven can do is provide an environment that encourages and is directed toward it and teaches the keys that unlock true Initiation on every level instead of just the physical. The real work is up to each one of you. This book is designed for a working Coven or group of people over a period of eighteen months. My first book "Complete Teachings of Wicca Book One-The Seeker" takes a period of about 6-12 months training and preparation prior to the second book of the series; The Witch, which will take another 6-12 months to complete. This will cover the entire Wicces stage, up to and including pre-Initiation into the first stages of our Priesthood. Some people will take longer, some shorter, it doesn't really matter, if you remember to 'fit in' with the rest of your Coven, remembering it is not a race, allow the Coven to grow together, slowly and devoutly. This is one of the most important parts of your Wiccan work, the ability to flow with currents of life outside your own. You will be using different tools from different cultures – one of which is RITUAL.

In ritual it is important to create a total atmosphere, so for outdoor work, you each make an ankle length green robe and a cape with a hood on it. This regalia will have either silver trim for ladies or gold trim for males and is tied with a nine-foot green Singulum (cord) around your waist. Each person should make his or her own robe and no other person can wear your Ritual Regalia. This is the first of your Magickal Tools, the more you put into making it, the better it will work. Lady Elizabeth, High Priestess of the Temple of Hope, a longtime friend of mine places a strand of her hair into the hems of her robes and capes that she makes for others, adding a little of her Magick and energy for their journey, this is her form of Sympathetic Magick.

The Wicce lays the foundation for self-control and for this reason it is important that this work is done without the use of hallucinogenic drugs or alcohol. Drugs can cause your Aura to shake or pulse violently and this can undo months of hard work you have done arranging the energies of your aura. This effect is then passed onto the other people you work with and their work is affected as well. It is possible for an Alchemist to 'treat' an herbal hallucinogenic like marijuana so that it fits in with the energy of a specific day, but even this is too much for the extremely delicate work done at first. After Initiation, it is up to you whether you use drugs or not, but before that time, be fair to the people you work with. Magick is directing all your energies into one harmonious flow. The MOTIVE is where your actions are started from so if you set this level in a positive and constructive manner, then all the energies that are affected will be positive and constructive. To consolidate the power of this book as a Talisman it is necessary (as with all Magickal work) to direct the energy invoked. The easiest way to do this is with mantra.

"May the Energy of the Work just done,
aid in the development of
Love and Understanding in all Things!"

Mantras can't work as well, if you visualise them as hard work, or laboriously repeat them as a dirge. They are joy filled statements of fact to be visualised vibrating and vitalising each cell in your body, mind and soul.

I
The Magician

No. 1 The Magician – Asar/Osiris Natural Magick-Thoth the Atlantean

The Medicine Woman or Man (Magus or Sage)

I will generate the Enlightenment Thought that I attain for all others and myself.

Everything in Nature is in some way or form linked to everything else. There are physical links of time, space, colour, shape, size, etc. There are also "different" links; that bind a Tool to a craft, the cause to the effect (and vice versa) and even more abstract links of similarity and/or purpose. Nature, just as people, categorises and systematises its actions, via these links. They are all ways for each thing to make its presence felt by the things around it, or if you prefer, the links are the way each thing includes itself in the flow of time/or change on any given 'level' of Nature. Magick goes searching for those links and then gradually develops, first awareness, then through practical application an understanding of their true purpose.

Everything is reaching for some form of development or ascension; not just people, or for that matter, not just what is normally called living; and during that development, each thing adds to the picture of the whole. Each part of each particle of Nature, adds its contribution to the definition of what we call reality. The extent of that definition that each thing has (of itself and reality) depends upon the limits of the *"languages"* that each thing uses. The definition a rock must be very different to the *"real"* (?) world that people see. Even among people, what's called true by one is obviously false to another, or is it?

What we see as REAL is only ONE of the MANY definitions of reality. To have a totally real image we would have to understand Nature from as many different angles as Nature itself has developed. We see the definition that has been agreed upon by the society we live in. This isn't a wrong definition, simply incomplete. We don't see its incompletion until we experience something that is outside the usual stream of conditioned perception, and even the personality of the individual will try to 'get around' what it's experienced by many varied and sometimes quite elaborate rationalisation's. So how can you tell which is the right way to see the universe?

The answer must be by looking at as many different Truths as we can and then trying to find a basic *'system of relationship'* between them all. This system must be flexible enough to be applicable to any situation, yet it is to be simple enough to use easily. People have used many such systems ranging from logic to faith.

There has always been rivalry and competition between these different schools of thought, especially in the Western world where LOGIC dictates that if something is TRUE then it can't possibly be FALSE. There has always been this rivalry, but only in the minds of the people concerned. Nature agrees with them all, because Nature is All. In other words, the tribe creates more and more links to the 'real' world from the imagery - God until, for all practical purposes, the God does in fact become a working, moving, change causing reality. Later in this book, we will see how thoughts not only have form and continuity (the 'ideas' and the stream of thought) but they have ENERGY and MASS as well and this is both changed by the environment and causes change in the environment (which is one way of defining something that's real).

Magick is learning to use this ability to pool the forces of our minds, to change our environment to one that suits us better. This is not 'new', it's the way mankind has always developed. First, someone develops a concept (puts together things/experiences from outside him or herself and then expresses them in a different form) then this concept gains energy from constant use, then this energy is 'focused' (anything can be used to focus this energy, but some things have been used before and are therefore already REALISED and easier to use) to form a new "God". These Gods don't have to be metaphysical, or even religious; we all know the power of the great god REASON, or the even the greater god MONEY! These gods then exert a certain pressure on us and often through us.

Gradually we learn more and more about where we want to develop and how to 'fit' that development in with the already existing stream of events. Our concept and use of God-forms is developed not only by us, but also by the development of the whole universe. As our description of reality comes closer to the description Nature gives Herself, we say we are becoming ENLIGHTENED. This is just another way of stating what Wicces have known for millennia; that if you take an active, positive interest in your development, Nature responds by allowing you greater freedom from Her own ways of forcing development (which are sometimes rather rough). It is easy to see Nature as 'already developed' and life gradually being molded into a pre-determined pattern, but this is in fact a two-way exchange. The microcosm (us) is developed by the macrocosm (everything else), but the macrocosm is just as really developed by the microcosm.

The God-forms we create, out of political parties, social ideas and the absolute faith most people have in material sciences, are extremely powerful thought forms. They can and do affect the whole balance of energy, not only for this planet, but the entire solar system, and more. Here again, these systems/ideas are not wrong, they are incomplete.

Their one-sided truths coupled with the force of millions of minds that give them energy have led all of us to the brink of yet another disaster in our long history of disasters. We are destroying the delicate balance of life on this planet through the technology that we created and now can no longer control. Obviously, we can no longer afford to devote our life's energies to such dangerously destructive gods. Equally as obvious is the fact that you can't change the world overnight, so the human does neither.

The solution is much simpler. All we need to do is **BALANCE** the more destructive side of our social gods. They are destructive because they give a false and frustrating picture of what you need to make you happy.

Modern man (in customary fashion) recognises half of his needs, physical survival and sexual/social contact. The half we don't work with, we 'hand over' to the system. The next two drives/energies, that we give/sacrifice to our technological gods are;

1. **Self-esteem;** in this drive is held the power to CREATE; it is necessary for the artist to believe she can create a 'special' part of her environment. In our society it is almost a sin to enjoy your own creativity. Many artists have been lost to the world because their artistic drive is suppressed and channeled to give still more energy to religious and political systems.

2. **Self-knowledge;** our learning at schools, socially and in work situations is directed towards satisfying the first two drives that opt towards fitting in more and more with social values (material successes, careers, etc.) the niches or roles people find themselves in, gives less and less opportunity for self-expression and therefore self-knowledge, yet this is perhaps the strongest drive of all. It is the object, the reason for all three of the other drives (physical survival, sexual/social contact and self-esteem).

In people, Nature is trying to develop part of Herself so that she can fully realise Her own beauty and unless we try to recognise and work with the whole of our internal and external environment, She will allow us to destroy ourselves. But we have got the choice. Mankind knows lots of ways to bring about the sort of harmony I've been talking about. We are going to use a few of them in our work on Magick. You will learn to become more sensitive to the patterns and flow of the energies that surround you and make up your own body and mind. Once you become aware of your own 'inner strengths' you must be prepared to take responsibility for all your actions.

You make your own moral code – in Magick there is no supreme Father or Mother that dictates right and wrong, you need to be continually developing your own values. Which means you must practice the art of being honest with yourself. This is harder than you think. It is very difficult and takes some time to undo society's conditioning and you must be very careful of what you throw away. You also should remember that **you do need other people and that they need you.**

To generate enough energy to change the influence society's definition of reality has on you, means you must work with a large group of people. This generates quite a few problems, so you must, right from the start; try to develop your ability to trust. Believe it or not, this is NOT NECESSARILY difficult, if you start with YOURSELF. In Wicca we have a sacred line; "I come with Perfect Love and Perfect Trust!" It does not necessarily mean that you have absolute love and trust in those around you, but you are aiming towards that goal. There is also another saying: "It is a hard road, walk it with pride!"

PRACTICAL:

"Sit or lie quietly in a comfortable position, in a clean room, where as much light as possible has been blocked out (also take care against moving or deep shadows) with perhaps some soft classical or meditational music playing softly in the background. Breathe very deeply and be as relaxed as you can. Try to get your breathing to come from deep down in your stomach, breathe with your stomach and not your chest, (as it is pushed out, it pulls the diaphragm down and expands the lungs to form the in-breath and vice versa). Try to get it to be very even with no sudden gasps.

When you feel you are sufficiently relaxed, let your mind wander very quickly, but smoothly backwards over your day. Don't dwell on problems, just simply acknowledge them and pass on. Do not get stuck in the good parts either, just look, do not think about things too much. When you get your waking up and realise its time then slowly come back through the day and as you come to what you think are the key points in each situation. Try to think of the intensity of the moment whether you are taking in energy or giving it off. (I.E. if your minds direction is in on itself or out to the environment then try to translate the feeling into colour).

Take each of these focus points one at a time. Don't spend too much time on each. Don't work it out; just try to evaluate each point by seeing its colour. Not easy at first, but it comes with practise. When you have looked at the whole day, try to choose one colour that you feel was the main colour that stood out that day. You will find that they have a particular colour pattern which will show you the type of intensity of the links you use to keep yourself in this 'level of reality', don't try to see them as a pattern rather than reason."

To record your results, you should start a Magickal Journal, (as in my second book "Complete Teachings of Wicca, Book Two-The Wicce") and date each thing you do, this Magickal Journal in which you will put a record of the colour and anything you feel is important, that you didn't fully understand, or that was seen from a different angle (including new things). This Magickal Journal should have a black cover and should be SEALED (see illustration below) front and back. When you are not using it, you should keep it above shoulder height in a safe place.

If you decide to get rid of your Magickal Diary, or any Magickal Tool, you should burn it, while at the same time visualising any links between you and it dissolving completely.

 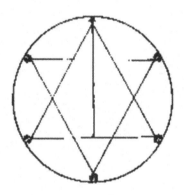

FRONT: Put your name in
Theban in the Centre
Of the Pentagram

BACK:

The names around the Circle on the front are (Greek) Hermes Trismegistos and (Egyptian) Tehuti – Thoth - this is the name of the first Shining One/Teacher and High Priest/ Psychopompos of Ancient Egyptian Magick.

"May the energy of the Great Work just done,
Aid in the development of Love and Understanding in all things".

II
THE HIGH
PRIESTESS

II The High Priestess – Aset/Isis
The Elements and their Elementals-Key to Wisdom

*"I will generate the Enlightenment thought,
so, I will attain success for all others and myself"*.

You can see that REALITY is sort of a compromise. What is real to you is the result of your links to Nature and in return Nature's links to you, like a Magickal umbilical cord. This is the meeting of the two 'opposite' forces, the MICROCOSM (micro-small, Cosmo-universe) which is you, and the MACROCOSM which is everything else.

This sort of interaction happens between All life in Nature. Even things we normally call DEAD perceive and interact with the things around it. A drop of water in a cloud 'feels' the forces of warmth from the Sun pulling it upward and the attraction of its own kind pulling the cloud closer and closer together until it becomes dense enough to feel the pull of gravity and fall as rain. This may be a very simple physical/chemical form of perception, but it is a meaningful communication. The water both CAUSES change and is itself CHANGED. It shares its reality by both giving meaning to its surroundings and taking meaning for it.

There are many levels of perception, all blend into each other and all interpret the same BASIC laws of Nature to form the basis of their sacred communication. At the same time, each level sees things slightly different to every other level. There are different degrees of importance placed in different ways upon everything that exists, and it is this giving and taking of importance that causes the webs of links that create the different levels of Nature.

Every form of interaction requires four factors or 'Elements'. For example, for this book to be real to you, there obviously should be you (Earth), and the book (Water), (2 factors), and there must be some 'point of balance' or interaction, the 'link' between you and the book (3rd factor-Air). There also must be some sort of framework on which these 3 factors can interact (4th factor-Fire).

These four Elements are difficult to see at first, especially for minds trained to think in logical patterns (LOGIC is itself a type of framework on which the forces of RIGHT and WRONG, TRUE and FALSE interact to give birth to one sort of knowledge but not all knowledge).

To make these factors easier to work with, the ancient Alchemists used the symbolic descriptions of the four states of matter or Elements – EARTH, AIR, FIRE, and WATER.

- **AIR:** is the subtlest Element. It is to what water is to fish. We don't see it because we are in it. In Chinese Medicine, the SKIN is the Element of AIR because it defines all the other bodily systems. This Element is called the INTRINSIC factor; it is implied by the other three. For example, an iceberg is solid, so it is Earth – a river is liquid, so it is Water – steam is heat, so it is Fire – the water ($h2O$) is the intrinsic, Air factor. Air is the basic idea that gains energy (fire) and is focused (water) to become matter (earth). The North American Indians see the Four Elements as four directions in their Medicine Wheel like the Wicces Magick Circle. The East, which we use to work Air, is the "FAR SEEING" place. You can think of this element as Illumination and new beginnings, it is of the MIND and the MENTAL WORLD.

- **FIRE:** comes into being when the Air Element gains a direction (energy). It is the ACTOR factor, the EXPANDING forces of Nature. In the body it is the HEART and BLOOD. If the Air factor is the INTELLIGENCE that underlies all things, then the Fire factor is the 'living' organism. Each of us are points of Fire that use the five senses (the Water Element) to penetrate down to a physical level (Earth). Fire is characterised by heat and pressure and as the principle of penetration it is the creation of the polarities of light and darkness. The Native Americans see this direction – the South – as the place of "INNOCENCE" where you can clearly see the energies of your heart of hearts. To the Wicce it is similar and is the SACRED HEART, the place of EMOTION and of DEEP LOVE.

- **WATER:** is the opposing/controlling factor to fire. It takes FIRES energy and gives it a focus. This gives the first semblance of form, because it is the first of the YIN, inward acting forces. AIR and FIRE are outward acting - YANG forces. The ability to condense into a liquid is due to Water's ability to recognise itself and to group together to form mass. It is cold and contracting, slowing down, and flows rather than explodes like fire. This direction – the West – is called "LOOKS WITHIN" so it is the introspection of water recognising itself. To the Wicce it is the world of Magick and the PSYCHIC world of meeting with ones HIGHER SELF.

- **EARTH:** is the densest Element. It generates the pull of inertia to create solid form. It is the IDEA Air changed by the action of FIRE and WATER into the FIXED pattern of physical matter. This matter then used the other elements to cause a constant stream of change, which we call time. The direction – North – is the pattern the other Elements expressed; and could be "WISDOM". To the Wicce it is the PHYSICAL REALM.

If we go back to the idea of this book's 'reality' to you, you could say that the passage of time is the AIR factor, because time is the framework on which we can see the changes that make up perception. The FIRE factor could be you, because you are the ACTIVE principle, the one that is doing the perceiving and the strongest "centre of consciousness" (at least from your point of view). The WATER factor is the book, the object of the FIRE'S actions, it's the thing being perceived or acted upon. Which is the other end of the link that is thrown out by the pressure of FIRE'S energy. The EXPERIENCE you have of the book is the EARTH factor – the result of the interaction between you and the book on a matrix (framework) of TIME.

The Elements could then be two sets of polarities set at right angles to each other.

Air = time

You = Fire + Water = this book

Earth = experience.

FIRE and WATER express the same energy, with opposite directions.

AIR and EARTH are the same form, with what we could call opposite densities.

The Elements need to be seen and worked in languages other than words, which tend to be misinterpreted and are inadequate when trying to understand these concepts. The ancient Shaman and Wicce never had names for these instead it was sacred symbols or sigils of design that represented their Magickal forces.

- AIR could be viewed as an unbroken circle without beginning or end and with a uniform pressure throughout, there are no points or edges. Make a card for yourself out of black cardboard (4" by 5") and paint a white circle on it 3" in diameter.

This card will not only give you an image of the AIR element, it will GENERATE an AIR "aura". As you use it, it gets gradually charged with your energy, the energy of the links you form as you concentrate on the card. The best unit to use is the Chinese inch or POUCE. This is the distance between the ends of the first and second knuckle creases of your index finger. It represents your basic 'note' or vibration.

Now erase the circle

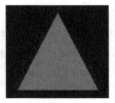

- FIRE is an upright equilateral triangle painted in red on a white card (4" by 5"). This portrays an upward flow of energy, the penetrative masculine dominant force. The triangle is set inside another 3" circle, which you should do in pencil and erase once the triangle is painted in.

A receptive Chalice or crescent shape symbolises WATER. Its colour is black or silver. This shape and colour shows energy that 'folds in' on itself (points are where energy leave and enter a shape). This is done on another 4" by 5" white card, by drawing another 3" diameter circle, and then using the same diameter making another circle to cut the first to form a crescent. Then rub out the extra line.

Erase this line

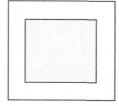

- EARTH is a yellow square (3" by 3") on the same sized card. This shows a field of energy that is fixed by the equal flows of energy from its four points.

These shapes and colours can maintain a constant type of energy, in much the same way as something you wear all the time that gradually gets some of your vibrations instilled into it.

Set yourself up in the same way as you set yourself up for your diary work, remember to use deep abdominal breaths (Goddess Breaths 4x4) and try to become as deeply relaxed as you know how to. Have the cards on your lap with Earth on the bottom; Water next, then Fire then Air. When you are as relaxed as you can get.

"Start to imagine your body becoming pleasantly heavy while your mind becomes pleasantly light."

Repeat this suggestion repeatedly, all the time concentrating on ever deepening, ever-slowing, always smooth and relaxed abdominal breathing. Tell yourself that you can produce in yourself a light trance state, one that is very easy to control and involves no loss of awareness.

Say: (in a soft but audible voice) "that you will recognise this light trance state by waves of relaxation that very pleasantly flows over your entire body. As you breathe in (through your nose, always) you breathe in energy that fills the lungs (AIR) and is taken by the blood (FIRE) to fill the body with a warm glow as you breathe out, the energy is pushed gently out of your body and with it let goes some of your fears (the negative emotion of WATER) and any fixed pattern of thinking that might hinder your work. Try imagining breathing in white which becomes red and breathing out black that becomes yellow, or you can combine both pictures, which is even better."

If you do all this and still don't feel that you are relaxing, try again and don't forget to reinforce the mental suggestions, keep trying. Half an hour at first, then gradually make it a little longer, but do not overdo it. Relaxation is an art that most people in our society, have forgotten, so it takes some people a little longer to remember how. I recommend recording your own voice leading you through these relaxation and meditation exercises, it makes it a lot easier for you.

Once you are truly relaxed as much as you think you can, let your eyes focus on the AIR card, do not try too hard, remember the key is RELAXATION. Then try to translate seeing the card turn into FEELING. Imagine that you have beams of energy coming from your eyes and these beams can feel just like your hands. (At first this feeling is like remembering feeling with your hands) then once you can feel with your eyes try to HEAR what the cards sound is. At this stage your imagination should be doing most of the work, don't fall into the trap of testing the reality of what you perceive yet." You can do that later, once your body has re-learnt to use this type of sensitivity. Children use it all the time. "Then try to imagine seeing the cards TASTE. This is difficult for most people to do, so you will probably need to try over a period of many weeks, every night. Constant attention is better than spasmodic concentrated effort, once you have gone through all your senses with the AIR card, then go to the FIRE card and do the same thing. Then WATER and finally EARTH."

This exercise is designed to do several things – increase relaxation, show you more about the Four Elements and how they interact; and it is also designed to exercise your imagination. It is your strength of imagination/visualisation that is your main tool in the control of the Wicces Magick energies, and it is your understanding of the Four Elements that enables you to recognise and fit in with already existing flows of energy.

Record your results in your Magickal Journal. Try to work out what Element you work best with and which one you have the most trouble with. You can alter the time spent with each card/concept so that you spend more time on the ones that you have trouble with. You can concentrate on/imagine breathing the appropriate colour as well. Your aim should be, to be equally at home with all your four types of energy.

The Australian Aborigine's say that we are born with one, two or sometimes three of the Elements (your birth chart) and your life purpose is to learn the others so that you become a full and balanced Centre of the Earth's creativity.

Another exercise you can try at this stage consists of taking simple concepts and working out their Air, Fire, Water and Earth Elements (all Elements are in all things, usually one or two predominate to give the thing its character). You should record this in your diary as well.

In the KABBALISTIC schools of Magick the Four Elements are symbolised as TETRAGRAMMATON, which is written:

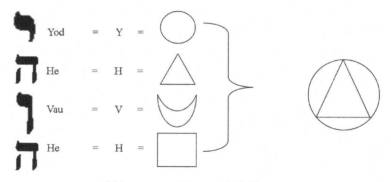

This expresses one Tetragrammic Reality.

In Hermetic Magick the symbol is a silver upright Triangle inside a gold Circle (the true sigil of the Isarum Wicce) where the three points of the triangle are positive, negative and neutral, and the circle itself is the intrinsic factor. This is the original symbol and Magickal seal of the Wicce, given to them on their Initiation ceremony. In Christianity the three parts of God the Father, Son and Holy Ghost, represent the same symbols. In Mahayana Buddhist terms, the four Elements are known as the solid, liquid, radiating and gaseous principles, In other words the qualities of inertia, cohesion, radiation and vibration.

The Earth Element shows a horizontal direction, a downward direction expresses the force of Water, upwards shows Fire and zigzag shows Air. If you look for them, you will find these Elements at or near the basis of just about all our great philosophies and religions. It helps if there are other people doing this work at the same time, as there will be parts that you won't see by yourself. You need to throw these ideas around quite a lot. The four Elements represent the interaction needed for an entity to become self-aware. You will notice that all four Elements interact with each other. This internal interaction is known as the FIFTH element, Ether, Akasha or Spirit. The Chinese call this Element wood, as it is the Element of life. In Alchemy this Element is regarded as a composite of the 3 types of action (called essentials), Mercury – the spirit, Sulphur – the binding force; and salt – the physical form, the seed.

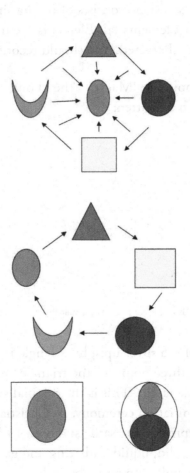

Once this Element is incorporated into the cycle, the order of Elemental changes to allow the entity to act outside itself. The Zen (Fire-Red) penetrates to this level to animate the body (Earth-Yellow) that is its own ashes. These ashes create the soil of the earth, which attracts to itself an atmosphere (Air-Blue) that becomes the vehicle for clouds (Water-Black) which causes growth (Wood-Blue), which is used as fuel for the Zen (Fire-Red) to create the body (Earth-Yellow) and so on.

Wood is the most complicated of all the Elements. In the body it is the LIVER and the liver has over 200 functions, all to do with the blood. Its shape is the shape of an egg and its color is green. Make your fifth card (a large circle beneath a smaller circle both with dots in their Centre and both joined with a circle around them. And from this you can see that Wood has two centers – the top, smaller circle represents the MICROCOSM and the larger base circle represents the MACROCOSM. Wood appears when one TETRAGRAMMIC reality interacts with another TETRAGRAMMIC reality. Western Wicces call this Element Ether/Spirit. The Indian systems give it the name Akasha.

"May the Energy of the work just done,
Aid in the development of Love and Understanding in all things"

III
THE EMPRESS

III THE EMPRESS — GREAT WHITE BUFFALO WOMAN

The Laws of Nature-Key to Space Born

*"I will generate the Enlightenment thought,
that I attain success for all others and for myself".*

The "Laws" of Magick are probably the most misused/mistrusted and misinterpreted statements you're ever likely to run across. They are seen on the one hand as mystical, and so 'deep' and impractical that they can never be understood. On the other hand, they're seen as an excuse for totally destructive action, especially the famous Third Law. They aren't a code of ETHICS or MORALS. Every Wicce must become aware of the fact that SHE is responsible for her own actions. We make our Gods. We put values of right and wrong on actions and things. The Laws are simple tools that are in themselves neither constructive nor destructive. The only way to understanding them is to PRACTISE them. There are four basic Laws (the mind, like everything else, is subject to the basic laws of interaction) the first of which is:

"MAN KNOW THYSELF"

This Law deals with the most basic problem of perception. How you see yourself has a direct effect on how well you relate to the things around you. All your previous experiences, in fact your whole cultural background (including your parents and friend's backgrounds and even your past lives) make you attach various degrees of importance to the things you see. We saw in the first chapter how people can be subject to the same external stimulation (a walk through the park) and come up with totally different experiences. We ALL have this readiness to see what is important to us at the time and ignore the rest, yet we are the TOTAL of our EXPERIENCES and unless we act from our whole self our experiences become "one-sided", limited and gradually FIXED. The Wicce can't afford this. You are going to be doing things that are alien to your normal conscious stream of thought and you must be able to see these new experiences from a balanced point of view.

Most of the more meaningful EXPERIENCES that we have involve OTHER people, yet we know that both sides are going to see things with a certain bias, which will cause misunderstanding. To get around this problem we learn as children to play certain games, we take on roles that enable us to get what we want, and to win approval and acceptance. Unfortunately, as we grow up these roles become more and more complicated and demand more and more of our energies until finally we become so immersed in these 'reflected' identities that we become cut off from our real self. Or to put it another way, we become neurotic. Gradually, at first and more dynamically later, the false identities that originally were only games become accepted as the real self. These identities are amazingly complicated, and their drive's and desires are synthetic and can NEVER BE REALLY SATISFIED.

They are the result of incorrect and incomplete communications, which are deflected back to us from a society built upon fear and aggressive competition. It is any wonder that we feel insecure and disillusioned at times? The problem goes even further when this feeling of alienation, causes us to 'cut off' from Nature. The food we eat is processed so much that very little of the Natural 'vital energy' or "life-force" is left. As we starve our body of proper food, our senses become even more dulled, so that our communications become more and more limited, and we become more and more ill, and eventually die.

Each of the major organs, mental as well as physical relate to a certain Element, and each Element has its own taste. In our society we use so much salt and sugar that they become the only things we taste. The SWEET taste relates to the Earthly Element and in the proper proportion, promotes insight (the ability to see your own patterns) but in excess it destroys that insight, causing the mind to become OBSESSIVE and in its efforts to give itself meaning, it becomes dogmatic and inflexible. The SALT taste relates to the Watery Element and in the proper proportions enables you to focus your energies to be able to accomplish your dreams. In excess it destroys this ability, which leaves you with a lack of confidence that develops into FEAR.

Later in this book we will be doing some work on diagnosis and treatment of disease, but for now take a good look at your eating habits. If you want to learn to be able to generate and direct your inner strength, your body needs to be fed good fuel, and by this, I mean the RIGHT FUEL. Not only food, but also exercise and breathing are important as well.

As a Wicce you should learn to see past the complicated meta-identities (reflected identities) that you have built, down to the basic drives of the true self. If you look at the exercises we have done so far, you will see that they are designed to show you your specific Elemental make-up and to help you correct any imbalance. Bear in mind that although it is possible to get back to the pre-neurotic personality, it isn't always wise. It is very hard, if not impossible, to live as a totally non-neurotic person in a neurotic society, what we can do is use the games where necessary and at the same time, try to see that the four basic drives are brought more into balance. These drives are:

1. **SURVIVAL** – both as an individual and as a complete integrated society.

2. **SEX** – including love, social interactions, family life, physical sex, art, in fact any sort of communication.

3. **SELF ESTEEM** – the 'feedback' from your communications should give you the ability to look at yourself and like what you see. You don't have to be perfect, no one is, but you can arrange your life so that things are getting better. Look for your strengths and weaknesses, and then **DO** something about them.

4. **SELF KNOWLEDGE** – again, you don't need to have perfect self-knowledge, but you do need to feel that you are at least beginning to see your potential and actual beauty. EVERYBODY is an artist in some way or another. You must TRY to develop your natural creative talents. I've met lots of people who say they can't until they have tried. True, some find it harder than others, but we are all part of Nature and Nature is the perfect artist!

The next Law of Magick is:

BE IN ALL THINGS!

This Law comes second because we can only KNOW other things to the same degree as we KNOW OURSELVES. If all you know of yourself is physical, then your knowledge of everything else is confined to the physical level. Some things you're more comfortable with than others, certain colours, different times of the day, seasons of the year, or even people. This is because those things create their 'links' use the energy and are compatible to the type of links you throw out. In our society, males are given a certain image to grow into, that teaches them to concentrate on their 'masculinity' (?), the role of the hunter and provider. This role tends to foster an outward movement of the mind and an inclination to see OBJECTS (single and separated focuses of attention) rather than relationships. This in turn makes the mind function more and more from the INTELLECT. Women, on the other hand, are given an entirely different role as that of the mother and wife, which generates an 'inward' movement of the mind. This role teaches an inclination to see patterns of relationships (the objects become, a background) and this leads the mind to function more and more emotionally. These roles no longer FIT in our present stage of development. We must get back through all that conditioning to be able to see things from a balanced point that incorporates BOTH emotion and intellect.

This can sometimes be very threatening, because it means questioning your whole sexual identity. Some heterosexual people have found they have homosexual feelings. Some homosexuals have found they have heterosexual feelings. I tend to think that we are in fact all bi-sexual, but the way in which we express that time. Keep your mind open on this question and in that way, you can stop too much pressure building up either way. In your past lives you have been female sometimes and male at others. Someone who is your parent in one life will be your lover in another life, etc. this doesn't mean that relationships have no value. This may be the most productive way for you at this time, or it may not, but part of the problem of our expanding awareness is relearning ways of handling the energy that is generated through deeper communication in an essentially tribal community. These energies can be directed into growing rather than owning relationships but only if we learn to see deeply into our potential and actual beauties and strengths. We must experience ALL things to understand all things, this is our Spiritual destiny to eventually become one with everything, it is the essential goal of the trained and learned Wicce.

To be able to put our 'being' into all things means being able to experience outside things, not only from our point of view but from theirs as well. Magick uses the 'links' we put out as a vehicle of our senses. You are already doing half the necessary meditation to illustrate what I mean. When you can use your eyes to touch, hear, taste and smell your cards, the next step will be to set up a flow of your 'life force' through the card to create an extra strong link.

"Sit at a table with the cards in front of you. Relax yourself as much as possible and then go through the AIR card, once you have gone through each sense, turn your attention back to your BREATH. Your back must be STRAIGHT so that you can breathe properly. Don't let your shoulders drop forward, let your breath sink very low and become very RHYTHMIC then place your hands on the table, one on EITHER SIDE OF THE CARD and try to imagine a gentle tide of energy that flows OUT of your right hand as you push your abdomen IN to push your breath OUT (not hard but firm). Try to deepen your concentration and bring energy IN through your LEFT HAND as you allow gravity to pull your abdomen down and expand your lungs so that you breathe in, this movement is the Deosil flow and is the flow of all positive life energy.

Try to concentrate your vision on the CENTRE OF THE CARD but do not STARE. Be gentle. When you see an AFTER IMAGE you will recognise it when you see it, gently shut your eyes and try to feel what the CARD FEELS. Allow yourself about 5-10 minutes of time (put a CD on in the background of some relaxing meditation music so that you will know when your time is up). When you can get some sort of feeling from the card. You can THEN strengthen the effect by using a MANTRA. This is a sort of verbal MANDALA, A spiral path of your mind to travel on. This one is very old; variations of it have always been around.

> "All things in all times,
> In all places is one thing,
> That thing is LOVE".

The Third Law is:

DO WHAT THOU WILT!

The greater your experience of the first Two Laws, the more you understand that you and the universe SHARE a common reality. You need it and it needs you. You become more and more aware of the EASE and BEAUTY of HARMONY.

The THOU talked about here, is both you as a single entity and you as an animal dependent on interaction with other people and things. If you are DEPENDING on these things, then you simply can't afford NOT to foster their growth. The greater THEIR ability to interact with YOU, the greater becomes your overall experience, therefore the wider your universe, the fuller your life – the greater your development. If you put out constructive links, Nature responds in kind (Like attracts Like-which is the Law of Similarity). The reverse applies as well; if you kill ANYTHING (mental or physical) then you are ROBBING YOURSELF and therefore going against your WILL and the very WILL of Nature.

Remember, we are talking about the will of the TRUE SELF, not the reflected identities that society has given us. Nature (your own nature) will not allow you to develop past this level unless you convince it that you can handle the responsibility of more power. The use of this law is a sort of test of the other people (our greatest source of experience/reality). Choose a 'special place', a 'Magick Circle' to work in. It should not be used for anything except Magickal and spiritual work. Set it aside for group or solo rituals EXCLUSIVELY.

There should be a soft floor the colour of rich earth if it is indoors. Its walls hung with purple drapes (no corners) symbolizing the union of fire and water and the ceiling should be blue, representing the clear blue sky (air). It should be clean and kept clean. Only enter it SKYCLAD or ROBED and UNAFRAID. This room symbolises your Magickal self and the purer/more complete the picture; the greater will be its efficiency.

Once you can do the Lesser Banishing Ritual of the Pentagram (this ritual is in full in "Complete Teachings of Wicca – Book Two – The Wicce" easily, then taking people who are not linked (by working with you) into the Magick Circle becomes less critical. Even then remember that if you affect the Magick Circle you affect all who use it. The lighting of your Four Etheric Candles (bees wax), one at each compass point and two altar candles representing the Goddess and God of your choice.

If you are working with a group of Initiated Wicces, you will use the FIRE TEMPLE, because it is necessary to CLEAN your energies before you start to build them into a working Tool. The Elements 'correspond' to these four directions called Watchtowers. The east, the rising Sun, the beginning is AIR. The South Pole of a magnetic field is negatively charged (therefore positive action. Electricity goes from the negative charge to the positive charge). Seen clairvoyantly the South Pole of a magnet is red, so the south is FIRE. The West is the setting Sun, the end of the day, the controlling forces of WATER. The North Pole is positively charged (therefore negative/reception action). It is the influx of the ETHERS (energy flows), the power to pull in the other planets' influence to fix or 'bring through' the EARTH Element.

Place something appropriate in each Watchtower – a blue disc for Air, (in the temple there is the Thurible (incense burner) as the Lesser Tool of the Wicce and the Wand as the Major Tool of the Priest or Priestess), a red triangle for Fire (Etheric Candle Flame as the Lesser Tool of the Wicce, and the Athame (Wicce) or Sword of the High Priest/ess as the Major Tool, a green crescent/Chalice for Water (Chalice as the Lesser Tool (Wicce), and the Cauldron (High Priest/ess as the Major Tool), a yellow square for Earth (Pentacle as the Lesser Tool and Major Tool of the Wicce), as it is the SACRED KEY to the mysteries of the Epagomenes (the secrets of the Pentagram and the Magick Circle). These colours are used because of their 'ease of association' with their appropriate Elements. They draw in the same type of links and 'feel like' those Elements. The other colours (white for Air, and black for Water) are more 'internal colors'.

Make a circle by either drawing it in white, or a little stronger is a cord soaked in salted water, which acts as a conductor for energies to be shared around the Magick Circle. Use both if you like. I have a sacred 90-foot white cord that I took to the ocean and soaked it in the salted water of the sea. It is used for very advanced workings in my Magick Circle (although it is dry it still contains the pure salt of the ocean and the water, I do often take it back to the sea for refreshing).

Use a symbolic start to all your Magickal Work; one of the best/easiest to use is the Equal Armed Cross. This is a symbolic (after a while actual) division of your Life Force into its four separate Elements, then a bringing together in the middle, because you are beginning your Work, you should use your hand in the form of a Wand (Air principle). This Wand is a symbol of potential sexual energy and is formed by making a fist with your right hand with your thumb in between the first and second fingers. With this you touch your forehead and say – "IN ME IS THE GODDESS" Then take your hand down to your genitalia and point to the ground and say – "AND MAN" Take your Wand to the left shoulder and say – "CERNUNNOS" Then to the right shoulder and say – "AND THE SHINING ONES" Then bring both hands together at your Solar Plexus and say, "FOREVER, SO IT IS".

Cernunnos (pronounced Karnayna, written this way by the Romans) means all our fears, and The Shining Ones (Angels) means all our Hopes. It is the same with the word Witch, which was first recorded in 720AD by the Romans, when they heard the word they wrote it as witch, where in fact the Saxon word is written Wicce and pronounced (wish).

This ritual helps to sort out your energy and strengthen the polarity and direction of your aura. The initial acceptance of your whole self is very important to your future work. You should practice it twice a day. When you get up, and again when you retire for the night.

Arrange yourself as near as possible with the sexes alternating, so that in the Magick Circle you have the opposite sex on either side, unless you are truly one with your sexuality and balanced as a sexual being. This makes the flow easier and Natural. Enter always from the North-East, or even East if possible and acknowledge each Watchtower as you pass, then the first person sits just to the left of the Air Watchtower (so fellow Wicces can still come in to your Magick Circle) and each Wicce sits to the left of the one prior until your Magick Circle is complete. Then about 5-10 minutes given for each person to centre him or herself and relax, set their motive and generate the emotion of just being there. You can use a chant as a long line of Wicces and Buddhists alike have in the past. If you say the Chant aloud and in unison with each other it keeps the evoked energies focused and slowly building. It also generates emotional connected involvement, so you include it as part of the beginning of every ritual. We always after the Wicces Rune say the Invocation of Bacchus: "I.O. EVO.HE. BLESSED BE." (Ee-oh-arvo-hay)

When ready, slowly and very gently join hands, left hand facing down and right hand facing up this is the natural Dragon flow of energy (the flow of the dragon within), and begin your Chant (as above), try to generate a good continual flow of energy. In with your breath through your right hand, which should be palm facing upwards, and out with your out breath, as you say, *"Blessed Be"*, through your left hand, which should be palm facing down. Close your eyes, as this flow draws energy up out of the Earth as well as sharing the energy of the Wicces in the flow. Let your breathing sink deep inside your body, using your abdomen, and not your chest. Then visualise the energy of the Wicce on your right flowing into you as you breathe in, and down to your *"centre"*, the bottom of your breath, which you should feel rather than force. The best place is the "ONE POINT", three fingers below the Navel, (The Sacral Chakra). To purify and harmonise this energy you distill it into three Alchemical Essences.

Visualise a small (the smaller the better) WHITE SEED at the THIRD EYE, as you breathe in. Visualise the ETHER filling the SEED (the flow comes from the Third Eye of the Wicce on your right) and as you breathe out, use the Chant as before to vibrate the SEED so that the flow of pure SPIRITUAL LIGHT (Mercury) flows continuously around the Magick Circle Deosil from Wicce to Wicce, and you are all becoming Male, Female. Feel the others flowing through you, when you feel that the Mercury is collected, let your tongue relax, and then stop your voice.

Let your lips form the shape and LISTEN to the sound of the BREATH. Then let it become a deep satisfying YAWN. You can tell when you are really and truly yawning by the tears that form; these tears are the Mercury (which rules Water) of the eyes.

Once the Mercury is distilled you then distill the BINDING FORCE, The Alchemical SULPHUR at the THROAT (the Binding Force between the head and your body). Visualise a small BLUE SEED at the centre of your Throat, then visualise and share it around the Magick Circle as you did with Mercury. Use the Chant "AH", when you feel your Auric Sulphur is focused at the Throat let your shoulders completely relax, and let the sound come out as a deep satisfied SIGH. Let the energy of the Sighs BUILD and distill the Sulphur to the Seed.

Finally bring your Consciousness down to the Middle of the Chest to your HEART and visualise a small GREEN SEED, the ALCHEMICAL SALT. Share the vitalised Essence as you have the other two. Using the Mantra "YAY". This time when you feel the Salt crystallise in the GREEN SEED allow the Chest and Heart to resonate a low HUM, a purr of contentment that comes from deep down inside.

Contemplate the THREE CIRCLES of LIFE FORCE flowing around the Magick Circle, sharing and being shared by all Wicces. (Do this for as long as you feel it needs). When ready visualise a CLEAR SHAFT of Light coming up from the centre of the Earth up through your body and out of the top of your head. Once this idea is set then visualise any disturbed or unharmonious energy being collected at the level of your Heart as you breathe in, once all the unwanted energy is collected as a BLACK LAVA ROCK (Obsidian) and then condensing it, raise your hands high above your heads. Then clap loudly and shout, "SO BE IT" whilst visualising the Rock flying off into deep space leaving your energies clear and distilled. Each Time you say "YAY" from now on you can visualise it as a distillation, the THREE SOUNDS are the THREE ALCHEMICAL ESSENCES.

This distillation will sort out any energy that is within your Aura by using your body, neck and head as separate resonating chambers. It also works on the land that you are on so that the more you do it; the more you harmonise your environment. It's like using a small acupuncture needle in your hand to affect the energy balance of your whole body, in this case you are the needle and the body is the Earth. It's a good idea to distill all your flows, but it is not entirely necessary. Perfect the technique, and then use it when you feel the need to purify and/or clarify.

Allow about 5-10 minutes of this, and then try to imagine you ARE the flow.

"Shut your eyes and imagine going around the Magick Circle through each of the Elements as they are expressed by the Magick Circle. Visualise the division between your auras dissolving so that you share your energies evenly. This is part of the ALCHEMICAL DISSOLUTION and an important part of developing AURIC SENSITIVITY. Allow yourself another 5-10 minutes of this, and then slow the spinning down. Come back to your own body and then slowly open your eyes when you are ready".

When everyone has their eyes open you all break the flow, GENTLY, at the same time, and then leave in the order you came in. You ALWAYS move Deosil and you must also acknowledge (thank) the Goddess and God, and the Lords and Ladies of the Watchtowers by the fixing chant to balance the generation chant. Then continue to the northeast where you entered and exit from there. Repeat the cross as your ritual re-birth into the everyday world. Use this ritual to create your initial link to the Sun, do it each week on a Sunday. A good way to thank the other people in the flow is to touch foreheads by leaning and giving weight but no pushing, and visualising the edge between your spirits (Mercury) dissolving.

Let yourselves sink into each other then roll away, don't pull back as you say BLESSED BE. Touching is an important part of your Magickal work.

The Fourth Law sums it all up/contains the other three. It is their final aim.

LOVE UNDER WILL!

Love is the equal sharing of experience. It is neither EMOTION nor INTELLECT, but both in a perfect union, first learn the difference between the two. The apparent contradictions are due to their opposite actions. They cannot and need not be the SAME. They make up two parts of a whole picture. The intellect is how we affect our environment, and the emotions are our adjustment to our environment. Once you can balance these forces in yourself (the active and the passive) then you can gain access to both at once. This brings your attention to the present moment (the intellect thinks ahead, and the emotions look behind) and produces true INVOLVEMENT, which satisfies all FOUR BASIC DRIVES and develops your artistic vision, the ability to express yourself as a creative force. This creative force is the Wicces Will – her ability to shape her environment. So, the creative WILL develops the ability of LOVE.

"May the energy of the work just done,
Aid in the development, of Love and Understanding in all things and myself".

MEDITATIVE STORY ON THE TRUTH OF BEING!

"In the beginning; was the Goddess! And within the infinite stillness of the Unformed and Unmanifest a note was sounded. The TONE issued forth an endless vibration besetting countless other tones in support, and the mind of the Goddess through LOVE saw the Image and was given LIFE. And the SPIRIT of the Goddess was given dominion as the CREATIVE PRINCIPLE of all that was to come for all eternity.

CREATION continued and this omnipresent image of the Goddess, the MOTHER/ FATHER of creation began to contemplate itself as an INDIVIDUAL BEING and sparks of CELESTIAL FIRE were thrown throughout the boundless UNIVERSE, forming CENTERS OF LIGHT, of SPIRIT CONSCIOUSNESS. I was one of those FIRELIGHTS, a point of INDIVIDUAL AWARENESS in my Omnipresence. I knew myself to be a Goddess, I knew myself to be me! Creation continued, and I sought to express the fullness of my BEING conceived in LOVE the precious idea of MYSELF in expression comes forth into MANIFESTATION as a LIVING SOUL. I am! I am! I am! In time, a part of my SELF EXPRESSION descends into the dense lower world for the experience of it I let myself play with CREATIONS and identify with them. I am descending deeper and deeper into Materiality. Mother help me! My Consciousness of you is fading. Father the Light is gone. There is darkness! Where am I? Who am I? What is the purpose of my Life? I am a far country I have spent all in search of MEANING and I am in want. I have come under the bondage of others, and I feel the swine in the fields and the ANGEL of the presence says:

You are so much more than you think you are, stand up seek the Mothers Kingdom your true estate, begin the journey home now!"

I turn within and seek MY SELF Through the Tunnel of Mind I travel moving across the emotional sea of my subjective world ... Be Still! I speak. Let the troubled waters be as glass reflecting only the memories of gladness, ecstasy, jubilation and joy. Let all others be dissolved and my fading

Nature responds and joins me on the Journey to the Light. There is a DOOR before me and I sense with mind and heart that it is THE WAY to the CHAMBER OF TRUTH

Slowly I reach out and open the Door and suddenly I am engulfed in a blazing golden light! Above me, below me, behind me, beside me through me is the LIGHT OF SPIRIT

O Beautiful me, O Abundant me, the Harmonious me, the Glass me, the Forgiving me, the Creative me, the Whole me, the Perfect me. Slowly this HIGHER SELF fills my consciousness with itself and my awareness of two separate entities is fading away Now there is only the single I and from the I a voice speaks."

IV
THE EMPEROR

IV The Emperor – Great Spirit
Evolution is Goddess/God Creation-The Dweller of Unal

"I will generate thought
that I attain success for all others and for myself".

One of the most basic problems any practical system dealing with REALITY must face is the BASIC ORIGIN of everything.

There was a space before anything, even time existed. This space had only one dimension - position, and one quality - potential. All that existed was a point, whose circumference was equal to its diameter, so small or large that every point inside it could be called the centre; anything, even the IDEA of anything coming from this or these centres, had the quality of PENETRATION and SPIRALLED out to cause the circumference to expand. This expansion caused "SHOCKS" - equal and opposite reactions, vibrations to flow back to the centre; these forces have the quality of RECEPTION and they spiral in on themselves. The closer these forces get to the centre, the greater becomes the pressure from the forces of penetration. Until the pressure becomes so great, the point where the two forces meet is placed under such great pressure that a great solid "WALL OF BALANCE" is formed and the twin polarities of matter and energy appear on the 'level' below.

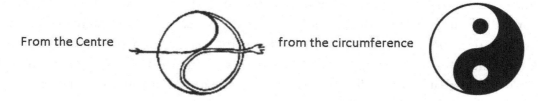

From the Centre — from the circumference

This is the basic shape of matter = YIN/YANG.

This action of creation happens all the time, it is happening now, life is always beginning and never ending; it disappears on one level only to emerge transformed on another, as with death.

The **AIR** Element (MIND) of the universe, the matrix on which all else appeared, is the space before everything else. It is INFINITE and contains all the Elements as POTENTIALS. There is an absolute LACK of division at this level and the first stirring of change is rejected violently to be born on a more 'dense' subtler level.

The **FIRE** Element (The HEART) is the Creation of Change/time and the first AWARENESS. This could not exist on the AIR level because perception is the experience of change. The Air factor is potential – the Fire factor is animation. It's at this 'level' that everything divides into active and passive – the YIN, receptive forces and the YANG penetrative forces. The intersection of these two forces produces a newfound AWARENESS, which is the UNITY of the Air Element transmuted to fit in with the new Laws of Change. This awareness is INFINITE – not the detailed, different seeing, perception orientated function we normally call AWARE. At this level, matter and energy are not yet 'separated' as they are on the EARTH level: YIN and YANG forces are the two directions of the SAME action. They are GOD (air) looking in on itself – YIN forces; or looking OUT at itself – YANG forces. Although there is no conception yet of individual variation's, this Element is TOTALLY aware.

It is one of the Wicces aims to cross the Abyss which separates the Fire of the infinite mind from the Water of her or his own individual mind. This level of force, plus the air level of "form without shape", is what is usually termed the GODHEAD – it is the Trilogy that is symbolised in our major religions and mythologies. Its symbol is the TRIANGLE INSIDE A CIRCLE – the Fire penetrating through from the Air, the true power and symbol of the INITIATED Wicce.

Make another 4" by 5" white card and on this one, draw a blue circle and in this put a red triangle – to give the talisman more strength it is a good idea to 'symbolise' the Circle as a Snake swallowing its own tail (Arborous) – this makes it a more 'living' energy, because the image of the snake relates directly to our instinctual level – to evoke out of your race memory this feeling of birth that is the primal FIRE experience, it is where your mind is 'focused' during the first years of your life, this is the main reason I have used it and the main symbology on the covers of my Books. Don't try to cut corners – go through the whole procedure that was used for the other cards – the direction you should face for this is SOUTHEAST between Fire and Air.

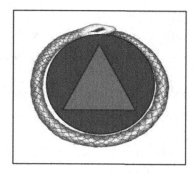

To understand how the forces of YIN and YANG produce the spectrum of colour that characterise the more complicated WATER Element (The MAGICK OR SOUL), that in turn, produced the solar system, we need to obtain a clear glass prism, 3 inches long with three surfaces, two of which meet at an angle of 60 degrees. The prism should be used with this angle of refraction downwards. The upper surface should slope slightly towards you.

You should look for the new image below where you think it would be. You will notice that whenever a black and white area meet, colour is created (Magick). Look through the prism at a narrow white band on a black background.

4 inches x 5 inches

First hold the prism close so that you see two distinct bands of colour with a white section in between. You see that the top colour against the black is red – then there is a band of yellow – then white – then under that blue – then violet and finally black again.

The prism displaces the image so that the two layers of darkness (different intensities) are pulled down like semi-transparent shadows over the white. The darker shadow obscures the white so much that the light only comes through as red – the lighter shadow allows more of the 'penetration of yang' through to form the colour yellow. This can also be seen when a dark cloud passes in front of the sun. Its colour changes from brilliance to yellow and through to red. The colours of the sunset are caused by the angle that light shines through the atmosphere at that time of day and the darkness of the oncoming night 'radiating' (darkness radiates just as light does) over the lighter colours of the day (just as the prism).

Underneath, the white is pulled down in the same way. The first layer of light is strong, so the colour produced is the darkness overcome strongly by the light to make blue. This is what happens during the day. The Sun lights up the air, which spreads like a veil between our eyes and the blackness of deep space – the clearer the day, the less dense the veil, the stronger veil shines through and the deeper the blue of the sky. At night there is very little light, but on a bright night, when the air is a little damp, it disperses enough of the polarised light of the Moon so that the Veil is strong enough to produce a deep violet, this is also seen towards Dawn. Try to really see the way the two forces act upon each other – they are of equal importance – each has its own strengths. The Yang radiating colours of red and yellow are essentially white modified by the Yin forces they seek to escape – the Yin cooling colours reflect the Nature of darkness that absorbs the light into itself to create the blue and violet.

If you pull back a little so that the bands of colour merge into each other, you will see the yellow and red merge to form orange, the blue and violet merge to form indigo. Where the two bands meet in the middle the blue and yellow give birth to a wonderful green. This is the seven-fold manifestation of the scale of darkness. It is produced by white light on a black background. The Sun in the centre of the Solar System is the YIN force, the 'contained organism' of the Solar System.

"POINTS OF MATTER" emerge from the infinite Air principle in an evenly spaced pattern.

The influence of WATER forces – the reaction/contraction caused by creation – drawn from these points of matter get closer to each other to form gigantic clouds of gases. These clouds condensed even further to produce Galaxies, and these condensed further still to produce Solar Systems like our own – clouds forming in less dense clouds. The Sun and Planets are the results of one of these clouds sorting itself into layers of density (or different Solar System colours). The cloud was spinning so the layers of density formed due to centrifugal force. Mercury is the closest planet to the Sun and 80% of its mass is iron. Venus and Earth have progressive densities. All the planets are the same age, 4.6 thousand million years old.

The Earth has OXYGEN, which is relatively heavy, and HYDROGEN that is a very light gas. This is since the Solar System has more than one source of energy or 'SOLAR WINDS'. Jupiter, the giant Planet, gives off 2 1/2 times as much heat as it receives from the Sun; this makes it appear as a miniature Sun itself.

Jupiter's Solar Winds exert enough backpressure to allow oxygen and hydrogen to be together on both Earth and Mars (Mars is like the Earth was 200 million years ago – just as oceans were forming – although its actual age is the same). Saturn supports this action of Jupiter and forms another 'wall of balance', which is a transmutation of the one that causes the Birth of Fire from Air. Each of the planets as we come in to the Sun, gives us a progressive development of the balance of energies or colours between the forces of light (the Sun) and darkness. The forces of darkness are the forces of infinite light as opposed to the Sun's relative light. These are the forces that are focused by the three-so-called transcendental (above this Plane) planets – Uranus, Neptune and Pluto.

In the early 1980's the Planets all lined up in a way that caused these two forces to generate considerable energy. We can use this energy to wake up our latent ability to channel planetary forces via the energy centres or Chakra's in our bodies. There are over 10,000 of these psychic centres in our bodies. We will be using the centres that relate to the Lymphatic system, because they do the cleaning and clearing that is necessary to our Magickal work. They can also handle the inevitable mistakes made while you learn to play the subtlest of all instruments - yourself.

A rainbow is a field of light acting inside the Earth's dense auric fields. If light manifests in free space it folds in on itself with a sort of spiral within spirals movement that balances its energies into a stable (?) form. Yellow is the strongest concentration of YANG force and it exerts a pull on the existing order of the spectrum to fulfill its desire to expand. This causes red and yellow to change places.

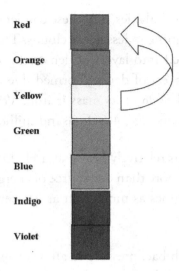

Its complimentary colour represents its counterpart in the YIN forces. This colour is purple. In the spectrum it is the combination of indigo and violet. This splitting is characteristic of the way Water Controls Fire.

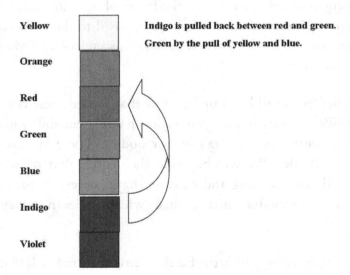

The violet (more yang of the two) is the point of balance (Saturn); the indigo is pulled back by the Yin forces (blue) as well by the need to contain the Yang forces (yellow) at the centre. The yellow – the Sun, the indigo – Earth and the violet – Saturn, become the central axis on which the other four energies act.

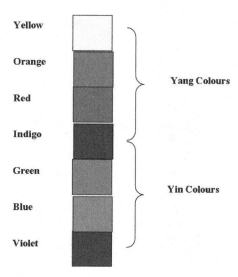

Indigo is a mixture of blue and red – they are EXTERNAL colours of the centre – the ones indigo uses to express it. With the indigo as the centre, RED and BLUE become the YANG colors. This causes another internal stirring and red and green transposed.

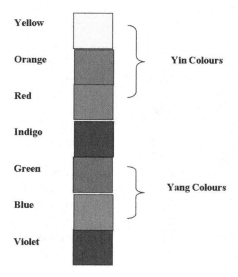

This internal action of YIN and YANG and vice versa is the way the contracting Water Element uses the forces of Fire to fix the form of matter – Earth. If you learn to imitate this action you learn to control the links your mind uses to fix itself in this reality. The colours we attribute to the planets follow this "Alchemized" pattern.

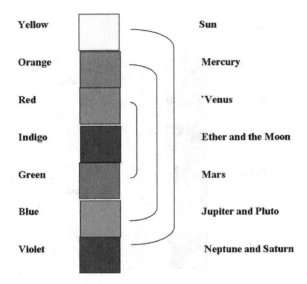

The Earth is the internal concentration of ZEN (a Chinese medicine term which means *"living force"*) and the other colours are arranged around this in complimentary pairs. You can see this same pairing of complimentary actions if we look at the seven major metals. These are also related to the nine Planets or colours.

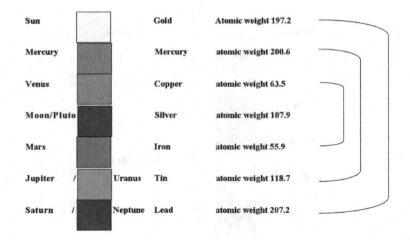

If we arrange them in a circle according to their atomic weights and with gold-Sun at the top, we get an interesting arrangement that illustrates the same pairing as the colour. The manifestation of these apparently vastly different levels of reality follow the same Laws – what you learn from looking at one level, you can apply to another level, they all follow the same pattern of evolution, just as we do.

We now have a picture of an infinite potential being evolved by its own inherent Nature to form the worlds around us. We also begin to see how much WE are the centre of Nature's energies. Our awareness is the result of a focusing of the creative and generative forces of Nature; we have evolved into a fully portable centre of experience.

Mercury has the atomic weight 200.6. The Earth is the internal concentration of ZEN and the other colours are arranged around this in complimentary pairs. You can see this same pairing of complimentary actions if we look at the seven major metals. These are also related to the nine Planets or colours.

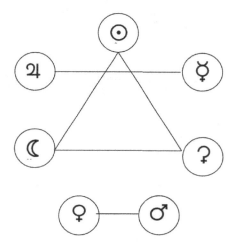

WE direct that experience because we ARE Nature enjoying a new level of realisation using our senses. Therefore, so much can be healed in us simply by developing some form of artistic expression. Art develops the ability to focus energy into a pattern; this ability is the same ability that uses the energy that comes to you all the time. You can learn to focus your energy into a pattern that heals you – you've already seen that shape and colour are more than symbols – they change/direct our experiences and the more you become sensitive to them, the more you can USE that energy in your Magickal endeavours. There are four main levels of manifestation:

The AIR level is the *unified potential*.

The FIRE level is the separation into *positive and negative*.

The WATER level is the development of colours and patterns, which means new ways of *balancing energy to create different forms*.

The EARTH level, what we normally call *solid reality*, the 'result' of the other three levels.

Each of these levels has within THEM four levels as well and each of them has four levels or Elements and so on.

"May the energy of the work just done,
Aid in the development of Love and Understanding in all things".

V
THE HIEROPHANT

V The Hierophant — Thoth Tehuti (Hermes Trismegistus)

A Universal Map-Key to Magick and Listening to Learn

*"I will generate the enlightenment thought
that I attain success for all others and for myself".*

For anything to exist for us, it must have DIMENSIONS, so that our senses can define it. These develop and gain reality just as more concrete things must.

The point has the first dimension — POSITION.

As this Air factor is expanded by Fire, it 'produces' itself at right angles to itself to produce a straight line.

Fire is the polarity of white and black, which are the 'two ends' of the same Pole — light. The straight line has position (circle) and length (triangle). The development of *'length'* is the first action. The line is only "transitory", as soon as it comes into being it projects itself, not only in the direction of the action, but also at right angles to itself. This creates the third dimension of width and the shape of a square. The projection of the line creates the idea, therefore the desire to explore/expand into above and below, the results in the focusing of fixing (Water) of a square *"Plane"* or area.

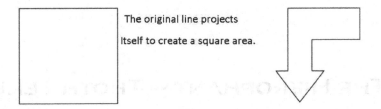

The original line projects Itself to create a square area.

This square has five factors or points in a specific relationship – the four corners which exert a pressure on their point of balance, and the centre.

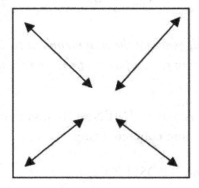

A picture of external points working on or coming in on the centre. This action/energy not only focuses or limits the expansion of Fire; it causes another development at right angles.

A

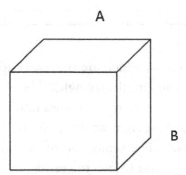

B

Where A is the original square and B is the new polarity. Here we have the final fixing of matter – the Earth Element – the creation of depth – the solid form. This is the state we normally call our three-dimensional world. The Air factor, position, is not usually recognised, but as a Wicce you must learn to see and work with the Air/intrinsic factor.

The first Element – AIR – which is symbolised as the circle, the point, boundless infinity, the sky, the skin, the basic AXIOM can be simply expressed as a single sphere, whose colour is BRILLIANCE (all colours).

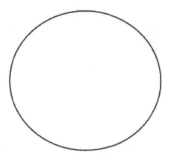

The next level – FIRE – shows this PRIME MOBILE splitting into polarities. This is the creation of past and future, father and mother, white and black, right and left and is expressed as two spheres or points that hang balanced from the Air Element.

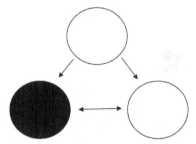

These two levels or actions make up the infinite unbounded levels – what is traditionally called the GODHEAD?

The third level – WATER – shows two 'sets' of polarities that interact to form a centre.

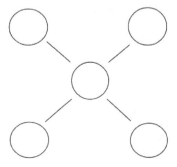

The top 'set' of polarities represents the polarities of the fire level acting most strongly on each other.

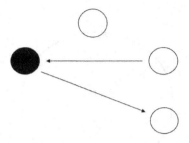

The white shines out using the black as a background on which to be seen, to create blue, the colour of the first of these spheres. The YANG right side acts first, upon the YIN left side, then it reacts to the right side and so on. On the left side black is the dominating force and it allows little of the background light to shine through, so the colour of this sphere is white, overcome strongly by black to create red.

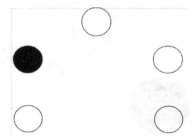

These two colors are the basic colours of polarity. They are the colours seen at either end of a bar magnet when you look at it clairvoyantly (through a flow of your spirit). The lower polarity is the focusing of those forces. These two spheres are the 'complements' of the upper polarity.

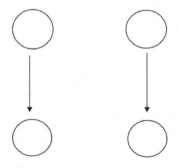

If you look at the colours diagonally you see that red needs yellow to become orange, and blue needs yellow to become green, so the colour of the central sphere is yellow. The five factors of the Water Element are now set out in an order of internal balance that acts in on its centre.

Red, blue, green and orange combine their forces to cause yellow (which is always expanding) to manifest physically as its complementary balance, which we've seen as the two colours indigo and violet.

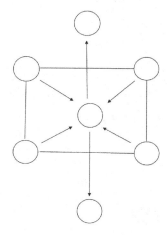

These two spheres are the EARTH image; the way the Earth Element 'translates' the image of the polarity of the Godhead and physical manifestation – energy and matter.

The Water Circle of force acts upon the yellow (which is white penetrating black most strongly) and forces it to act in on itself. This pressure becomes so great that yellow creates the Earth level from its need to create or find its complement. It is so strong that it takes two colours to compliment it. Yellow is Yang to the other colours. Indigo and violet are Yin to the other colours, but Yin and Yang to themselves are next to each other in the created scale of colour. So, they provide the necessary solidity to fix the Akasha of yellow. Violet is the most external, so it is the lower sphere, the basic four Elements/states of matter. Indigo is their reflected energies. Reflected not only from Earth, but the Sun as well. They are expressed as two Spheres one on top of the other. The lower divided into the four Elements. The upper sphere is divided into the two types of actions or energies.

If we put together these four different levels, we get an extended or exploded picture of the interaction of the Four Elements. The glyph is a map that shows the stages of development everything passes through to become real Brilliance

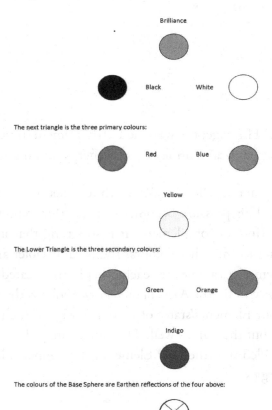

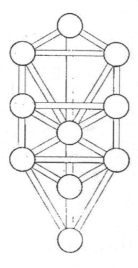

Most of the work you will be doing as a Wicce and entering the Wiccan Priesthood involves the two Earth spheres; and as indigo and violet are too close for our Spirit to be able to penetrate, we 'symbolise' these two spheres further when we work with them.

The Earth sphere is four different Earth colors.
The Sphere of the Moon is purple with blue marbling.

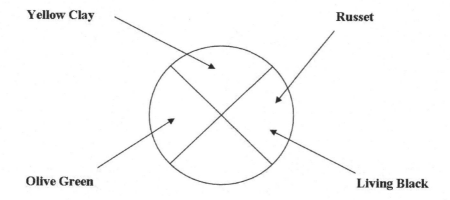

These colours are easier to work yet keep a pure picture of the Sphere's action. The Tree is also a picture of the Solar System. If you stand on the Earth, look towards the Sun, you see first the Moon, then Venus, then Mercury, then the Sun.

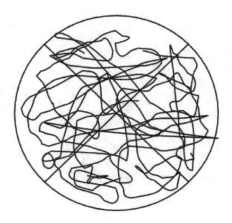

Mercury and Venus are planets below the Sun. Mars is the next planet on the way out from the Sun, and then comes Jupiter.

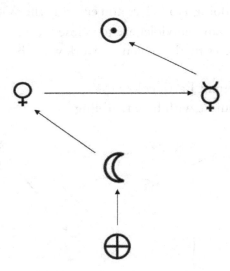

Saturn is the next sphere and it is the abyss between the Godhead, the Transcendental Planets and the incarnate MAN, the Earth. So, this Sphere is called in Traditional Magick "THE HOLLOW OR UNFILLED ROOM". It is only filled when we die and return from the Earth to the Shadow realms of Death or as the Buddhists call it, the BARDO or in between state.

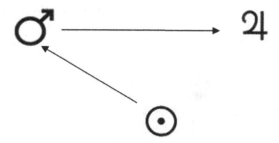

Because it is not possible to call on the influence of the Earth (Indigo) in the same way as we can the other Planets (because we are on Earth), we use Saturn (violet), its closest colour relative, to symbolise the Base Sphere, as the Earth Element in the body (the spleen) is ruled by Saturn. This is so we can use the different planet. To see where the sequence of the days came from we need to look at the circle of metals that we used before.

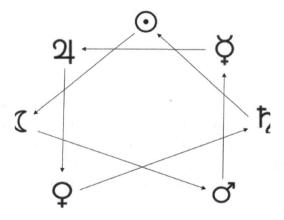

Start from the Sun; miss one to go to the Moon and so on to make a seven-pointed star, which is The Star of Aset/Isis.

Sunday	Sun
Monday	Moon
Tuesday	Mars
Wednesday	Mercury
Thursday	Jupiter
Friday	Venus
Saturday	Saturn

Get yourself another card, this time 15 units x 12 units and paint this diagram.

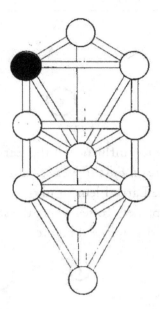

Use the correct colours and in the centre of each sphere put the symbol of the appropriate planet. Put a wash of pale blue for the Air level, pale red for the Fire, pale green for Water, pale yellow for Earth. Do the connecting paths in silver. This glyph is one of the most important tools that you will be using – but it IS a tool – NOT the product! You must keep it covered in black cloth (silk is best) and put a Seal (as on your Book of Shadows) on the front and back. It is the basis of the ancient Isian system from Saiss now adopted and called the KABBALAH. The map itself is called the TREE OF LIFE, the more you work with it, the more suitable/obvious the name becomes.

The Kabbalah was formulated in a different age when mankind was at a different level or stage in her development that she is now. We needed a God/dess to give us purpose and protection while we grew through our different levels of social systems. The closer we come to everyone seeing his or her own Divinity, the need for the individual to accept responsibility for him/herself grows. This is one of the reasons, the others I've already stated, that we need to change part of the Traditional Path. Traditional Kabbalah puts MERCURY as the bottom of the left-hand pillar in the tree and VENUS as the bottom of the right. This is because the development was the Sun's development (Gods development) not OURS. That way the first Planet seen would be Mercury, then Venus, etc. By changing part of the structure, not arbitrarily, but with purpose, we take back our responsibility. This should not be done lightly, it means consciously choosing to say that there is nothing you have any obligation over. You must choose your responsibilities because of your own values. For a society based upon conscious sharing of meaning you must begin to gain value from inside yourself. Then use your value to give strength to another people's value of themselves. Then they can use their strength to do the same for you.

We must make the next step. Working makes the choice with you as the teacher. Other things and people, including this book and the Tree of Life, are part of the forces that you draw in to yourself. They are mirrors for you to see yourself in.

The Hebrew names of the Four Worlds (the Four Elemental Planes) are **ATZILUTH** – Circle, **BRIAH** – Triangle, **YETZIRAH** – Crescent, and **ASSIAH** – Square. The Hebrew names of the spheres are descriptions of their qualities.

Uranus	KETHER	the Crown	the 1st sphere
Neptune	HOCKMAH	wisdom	the 2nd sphere
Saturn	BINAH	understanding	the 3rd sphere
Jupiter	HESED	mercy	the 4th sphere
Mars	GEBURAH	severity	the 5th sphere
Sun	TIPHERETH	harmony	the 6th sphere
Mercury	HOD	splendor	the 7th sphere
Mars	NETZACH	victory	the 8th sphere
Moon	YESOD	foundation	the 9th sphere
Earth	MALKUTH	kingdom	the 10th sphere

These names have a great deal of power and are designed to be used as talismans or *"Focuses"* of the energies they represent.

"May the energy of the work just done,
Aid in the development of Love and Understanding in all things".

VI
THE LOVERS

VI THE LOVERS – THE GREENMAN & GREENWOMAN

The Mind – The Solar System-Key to the Seven Lords and Ladies

"I will generate the Enlightenment thought,
that I attain success for myself and all others".

Our minds Evolution happened at the same time, following the same Laws as everything else. We are not simply what is held together by the skin and supported by the bones. This is only one layer or level of reality and you have many bodies/minds. Make yourself another Talisman (15 units x 12 units). This time it should be purple with a thin black border (to limit its action) and on it paint this Talisman.

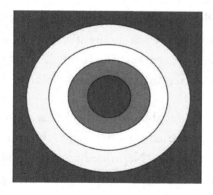

This outer circle is yellow or gold and 1 1/2 units thick (all the bands are the same thickness; the middle is 1 1/2 units in diameter) - the next is silver or green – next is red or copper and then blue or tin. Here the outer gold band represents matter, as we know it. The inner blue 'dot' represents the prime matter – the other two are Fire and Water.

Just as infinity is the 'centre of the universe' it is also the central, common and constant part of the mind. Imagine that you (physical) are standing on the outer rim and your mind reaches inward to the centre. As it gets closer to the centre, its relative movement is less and less, until at the very hub of the wheel it simply revolves on itself. As everybody else is also on the same rim of this wheel you can see that the central level of the mind forms a COLLECTIVE UNCONSCIOUS. The AIR level is without TIME, therefore INFINITE. It is the intrinsic source of the mind, "neither" active, passive nor neutral.

The awareness of this "Godhead" is the unity of infinity, it is totally abstract, it has no boundaries, no 'mirrors', to see that awareness. It is this force of awareness, which is the potential for everything else. Everything that exists is an expression of that awareness trying to 'see' itself. This causes the initial split of the mind into the thinker, Yang action and the thing thought about, Yin reaction the tops of the two pillars of the Tree of Life. This Fire action sets the pattern for the rest of the mind.

Realisation (the making of reality) comes after the thinker thinks, so the right-hand pillar of the Tree of Life is the future. Its action is essentially the 'creation of the future.'

The left-hand pillar is the reaction, so its motivation is always in the past. This fixing of the past is necessary for any sort of constant time stream, which in turn is essential for action and growth. This is a balance of EQUAL internal forces. It is self-aware, but it is not aware of finite interactions. Uranus, Neptune and Pluto are the spheres that act as the focusing forces of these energies in our solar system. Pluto or Hera (as is Her true Magickal name), is the Universal Mother, the thing thought about, the pregnant parent, we are all in the womb of the orbit of this planet; She encompasses and nurtures everything inside. Hera keeps her dark self, her shadow, hidden just as this planet hides Persephone, her shadow planet.

Neptune is the father of all else. He is the only Sphere that sometimes penetrates Hera's orbit. The number of Moons expresses the complexity of rhythms or types of energy tides on the planet. They focus forces like a lens does. Neptune has two Moons, which represent the created polarities, the active FIRE Element. They focus and express the prime polarity, so they present extreme pictures. One Moon has an almost perfectly circular orbit while the other has the most erratic orbit of all the Moons in our solar system.

Uranus is the perfect whole, the focusing force of the prime mobile. It is inside the orbits of Mother and Father because it uses them to focus, give birth to the logos (the macrocosmic counterpart of the Zen). Uranus has five large Moons, which symbolise the Five Elements of the perfected person. Around these five are a hundred tiny Moons, which give diversity to its expression. Its rings are there because, like Saturn, it is the meeting point between two levels of manifestation.

This new order of the Elements is the order they use to generate themselves in a living organism. Later we will use this shape to 'bring through' or 'clean out' energy.

This image is 'picked up' and translated/transmuted by Saturn. We've already seen how this planet is the 'meeting point' of the forces of the Sun acting out and the forces of the Universe acting in. It has ten Moons, the same as the Sun. it sees the Solar System, including the Godhead, the Three Transcendental Planets. The rings of Saturn are a 'TRANSLATION' of the pattern that Uranus reflects in from infinity. Saturn (violet) is half the polarity of the Sun (yellow), the sphere that carries the internal picture expressed by the solar system. Traditional Kabbalah puts this sphere 'above the abyss' as part of the Godhead and unreachable because it is here to the Abyss that the focusing force of the individual returns to during Death. You can work with Saturn as the base Sphere as it is the same pattern that is reflected in your own Moon and changed by our different positions – Saturn's colour is 'next to' the Earth's (indigo and violet). The Earth expresses this PENTAGRAM pattern internally, as us. The Earth is incarnate life; Saturn is the life between incarnations. They are the two sides of the life cycle, the base Sphere of the KABBALA that straddles the Abyss and is the vibration/colour of Saturn; it can help you greatly in the fixing of the base Sphere (the physical body).

The Air and Fire levels of your mind; the Godhead, generate a perfected pattern, but it is only through the re-active forces of Water and creation of diversity, that time becomes more recognisable to us and this pattern can be realised. The Jupiter level of the mind is the generator of the Water forces while Saturn is the focusing power of the Water forces (the individual mind). Jupiter is the life force of the zodiac contracting into us. From our angle this is experienced as an expansive force. Make a white card 4x5 units and put a black line in the middle.

This is the opposite card we used to express the scale of darkness. Use your Prism as before and you will see two groups of colour (forces) being born from the marriage of black and white. This time BLUE is the first colour to appear (Jupiter's colour is blue), below is violet, then black, the next colour is red, then yellow. As you go further away with the Prism, blue intensifies into violet and yellow darkens to orange. Then hints of new colours appear, a darker red, a redder violet, and a lighter yellow.

If the two dark colours meet, you might expect their combined darkness to create a greater depth of dark. The opposite happens! The colour that is created is a soft and gently radiating shade that is called peach-blossom.

Red and violet vanish when peach-blossom is fully revealed. On one side of it there is left a light yellow and a darker yellow and on the other side, dark blue and sea blue. These five new colours are the colours of the scale of light – the YANG forces, the 'expanded organism' of the universe. To be able to appreciate this balance of forces you should make another Talisman. A circular piece of white paper, 15 units in diameter, divided into 12 sections with the 7 colours of darkness and the 5 colours of light arranged in a colour wheel. This is the zodiac's arrangement of colours. Aries, the 'strongest individual' house is peach-blossom.

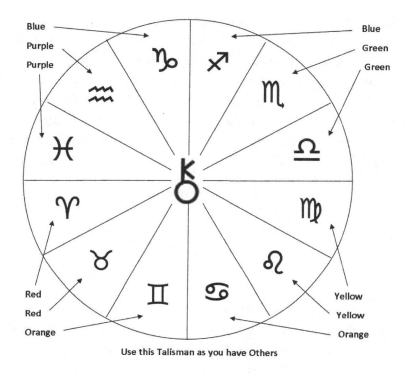

Use this Talisman as you have Others

This level of your mind is the director of your progression through your KARMA. The balance of the forces of this Sphere is different with each passing moment. Your 'birth-chart' can show you the type of energy that was available at your time of birth. These are the energies you used to bring through your Zen and they determine your manner of 'linking' to other things later in life.

Jupiter is a YANG expression of the Universal Mother, it is if you like, the way the feminine forces affect the future.

Mars is a YIN expression of the Universal Father; it is the 'memory' of all his actions and the way the Yang forces shape the past. It has two Moons that are small, irregular rocks that move very quickly around the Planet. To understand the importance of this, you should remember how much of your own biological rhythms are affected by our single large Moon traveling relatively slowly around our planet.

Your subjective realisation of time and space are greatly influenced by the Moons cycles. The Martian memory is a vastly different thing to what we call memory under normal circumstances. It encompasses chemical memory, racial memory and most important to the Wicce, it is the memory of past incarnations. This makes it the record of our Karmic debt, whereas Jupiter is the mechanism of our Karmic future. Red is the 'expression' the LOGOS has made since it became separated from the primal black and white. The life force of white is a memory through the darkness. Because of this it is the sum of your experiences in the past. This coupled with the Jupiter force (Jupiter is much further away – more the force of the cosmos) wakes up the parts of the mind 'above' the Sun. This is the first level of perception (remembered, rather than actual). The two polarities of red and blue make possible the creation of yellow by their creation of a 'field' of energy. BLUE draws Ether in; RED radiates the logos towards the Sun.

This 'field' or 'focus' of energy is the birth of the logos as an independent Sphere of awareness. This is the 'real' form of the Sun's radiations. A constant stream of tiny sparks of life. What we see as light is the physical translation of the Sun's breath. The Sun is the, yet, unborn child, the unity of infinity transmuted by the actions, first of black and white, then the more defining pressure of red and blue. It is NIRVANA – the peace at the centre. The colour yellow is the strongest Yang colour; it will 'even' shine out over a background of white. The metal gold is the most colourful and most noble of the metals. Just as the Sun level of our mind is the true source of the mind's colours and the artistic genius that is the Wicce inside us all.

The pressure of this yellow colour spreads the Sun's seeds of life out to the Sphere of Mercury. The orange colour is the sleeping force of Mars animated by the logos (yellow). It is the function of the intellect of the mind. The Messenger of the Gods, it is small and moves quickly around the Sun. **Mercury** is the first matter the Logos feels as it comes out of the Sun. It is like our Moon in that it tends to keep the same face to the Sun. The first perception of heat is felt on the Sun-side of the Planet and the first finite perception of cold is felt on the other. This action of comparison of separate states characterises this Sphere of the mind. Think of the enormously different and seemingly unrelated experiences of first the Sun and then Mercury, the greatest and the smallest. This causes the realisation of objects, and the intellects capacity of comparison.

The next Sphere of experience is **Venus**. This Planets gaseous atmosphere seems to be sensitive to every movement in the Solar System, it is a constantly moving, swirling pattern of 200 mile per hour winds, yet there are no Moons to pull it about to create tides and the Planets rotation is very slow, 243 days. The movements are the combination of the subtler tides of the other planets and Venus' own heat. Because of its atmospheric make-up Venus absorbs heat but let's none radiate away. Green is the central receptive colour that combines the forces of black and white in the scale of light. This shows the absorbing, sensitive character of this level of the mind, which causes it to see relationships and flows, rather than individual objects. It is the emotions – your adjustment between the Logos working 'down' and physical sensation, the Zen working 'up' as experience. It's the mind experience of CYCLES, arranged as the progression of the Four Elements. Plants use this Venus characteristic of reception and retention, through the colour green in their digestive process. The plants' cycles/rhythms are created externally by the progression of night and day. The realisation of Venus gives the Logos the need to finally 'incarnate' in a physical body.

The Earth is a Sphere of physical experience. The prime reason the Logos has for manifesting is SELF KNOWLEDGE. This is the first of the basic four drives. This is expressed as one "art" or another (an art is something that you become involved in on more than one level), for the expression to grow. This generates the desire for sexual or social contact and this generates the need to survive. Seen from the point of view of the Zen (the microcosm) survival is the first drive, which causes the sexual/social need to communicate. This communication brings about the need for self-esteem and this causes the development of self-knowledge. The drives are the result of the physical body trying to understand or realise (make real) the Earth translation of the Air Element's unity. To do this, it uses the reflective properties of the Moon.

The drives are the result of the physical body trying to understand or realise (make real) the Earth translation of the Air Element's unity. To do this, it uses the reflective properties of the Moon. The Moon reflects and polarises light from the Sun. Non-polarized light (Yang) vibrates in every direction around the axis, but polarised light (Yin) vibrates in one direction only, so that shadows in the daytime have light in them and Shadows at night are empty of light.

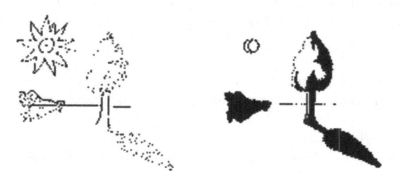

Using polarisation and reflection the four basic drives are built into reflected and multi-directional roles or meta-identities. We've already talked about how complex and limiting these roles can be. They can "cut-off" our access to the basic drives and this creates a sort of "PRESSURE" between the two. This pressure is what modern psychiatry calls a neurosis. As the Moon grows from its new phase, the greatest concentration of energy for the point where Yin meets Yang is pulled from the feet up, until at the Full Moon it has reached the top of the head. This past of the cycle works on the body's fluids, gently expanding the entire body, especially the internal organs and the muscles. This movement can be used to cleanse these parts of the body and their corresponding drives, which are survival and sexuality. These drives are the two most physical of the drives because they are Yin, the first or Yang part of the cycle draws energy through them. This idea of physical organs corresponding to mental organs is simply an extension of the Laws of Nature and the Laws of Thoth we have already worked with – AS ABOVE, SO BELOW.

The Full Moon reflects a "PERFECT BALANCE" to the Sun. The LOGOS, the non-polarised golden light, is given a new individual identity in the polarised silver light of the Moon. This is the final reception of the image of the perfected man that Uranus originally draws in from the Universe. The effect of this talisman should cause the second half of the four drives and Etheric (non-physical) body to be cleaned, as the physical body contracts, the Etheric expands due to the force of the Waning Moon. The energy descends the body during this part of the cycle until it reaches the feet at the New Moon. At this stage of the cycle, both the Moon and the Sun are exerting a pull in the same direction. There is no inflow of polarised, confining light and the freed energy rises then falls in the same day as the Moon begins to re-assert itself. The cycle starts again and regulates the tides and rhythms of our bodies. This is a natural cleaning action, but you can USE this extra flow of energy to re-set the balance of your OWN cycles.

It is important that you see that while each level or Sphere seems to be a separate entity, it is in fact a part of the whole system. Both the mind that is you the individual, and the mind that is the solar system, are made up of layers that exert different pressures in different directions upon each other.

The efficiency of the system depends upon how fluid this communication between the levels is and this depends upon their relative purity or cleanness of colour, the clarity of their language.

The vibration or auric colour each person has reflected the state of his or her body and mind. Look in the mirror at the coloured parts of your eyes, they should be evenly coloured, with an even close texture, this shows a healthy body. Most of us have a lot to clean out of the body; because of the food we've fed it all our lives. Fasting is one of the best cleansers and if you combine fasting with the Moon's cycle and conscious work on the Four Elements, you will find that you can use the "New Moon" (usually used to do this cleansing and integrating) to bring through a "HIGHER LEVEL" of energies.

Start the fast at the New Moon and for the first week eat only natural, healthy food; no meat, white sugar, salt or preservatives of any kind. Try to keep a balance of vegetables, fruit, grains, and beans. Have two cups of red clover tea per day, this is a blood purifier and the blood are the physical manifestation of the Zen. You should also have honey and ghee (clarified butter). These two foods, plus milk that has been milked in the morning and unprocessed, are used in Tantric Yoga to generate a slight Yang EDGE to the body's energies, which makes them easier to use. During this first week, you should try to become conscious of energy slowly rising with each day until it is at the navel at the end of the week. Each night you should 'WORK' your Earth Card and during the week always have some yellow article of clothing on. Try to concentrate on seeing patterns, being set up to receive Zen (fire), or being left in the wake of Zen. The Earth's patterns are the ashes left after the action of Fire and the contraction of Water/cooling.

The next week is Water. You can have the same food, but it should be liquefied – NO solids. You should work the Water Card during this week and feel the energy rising through the body to the top of the head. Concentrate on the forces behind the patterns, the colours and complexities that characterise this Element. At the Full Moon you should do a midnight ritual (preferably skyclad and in the open) to "EVOKE THE ENERGIES OF THE MOON". This is a simple Deosil flow (as you've done before), done inside a salt water Magick Circle (if you are working with Initiates get them to do the 'LBRP' of the Magick Circle). The males should use the Chant "I.O.EVO.HE. BLESSED BE" (the perfect description of the action of the universe) and as they breathe in (between this chant) the females should intone or 'call' AUSET (the Goddess of the Moon.) when it is felt that the flow is strong enough the right hand should be held up towards the Moon visualise/imagine a link growing from your fingertips to touch the Moon. Your left hand should be pointing towards the centre of the Magick Circle. Then you should imagine/visualise the force of the Full Moon pulling you through to the FIRE level of your fast. This creates a 'BRIDGE' between the physical body and the Sun through the positive use of the Moon's influence.

The Fire week of the fast should consist of clear vegetable soups and fruit juices. If you have access to Bach Flower Remedies (recipe is in my first book "Complete Teachings of Wicca

– Book One – The Seeker") they can greatly assist the action of these weeks' penetrative energies. The actual remedies used should be worked out for each individual case. Work your Fire Card and concentrate on the energy coming down to the navel. Try to see or feel POLARITY, the COMPLIMENTARY action of your Etheric Body.

The final Air week consists of pure water (try not to use treated city water), the best water comes from the high mountain streams, spring water or rainwater. You can also have honey during this week, but here again you should be careful of its purity.

You should be working with your AIR card and the energy should gently fall back to the Mother Earth and your feet. Your concentration should be upon the intrinsic Air factors of your personality, the real basic picture you have of yourself. On the day of the new Moon, when both the Sun and Moon are at the zenith together, you should do the opposite ritual to the midnight one, except that the flow is still in the same direction and the right hand is still used to project the link. In this ritual the females intone "I.O.EVO.HE BLESSED BE", whilst the males call down Ra (pronounced ray) the God of the Sun.

You are not starting to increase the strength of your links, so at this stage, you need something to protect your Aura until you develop the necessary skill to protect yourself Magickally. What you need is a FILTER that will make sure you don't push out too much of your own energies. We are using these to build a new increased communication between the Earth and Water levels of your mind. As your links increase their strength, they sometimes pull in too much, so you need a little control here as well. The SEAL that you used for your Book of Shadows can be incorporated into a single silver disk, which is worked, by you during your Wiccan work, that is if you do not have a Pentagram or Pentacle necklace. The best place is between the breasts, or on the wrist, with the Pentagram facing out

"May the energy of the work just done,
Aid in the development of Love and Understanding in all things".

VII
THE CHARIOT

VII The Chariot — Sekhmet the Charioteer

The Language of the Tree of Knowledge-Key to the Mysteries

"I will generate the Enlightenment thought,
that I attain success for all others and myself".

Life is extremely complex and ultimately simple, all at once. In fact, it can be looked at from any number of angles and always it appears different and yet the same. This sort of paradox appears within the TREE OF LIFE as well.

We can express the Tree in many ways – the 4 Elements, the 7 levels, the 3 Pillars and so on. Each of these divisions of the whole reflected in them. For instance, we could say there are 4 Elements and each of these Elements expresses the Tree, or we could say that each of the Spheres has a Tree internally and look at the Yin and Yang aspects of it. We can even draw the Tree in different ways.

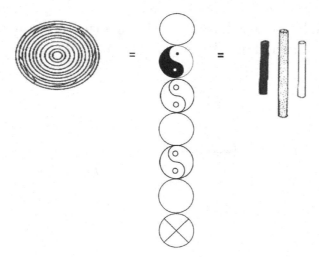

These diagrams are valid, and you should throw these ideas around yourself. The Tree and the Elements are wonderful ideas to build Chants and Talisman's from. The more you express or use the Tree, the more you will find that it fits EVERY situation. At the same time the concept of the Elements can be used to express the same situation, or you could use YIN/YANG, or the Chinese Five Elements (the four internal Elements plus WOOD, the Element of life) of the Indian TRI-DOSHA, the three types of universal energies; the cooling energy, the heating energy and the mediating energy. Each of these ideas shades into the other. Each had their own advantages and disadvantages as a system. They are all correct. It is simply that each person uses their balance of Elements to create links to the rest and this means we see the same pattern as apparently unrelated things.

There are some patterns that have been used by Wicces for Millennia and they have "GIVEN POWER" to these patterns by their use. The Tree of Life is an easy picture to use. It fits so completely onto the pictures we've looked at. Each Sphere or level can be singled out or worked by simply becoming sensitive to his or her different attributes and using them consciously, instead of having them use you.

The work that you are doing is to prepare your Aura (which we will study in the next chapter) so that the Tree of Life can be built into and out of it and its functions. This means that at first you concentrate on cleansing and becoming sensitive, later you gradually shape and take conscious control of these forces.

Its own 'LANGUAGE' characterises each of these levels, which is in harmony with its inherent nature. If we are to promote communication between these levels, and at the same time ease any tension or pressure that has been built up, then it is important that we recognise their different methods of communication and their languages.

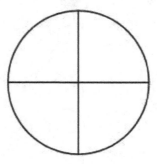

The Earth level is the physical form; its language or the way it uses its energies SHAPE. It is this basic shape that determines the Elemental quality of the energy used. CRYSTALS show this relationship of shape and energy. They are among the most basic forms that can be said to have any sort of life. Almost inanimate, except for the fact that they grow from definite shapes.

In our bodies the basic shape is provided and controlled by the bones, especially the backbone. It is immensely important that you take care of your posture by some form of complete exercise. The two best systems of exercise I know of are TAI CHI – a Chinese system of martial arts that concentrates on softness and the development of awareness and HATHA YOGA – the Yoga of physical postures. Both these systems concentrate on changing the shape of the body to produce different energies and are excellent ways to learn the language of the base sphere. If either one of these arts are developed, they will heal the physical body and satisfy the four basic drives. Go to a good natural therapist and particularly have your back looked at, and any needed adjustment done. A straight back is essential to breathe correct, which is the body's way of gaining Prana; the BREATH OF THE SUN we talked about before. So, practice Pranayama – breath control.

Sit cross-legged, or in the lotus position, right leg on top, which is the smallest circle made with the body and an upright spine, therefore it is the most intense energy focusing shape of the body. Your hands should rest palm up on your knees, with your thumb and index finger touching, this completes a circuit between the two Air acupuncture meridians, the lung and the colon. Keep your back straight and slowly lower your head, by gently rolling first the top vertebra, which relates to Saturn, the next Jupiter, and so on down until you have relaxed the entire neck down to the Sun (the seventh vertebra). Your chin should be resting in the notch between your collarbone and above your breastbone.

The first of the three-part complete breath is the ABDOMINAL BREATH. Place your hands on your abdomen so that your fingertips touch one inch below your navel, breath IN filling the lower part of your lungs – your fingertips will spread apart. This breath generates the two denser Elements Earth and Water.

The next part of the breath is the CHEST. Place your hands on your chest, above the breasts, again so the fingertips just touch. Breathe in filling your chest very deeply – your fingertips will move apart. This breath is the Fire and steam (Water and pressure) breath.

The last third of the breath is UPPER AND SHOULDER BREATHING. Turn your hands palm down, thumbs in to the chest and fingertips touching in front of your chest, breathe in deeply and stretch your arms out and back as far as possible, keep your palms down. This part of the breath deals with the Air and Akashic Elements. Then breathe OUT and bring your hands back to your abdomen and repeat. As you inhale, you should concentrate on the picture of Prana (small sparks of intense light) streaming in through your nostrils to fill your body with the appropriate energy. As you breathe out visualise the nostrils expelling negative thoughts and disease. Use this as a preliminary to ALL your ritual work.

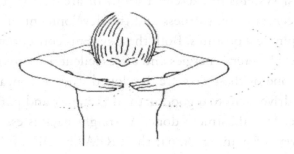

- Crescent *An incomplete circle represents the reception/reflection of the human spirit.*

The next Language as we climb the tree is the LANGUAGE OF THE MOON. It exists because of the twin pulls from the Earth (the four basic drives) and the Sun (the creative drive). The Sun's energy is tempered by its passage through the Spheres of Mercury (intellect) and Venus (emotion), and this polarity also exerts its pressure on the Moon.

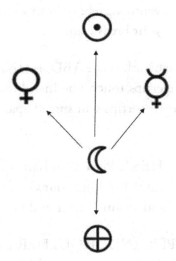

The Moon itself is a picture of constant change, Yin becoming Yang, becoming Yin, etc. the conflict of forces becomes the constant re-balancing and re-assessing of our emotional/intellectual communications between our four basic drives (how we feel and how we act). It is also the energy (Zen) that results from polarisation of light, or the creation of the individual personality. It is the field of energy or AURA that surrounds you because of the interactions between your mind and your body, the physical and non-physical levels of your being.

We can choose to see this as a field of eternal conflict, or a delicate, beautiful cycle that allows each of us the greatest scope of experience. It depends on your USE of these energies. This level exists only because of the apparent conflict, the two sides should be kept in balance, but not in agreement, they are not the same thing and they don't see the same thing, as we saw when we looked at the second law – BE IN ALL THINGS. This level is the most commonly used level of conscious communication, (the Akashic point of the Tree) and this leads to a further externalisation of this apparently unsolvable conflict, to give as our aggressive and competitive social natures. If you control the Moon levels of your body, you can control and satisfy all four basic drives by being able to become both YIN and YANG and able to balance the IN-flow of Auric energies with the OUT-flow of these energies. This is the only way to really prepare to work with both Venus and Mercury together.

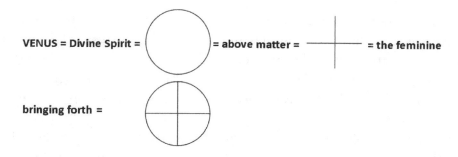

The first Sphere beyond the Veil is Venus. We go in to the source (the Sun) because we need to be able to keep a stable centre before dealing with the vaster forces of Mars and Jupiter.

This Sphere as we have seen, the emotions, our reactions, to experiences that the body has, via the directions of the personality. Its language is the internal awareness of cycles. The most basic cycle that the body/mind goes through is the cycle of day and night.

Because this is an internal cycle (no Akashic point) it is a cycle of the Four Elements. The Dawn is (circle) Yang of Yang, the beginning; midday is (Triangle-Red) Yin of Yang, the strongest penetration of Zen; sunset is (Moon-Silver) Yang of Yin, the cooling part of the cycle; midnight is (Square-Yellow) Yin of Yin, the least strong penetration of Zen (sleep-Blue).

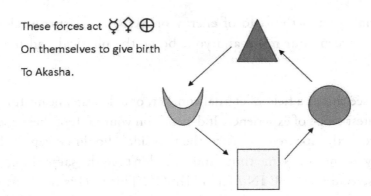

These forces act ☿ ♀ ⊕
On themselves to give birth
To Akasha.

Here, as in all even number cycles, the Zen is contained within itself. You could symbolise this by thinking of the personality (the Moon) between this cycle (Venus) and the physical body (the Earth). Venus is the bottom of the left-hand pillar; it is sensitivity, the moment that has just passed, and possibly the best way to experience Venus as a pure force is through improvising music.

Set up a ritual, to be done on a Friday, which uses the Moon and Sun rituals as its basis, but with one difference. Everyone takes in musical instruments (everyone can at least play sticks and hum), which you use, after calling the forces of the Planet down (do the ritual when the planet is in the sky, also we are not actually calling down the Planet, but I prefer the term Planetary Consciousness). The Goddess of Venus is always the Goddess of sensuality and physical love.

You can have special instruments for each quarter. Air is wind instruments, didgeridoo, flute, etc. Fire is sticks or any sharp clicking sound like clapping. Water can be jingling bells or even some instrument that uses the sound of running water (improvising something). Earth is usually seen as the drone or dull drumming.

Mercury: ☿ *the three basic symbols, the half circle (human spirit, receptive) over the circle (divine spirit) and the cross (matter).*

After Venus has felt the experiences of the body and personality, the Mercurial forces of the intellect can assess and analyse, then use these experiences. Mercury is the warrior, the way we affect our surroundings (or the way we use the Moon). It is the recognition of life (wood) as an Element, so it is a cycle of Five Elements. The odd numbers (triangle) are Yang, action, they stimulate and the even numbers (crescent) are Yin, reaction, they sedate. To stimulate any Element, do the appropriate breath an ODD number of times. Mercury is the MESSENGER OF THE GODS; it carries the image of the perfect person, which is reflected in by Uranus. It uses the force of recognition, (which is the function of the intellect) to create the idea of self and not self, which develops into the recognition of life and the creation of the Wood Element.

Individuality is the original idea that the Logos (Sun) realises because of its experience of Mercury. This direction of forces plus the idea of feeling and sensitivity (Venus) causes the Logos to incarnate (be born) to experience more fully. Make this Mandala using the Chinese names of the elements, start with fire and go around through Earth then Air etc.

ELEMENT	YIN	YANG
FIRE	HEART	SMALL INTESTINES
EARTH	SPLEEN	STOMACH
AIR	LUNG	COLON
WATER	KIDNEY	BLADDER
WOOD	LIVER	GALL BLADDER

Fire creates ashes that form the soil and nourishment of the Earth, which contains metal that the Indigenous Aborigines of Australia use to symbolise Air.

The Air is a vehicle for the cyclic movement of Water (clouds), or if you like, the metal gold (the Aboriginal symbol for this Element) forms a cup to contain the Water. The Water allows growth patterns, the Wood Elements to evolve. These can then burn to complete the cycle.

The intellect can only ever give you an understanding of something within its Sphere of experience. Once you see your place in the flow and patterns of life that surround and support you, you can try to learn first from experience, and then apply your intellect to understand that experience. This doesn't mean you can't use the intellect to direct the path of your experience, just remember that your experience is expanding and the intellect by itself is unable to formulate new meanings, experience must do that. You should call down the force of this Planet on a Wednesday. The God of this Sphere is Mercury, or to give him his Egyptian title TEHUTI THOTH, or HERMES TRISMEGISTUS (his Greek title), the three times wise, the wise Magician. Use this ritual to work your Mandala of the Chinese five Elements and use the power this engenders in you to 'link' Thoth, for he is your teacher and Mentor.

The Sun  Circle (divine Spirit) with a dot (seed of the Zen).

The Language of the Sun level is the central LANGUAGE OF THE MIND, it is the creative force, the desire to exist and be aware of that existence. The Solar Plexus and the Zen are 'HARMONIC VIBRATIONS' to the Sun. Our musical scale is based upon the same numbers as the colour scale, there are seven notes that occur in a repeating pattern, the same pattern appears in the planets, metals, even the days of the week. This rhythm is the most natural for wave formation; an ocean wave has a ratio of 1:7.

If the ratio goes beyond this, the wave 'crests' to create white foam. Both A and B represent the same point in a re-occurring pattern, so they have HARMONIC values.

This rhythm is expressed again in the Moon's cycle, where each part is seen from the Earth's four basic drives to become (4x7) a cycle of 28 days (calendrical month). The Sun level of the mind is the source of artistic vision, the greatest strength of the centre Zen and the perfect marriage of intellect and emotion. It is the central Sphere on the TREE OF LIFE, the point of perfect harmony between the finite planets below the Sun and the infinite forces above. It is what is called HEAVEN AND NIRVANA. Its level of action is mid-way between concentrative meditation – cutting off external awareness and concentrating on internal cycles (you can use

Venus to help this) and "MINDFULNESS", which concentrates on being equally aware of everything (for this you use Mercury).

Concentrative meditation is what you practice when you do ritual in a Magick Circle where the environment is consciously set up to minimise distraction and reflect the internal structures of your mind/body/spirit system. This environment directs your involvement inward, but how far or how deep the process goes is governed by your involvement or how much of yourself you put into the ritual.

Mindfulness is the opposite direction of thought and is practiced by you when you do ritual in the country (the best way to call down the planets, this ritual is in "Complete Teachings of Wicca Book Two-The Wicce"). Your mind is drawn out by the presence of Nature and the ritual (the Magick Circle) directs or "emphasises" the appropriate energy in the appropriate Watchtower, so your selective sensitivity is increased. The rituals you have done so far have all been evocations, bringing energy or Elemental qualities OUT from inside you.

Both these systems are ways to break the habit of looking at things automatically. Write down all the sounds you hear in the next 30 seconds you might write music playing, cars passing, people talking, tap running BUT THESE ARE NOT SOUNDS, they are the source of sounds. As soon as you hear something you analyse it and once you identify it, you either 'GO OUT TO IT', listen more intently (concentration), or 'TURN IT OFF' which is the same mechanism as mindfulness.

The mid-point is neither of these and yet has flavours of both – you must develop the ability to do both at once. When you do, you will experience a change in what Magickal Ritual truly means to you. In this state of mind, you are most aware of internal tides and flows and are most likely to be able to sensitise yourself to the invoked "FIELD OF FORCE".

The LANGUAGE OF THE SUN is not only becoming sensitive to the cycles of 7 and the rhythms this cycle causes and supports, it is a certain quality of awareness as well.

Mars ♂ *The circle of divine spirit and the cross of matter converted to the penetrating spear.*

The Martian level of the mind is the mid-level of the left-hand pillar; its language reflects both Venus and the Supernals. Its character is still the memory of cycles, but they are not only the finite cycles of Venus. Mars is the memory of your past and present lives and it balances this with its 'MEMORY' of the Supernals, the mid-point of these two flows produce force. Symbolically this is the 'BALANCE' of forces expressed by the changing seasons and the growth cycles of plant and animal worlds. It expresses the energy balance between you (the Sun total of ALL your experiences, since the beginning of your existence) and evolving forces of your environment. In a way it is a judgment of your harmony with Nature. The symbol of Mars shows the cross of matter, which is contained by the spirit on the Earth level, changed to force, and rising from the spirit towards the macrocosm. To be stable this force must be internally balanced.

On a Tuesday, the day of Mars, use your Elemental cards to form a large circle, large enough to sit in. Place a mirror outside the circle in the West (Water) Quarter, the past. Use your Four Etheric Candles.

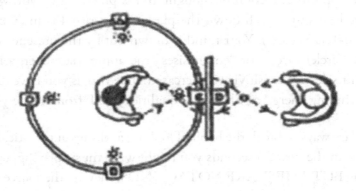

Once you have done a flow with each Tattwa card, you sit facing the mirror and devote 5 to 10 minutes getting your breathing correct and deepening your relaxation. If the planet Mars is in the sky at the time, you can call down its force as you did with the other planets (you NEVER call down a Planet that is not above the horizon). The God associated with this Sphere is PAN, – the God of Spring Forces which is the start of the Seasonal Cycle. Then, when you can, 'FEEL THE FORCE OF MARS, you set up a flow with your image in the mirror, through the candle in front of you, see illustration above.

Watch the flow of energy with your mind's eye, build a picture of the flow in your imagination, and then work the image as you did your cards. Note any change in the facial features of the image. After some practice (3 months usually), you will find that some faces 'APPEAR' more often than others. These faces are memories of your past lives and can sometimes give you valuable insight into what your 'MAGICKAL WORK' will consist of in this life (or where you get your energies for growth). The Mars force is traditionally seen as a wholly masculine force, but its feminine, more creative and less destructive manner (world governments are run by males and look at the mess).

Jupiter: ♃ *the receptive crescent with the cross of matter behind and below it.*

The Jupiter level of the mind reflects Mercury, the 'MIDDLE' of the right-hand pillar on the Tree. It develops the concept of the Wood Element into the colours of the scale of darkness and unites these with the scale of light, to form the Natural colour-wheel that expresses the forces of the zodiac (the macrocosm). It focuses these forces via its 12 moons, just as the Earth focuses the force of the Sun via our one Moon. Your birth chart, which you should do, or get done, will enable you to see just how strongly each of the Spheres (planets) were positioned at the time of your birth. This initial availability and balance of energy is what determines the way you 'link' to whatever you use as reality later in life. None of these forces are positive or negative in themselves. They depend on your use of them, that is, whether you flow with, or against, your own Nature.

The 'CONTROL' of Jupiter is the control of the harmony between your birth chart and how you do use energy. If you flow with your Jupiter Nature and use it, you will be able to develop in a relaxed and pleasurable way. If you constantly call upon your strengths to challenge or limit your development, then this backward movement develops pockets of pressure in the overall pattern of your flow. This pressure forces the Zen (awareness) out of the corresponding areas in our mind and body. The mechanism we use to bring attention to the problem is pain. If you learn to control pain on a physical level, you learn the basic mechanism for EVERY level, including the so-called "KARMIC" pain. Obviously, some pains are harder to control than others; the easiest one to start with is fatigue.

Set up a Thursday (Jupiter) ritual using your cards and a Magick Circle, as you did for Mars. Go through the usual procedure to call down the force of Jupiter. You can call on the Goddess Diana (usually associated with the Moon but used here as a "balance" to the forces of Pan). Then stand in the centre facing East – the beginning. Your feet should be slightly apart, rotate your hips so that your back becomes straight.

Put your chin in and lift your head as if you had taken hold of the hair at the crown and pulled up.

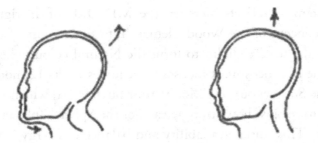

Raise your hands as if you were doing the top breath. This time you raise your hands up with the in breath and gently push them out (palm up) with the out breath.

Close your eyes and imagine that you have a small bowl of clear mountain water in each hand, the right-hand bowl is pure gold and the left is pure silver. As your arms become tired the muscles contract to create pressure which restricts the flow of blood and Chi. The more heavily polluted your muscles are, the quicker the tension builds. Usually at this point, your mind starts to pull back and screen off the pain. Let the pressure build, to create warmth (a buildup of blood and Chi), concentrate on feeling the buildup as warmth rather than pressure.

At the point where you feel it is about to become pain, use the warmth to relax your arm. Feel the warmth and pain flow out through your fingertips (the action of Chi is controlled by your breathing, as you breathe in the part of your body that is the focus of your Zen brings in Chi and vice versa). This exercise should be done for 21 deep full breathes, for the first couple of weeks, but you should then extend the time to 36 deep breaths, Then 64, then 84 and lastly to 108, (THE NUMBER OF THE MOON and the MAGICK CIRCLE). This level of control is what the Chinese art of Tai Chi calls PERFECTION. This is the Yin (defense) side of learning to use the Jupiter force of realising your potential. The other side of healing (growth) that is Yang (outgoing) action.

Lower your hands to your sides get your breathing very deep and rhythmical. Go over your body relaxing any part that feels tension or pain. Imagine a gentle tide of energy that flows like water, down the left-hand side of your head, then down the left-hand side of your body and the left leg, as you breathe out (breathe out for a count of 6 heart beats). Then, as you hold your breath out for a count of 3, the energy passes from the sole of the left foot to the sole of the right foot.

As you breathe in (for a count of 6) the energy rises up your right side. This flow is not confined to the surface of your body, it travels independently of your physical shape, and it is Psychic rather than Physical. As it reaches the top of your head imagine the energy building to a peak. Hold both the flow and your breath for a count of 3. Then allow the flow to fall with your out breath down the front of your body (hold for 3), then as you breathe in, bring the flow up your back. As you breathe out this time, let the energy fall all over your skin, down to your feet. Hold for 3 again. Then bring it up, (with your breath) the inside of your legs. Visualise the energy penetrating your mid-way between the genitals and the anus, then rising up through the centre of your body, to burst through the top of your head in a glorious shower of silver and blue sparks (Jupiter). As you hold for 3, visualise the colour changing to a wonderfully warm red (Mars) and this slowly becoming a golden yellow (the Sun). This golden rain falls like an egg-shaped umbrella over the whole body.

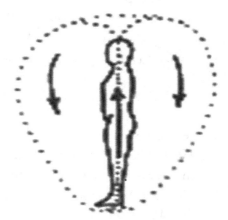

Vibrate/intone the mantra AUM for 5 - 10 minutes until you can feel where the weakest part of your body/mind is, and then concentrate the flow of energy on, around, and then through that area. The Jupiter level of your mind is not only the language of the Zodiac, it is also the ability to flow with 'THE WAY' of Nature. This Sphere is called "THE SPHERE OF THE SHINING ONES/MASTERS", because realisation of this level of yourself enables you to control your own destiny.

The cross of matter on top and in front of the receptive crescent.

Jupiter seeks to bring in and focus the forces of the Zodiac (the macrocosm) and Saturn focuses the forces of matter (the microcosm). To the Romans, Saturnus was a God of agriculture and social order. He is identified with Chronos the Greek God of time who was originally a Harvest God. The Egyptians called this planet Seb, the God of Earth and time. The rings of Saturn represent the "ring-pass-not" or the limit of solar influence. The planets inside the orbit of Saturn correspond to personal characteristics while the three outside of Saturn's orbit (above the Abyss) are impersonal characteristics, the Supernals. This level of the mind is the fixing of patterns, the ability to concentrate, or make realistic concrete plans.

We have seen how Saturn can be used to symbolise both the Earth level, which is the bottom of the Tree (one limitation) and on the other hand it can be used to symbolise the Abyss between the colours (crescent and square) and black and white (triangle). The Abyss contains the empty (potential) Sphere, which on the Tree represents man 'BEFORE THE FALL'. When you die the Zen retreats from Earth through the Moon, Venus, Mercury, the Sun, Mars, Jupiter, and finally rests in Saturn (the Abyss). This is traditionally seen as evil, because it has been the END OF LIFE. We need to sort through what we have learnt during our life and use this after the death period. Its perceived form (how you experience it while you are there) is decided during that previous life. It is true that to a lot of people this means hell fire and punishment, but it doesn't have to, as that is a Judaic and Christian concept not a Wiccan One! You can spend this rest period between incarnations in any or as many heavens as you like.

You are making the choice now.

Once the Logos/Zen has fixed the lessons and they have been assimilated by the Three Transcendental Planets, they stimulate the desire for incarnation again, so that there is further development and evolution. For two days before the Saturn ritual (on Thursday) you should eat very little (not a complete fast). To help build the necessary energy you refrain from any sexual expression for three days (from Wednesday). If you can do it, a speech fast of three or five hours before the ritual is great.

This ritual is a concentrative meditation, so you do it in the MAGICK CIRCLE. It requires a large amount of energy to be finely directed so you need the strength of your Coven, if you have one. If you are working with Initiates, they will invoke and banish the Temple for you. Choose someone to be the 'Principal Ritualist or Man in Black' (PR or MiB) or 'guide' (an Initiate could do this). This person will be 'acting' the part of the planet God Saturn. He should wear a prism hung on a chain as a medallion. If you remember how we have used the prism you will see why it is the "WEAPON OF THE ABYSS".

The PR selects four Principal Wardens (PW), 2 males and 2 females, who make sure the Magick Circle is set up correctly, the Candles are lit, and Incense is burning (use Sandalwood). The PW play the parts of the Four Elements or Watchtowers. Airs Warden should wear a blue cloak and take into the Circle a blue bowl containing warming herbal oil such as Eucalyptus, Lavender or Tiger Balm. South's Warden; cloak is red, and a red triangular dish should be made to carry the oil in. West Warden has a green cloak and the container is a Chalice. North's Warden wears a cloak of yellow and the container is a cube.

The PW's and the PR must visualise (imagine) that everything they say and do and everything that they hear and see is characteristic of the part that they are playing. They must see everything through new (Wicce) eyes that means being conscious of the part they are playing constantly, through the whole ritual. This is difficult but valuable training and each of the work group should, at various times, work each of the Quarters for a ritual. You should extend your regular Moon rituals to include healing (if you do the healing flow on a Sunday the colour of the fountain is gold all along) and the use of Principals. If it is possible, each person should have a shower (hot then cold) before the ritual.

The Principals enter the Circle first. Each goes in and acknowledges each of the Watchtowers and the Altar of the Mysteries, then stands in their appropriate place, facing the centre of the circle. Remember ALWAYS go Deosil in our Magick Circle. The rest of the Coven enters in the normal ritual manner. Then the generation Chant is started and kept up until the PR is ready to begin. The PR is the last to enter and she/he takes in a copy of the ritual, a watch, and goes to the centre of the Magick Circle. As each person enters, Air Warden anoints his or her forehead with a circle, using her right-hand index finger, which has been dipped in Consecrated Oil.

Fire Warden anoints the right wrist with her middle finger, in the form of a triangle with the point facing in to the body. Water Warden anoints the left wrist with a crescent, the points of which point out to the fingers, using the third finger. Earth Warden anoints each ankle with a square, using the little finger. The PR anoints the Wardens as they come in.

The whole Coven then calls down Saturn, using one of the Gods already talked about, or Anubis, the God of the Abyss, The Guide at the doors of death.

When the PR feels the flow is strong enough and there is enough room, he asks everybody to lie down with their feet towards the centre. The PR then says:

"Focus on your breathing and make it very deep and rhythmical. Take your time, the breath should be easy and make no sound as it passes through your nostrils. Relax, breathe gently in and feel the Vital Force that we have evoked here in this Magick Circle enter your body and fill it with strength, and your mind with calm and tranquility. As you breathe out feel the tension and discomfort flow out through the five points that were anointed. Take your time and relax. Breathe very deeply and rhythmically. You can move, but very slowly as you won't have to often.

Listen to the sound of my voice as you become more relaxed, you will find that the way you hear me will change. At first my voice will become easier to concentrate upon. It is pleasant to lie there feeling your strength and listening to my voice. Then slowly as we progress you will begin to hear what I say not as words but as a series of pictures.

You will find this a little strange but not at all frightening. Concentrate on your breathing, feel it becoming even more relaxed. Your body feels heavier than it did before. It is slowly sinking to a pleasant, soft, dark cloud. Your mind feels lighter than before. You are very alert and fully conscious, yet your body is more and more relaxed. The more relaxed your body is, the lighter and freer your mind feels.

In a short while you are going on a journey, this journey will take place entirely within yourself. But it will cover great distances and you will feel as though you have passed through many types of time. In a short while you will visualise or create with your imagination a door in front of you. You will go up to this door and reach out your hand and feel the doorknob. You will notice how cold and hard it is.

It will turn easily in your hand and the door will swing open, you will walk through and find on the other side a winding staircase cut into living rock that seems to go down through a spiraling tunnel. You cannot see how far. You will feel a gentle pull, a desire to descend to the star. As you go down you will notice that you can see quite clearly although there is no light. You will wonder about this as you go deeper and deeper down the staircase. Far ahead deep down below, you will see a faint light.

When you finally reach it and you will see that it is the end of the tunnel and it comes out into a gigantic cavern. So vast is this cavern that you cannot see the top of the other side.

The sand that you stand upon will seem to glow with a faint luminosity. On the shore you see a boat with a sail. You will go and get into the boat and then head out into the water. The shore will disappear behind you; you will drift for some unimaginable time here on this ocean. The water is black, the deepest black you have ever seen. You will feel warm and safe even though you are in this strange place. You will find that it is amazingly pleasant to be there unmoving. Relax, watch yourself, and see how every part of you is relaxed totally. Deep down in the water miles down in the water you can sense something moving. Slowly it comes closer, growing larger and larger. You can feel it being drawn to you. It comes closer to the surface, which will be starting to become disturbed; waves will begin to appear, as you wait.

You will feel only curiosity about what is coming. No fear. There is never anything to fear in this cavern beneath the Earth. At last the thing will break the surface. It will be gigantic, blacker than the water. But when you move into the blackness. Which you will find easy to do, you will see that there are thousands of lights, all different shades and sizes, ranging from hot red glows to hard points of brilliant blue or white light. You will be attracted and drawn to just one of these lights. As you move towards it you will feel strands of energy that come from the centre of the light and reach out to you and caress you and make you feel wonderful. The strands of light will weave a cocoon around you. You will feel yourself becoming stronger very shortly now; you are going to take this trip.

You will have ten minutes of normal clock time. But this will be long enough to experience every part in minute detail and then I will talk you back again."

PR allows for the appropriate time to elapse and she says:

"You are shortly going to return, but you will be able to return to this experience and gain strength from its time by yourself. You will return from the depths of the Earth, you will feel yourself getting stronger, deserving more and more to live and move and laugh and love. You will feel yourself rising through solid rock to return again to this Magick Circle and this field of energy we have evoked by our sharing. You will feel your mind enter and fill your body and your body will feel more and more alive and vital. You will remember the experience you have had, and you will remember having had it before. You will then, when you are ready, get up and thank the Principal Ritualist then each of the Wardens and leave the Magick Circle".

After everyone else has left the PR thanks the Wardens and leaves as well. Don't forget to write the results of this and your other planetary rituals in your Record Book. The language of Saturn is the force of EVOLUTION, the desire to experience, to be born the Prism that causes the colours. The ritual can be a rebirth, but you must remember that ritual is an art and you, not the PR are the artist and you have to develop, work your art. You can see that each of the levels of your mind has its own way of seeing what it considers to be real. A lot of what we see as conflict is simply a change of viewpoint.

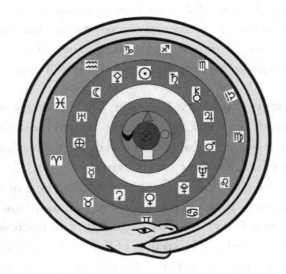

This Mandala/Talisman is a pictorial representation of their apparent differences. The centre is the Earth sphere, the structure of crystals and the perfect person, next is the Moon's sphere of interacting YIN and Yang, the Shining One of the day and the Shining One of the night. Next is the Venus sphere, the progression of the day cycle and the Four Elements, then Mercury, with its abstract ideas of the generative functions, then the Sun and its planets. After that the Seasonal cycle of Mars, plus the reflection or symbols of the Three Transcendental Planets, then the thirteen colours of the Jupiterian Zodiac. Around that is a black snake eating its own tail (Arborous) with 365 stars in it, which represent the ABYSS. The whole Mandala is an island on the sea of the YIN forces in the day of the YANG forces. The whole thing or the implied idea is the Air factor.

The only part that is constant, always at the top is FIRE. This is the Element that allows you to travel from one level to another. It is the common point in all the Magickal Languages. Simply stated it is your involvement, the animated form – the Zen (soul-fire).

You must become very familiar with the TREE OF LIFE. Take 11 pages in your black book and on each consecutive page, evoke each of the appropriate Spheres. Use their names, colours, planetary symbol and anything and everything else you can find out about that Sphere. Do each Sphere on the appropriate day and "BIND" (contain the action of) each Talisman you produce, by putting an edge of the planets colour all the way around the page.

"May the energy of the work just done,
Aid in the development of Love and Understanding in all things".

VIII
STRENGTH AND
ADJUSTMENT

No. VIII Strength & Adjustment
The Goddess Pele

The Aura and the Astral-Key to Freedom of Space

"I will generate the Enlightenment thought,
that I attain success for all others and myself".

In the previous chapters we've looked at a complicated yet simple pattern that seems to be repeated over and over in thousands of different ways. We've seen how MATTER is the result of the interaction of light and dark forces, how the future and the past are dependent upon each other and how the whole thing is a NEVER-ENDING development, each moment new and unique, an experience that can never be repeated. But each thing that happens changes the things that follow. These complex movements are governed by the same BASIC set of patterns. The colours of the rainbow are a picture of the mind and this is a picture of the solar system. Each form of energy that our body/mind system uses generates its own field, just as the Earth's rotation produces MAGNETISM. Each field can produce ENERGY.

Magnetism can be spun (in a generator) to produce ELECTRICITY. This communication between macrocosmic forces (the Earth's rotation) and microcosmic phenomena (generation of electricity) is reflected in our body. The physical and non-physical parts of our body exist in the same place, at the same time. They are the same light and can be mixed to produce other colours. Gold and the physical body have apparently no connection, but we know gold is a harmonic vibration to artistic vision, and vision IS a part of the body's function. All these things are the same thing, just seen from different angles, all using their own webs of experience.

Every time you touch anything, you leave on that thing part of yourself, part of your "LINKS", part of your field of energy or what Wicces term TADLOCKS. The links are the circles within circles, they are the patterns weaved by the WATER FORCES to fix the order of the physical body.

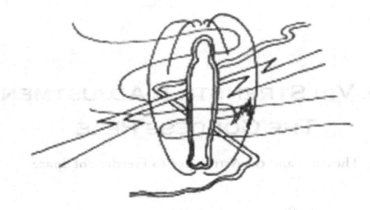

Some links are strong and used by many people. They can even take on independence and a form of their own once they are given sufficient life force. These newly formed forces can then react on the people who made them. This process is called charging or vitalising. It is the basic process behind all forms of Magick, conscious and unconscious. The links are either YANG, thermal, heating and expanding, rising in a column, with Widdershins (anti-clockwise or Moon direction) movements.

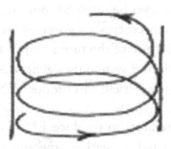

Or they are YIN, electric, cooling, and contracting, falling in spiral, Deosil (clockwise or Sunwise) movements:

These two movements are shaped and given colour to become the multiple types of links we create. Normally, the aura contains, and is contained in webs of thousands of different tides and flows, some are HARMONIOUS, but too often, they are CONFLICTING and CONFUSING directions and qualities. You have been working on sorting out these multiple sets and levels of experience and developing a greater awareness and understanding of the ways we use these links. You have created many new conscious means of experiences. These in turn will increase and develop your sixth sense - the sense of INTUITION (Venus—the First Sphere above the Veil). Sorting out your aura and arranging it so that it can take and give energies in a balanced and understood way develop your intuition.

The flows you have done - Deosil - have been to help you "FIT IN" to the specific forces that were being emphasized by both you and the macrocosm, the time of the ritual and your conscious concentration. The next step is to fit the map or pattern we've found onto and into our mind/body system. The easiest level to move or shape is the field surrounding the body, the aura. We must be careful only to bring into consciousness what already happens, so it must be found rather than placed. The back is the Yang (outside) part of the body (the Yang meridians in acupuncture travel down the back). So, this is the meeting point of your internal forces and the flow outside.

The external flow comes in the right hand and out the left. This means the right shoulder is the body's first point of contact; therefore, it is the blue, the most receptive, the Jupiter Sphere, of (Tarot) Strength/Adjustment. The Sphere of Mercury, the intellect or action, the force of our movement, is the right hip. The Sphere of Neptune, the Father of experience is OUTSIDE the body, above the Abyss on the right-hand side of the head. Our reaction to the energy/experience that has flowed through our body, Venus, the emotions, the Green Sphere is the left hip. Mars, the Sphere that recognises and remembers all your past experiences, the source of your force, the memory of your Death, the Red Sphere, is your left shoulder. Pluto, the Black Sphere, the Mother is to the left of the head.

The Sphere of Uranus, the image of SPIRITUAL PERFECTION, is the Air factor (the potential for all else) or the Wood factor (the real meeting point or point of one-ness). It is situated about 6" above the Crown of the Head.

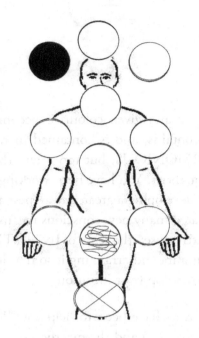

The Sphere of Saturn, the boundary between the Planets of personal experience and the Transcendental Planets is situated in the neck, the boundary between the body and head. This be the Wood Element (the meeting point) or the Air Element (the first personal realisation of force) the first in the body.

The SUN SPHERE, yellow, is in the centre of the body, SOLAR PLEXUS. This sphere be the centre of the Water level, or the Fire in the Middle Pillar.

The MOON SPHERE (the first of the Earth spheres) is the TOP OF THE LEGS. It is the Water Sphere of the Middle Pillar and is concentrated in the region of the genitals.

The EARTH SPHERE is the bottom of the legs closest to the planet Earth. It is concentrated between the ankles.

These spheres also relate to the drainage areas of the lymphatic system. Each area relates to a specific organ, which is a concentration of a planetary force.

The Heart expresses Mars and is in the upper part towards the left. The lymphatic sphere of action is at the nearest major joint, the left shoulder. The joints provide heat and friction so that the lymph can break down toxins and waste that are too much for the blood.

The Liver expresses Jupiter. This organ dominates the right side, so its sphere is at the right shoulder.

The Spleen expresses Saturn; its lymph drainage area is the neck and throat.

The Solar Plexus expresses the Sun; its centre of action is the centre of the body.

The right Kidney provides the pushing power of the body, so the action sphere of **Mercury, who rules the kidney,** is the right hip.

The Colon expresses Venus, on the right side is only the ascending colon, and while on the left is the descending colon, the sigmoid colon and the anus, so that there is a concentration of Venus at the left hip.

The Genitals express the Moon; their lymph drainage area is the groin.
The Feet expresses as well as caress the Earth.

The Supernals are outside the body around the head. The aura that appears to be the densest is of course the physical body. We see it as solid, but, if we were able to enlarge a single atom of this solid body to the size of an average room, we would see that atoms are about as solid as the solar system. The matter contained in the system takes up a very small percentage of the area. The carbon atom, the basis of our life cycle, has a central Sun (nucleus) with 6 electrons or planets in orbit around it, reflecting again the pattern of the spectrum. This pattern defines the limit or range of our perceptions.

Extra Red   **Our Perceptions**   **Ultra Violet**

This is obvious in areas such as sight and hearing (we all know some animals can hear more than humans). Our sense of SOLIDARITY is limited in the same sort of way. When we "TOUCH" something we don't touch matter, we touch the field of force that surrounds thousands of microcosmic solar systems.

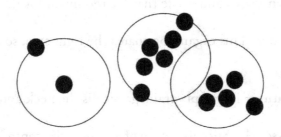

Different types of matter (CHEMICAL ELEMENTS) have different numbers of planets and different complexities of form and shape. They are also at various levels of development, in some, the particles are as well defined as the particles in our Solar System, while some are at a stage of Development that corresponds to the time when the Solar System was a cloud of gases, some are pure colour. Here again, our senses are limited. What I see and the things I touch are usually the same thing, these things vibrate in the same range, or at the same rate as my physical body (my sense organs). Therefore, my hand won't pass through the object, I can feel it, and it reflects light of the spectrum I see, so it is solid to me. If the object vibrated at a different rate, my physical senses wouldn't pick it up. It could slip unnoticed through the atoms of my body; the object wouldn't EXIST to my physical senses. Everything within the level of reality is bound to a framework of light, which has a constant velocity throughout and constitutes its basic vibration. If you change this basis you change levels.

The Etheric or non-physical levels of your body occupy the same space, but vastly different worlds. The interactions of these different worlds produce the AURA or field of force. The so-called physical form is the Moon level of the mind. It is perceived as surfaces and these are not the matter but the 'SURFACE TENSION on each system. To see physically you must focus your eyes on an object, but to see Aurically you must focus on the quality of the FIELD that surrounds it. Because this field is constantly changing, you usually get "flashes". These happen when, or if, the field passes through the same Elemental value as your field is expressing at the time.

If you wear a small bar magnet for a period, it will gradually tune in to your Aura and vice versa.

Just before you go to sleep at night, when your consciousness is on the verge of changing to the Etheric reality, the "DREAMTIME", put the magnet under a white sheet in such a way that you are not sure where it is. Then pass your hands 1/2" to 1" above the sheet until you "FEEL OR SENSE" that you've located the field.

Make sure there is no strong light; the best lights are bee's wax candles or Moonlight. Form a link with your breath and try to "SEE" the poles, one is red (the south-fire) and one is blue (the north-earth). Remember the Auric sight can be a tactile perception or a sound, or smell, or even a taste instead of a visualised picture, depending upon the circumstances.

You can also practice doing a few between your hands, fingers touching then slowly pulling them apart. Watch for the threads between the fingers. The lighting is again important, and the background should be white or some neutral colour. Daily eyewash of Damiana, Eyebright and Golden Seal will help your eyes accommodate the new type of vision and clear your Third Eye. In some ways the densest layer of the body is the Etheric Double. This follows externally the shape of the body and is internally the Solar System (the physical mind).

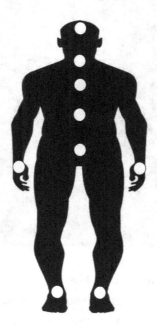

The relative position of these points of light (the planets)

Depends a lot upon the person and the environment.

This is the expression of the unit as an autonomous (atom unit) entity. In some ways, it's the real Earth level, but to "see" it, you must come from the negative (restrictive) Moon level, (our social personalities) to the four basic drives. From this standpoint, you can SEE each entity as its true solar self, a luminous being. The Chi Meridians of acupuncture act as the link between the physical and the Etheric forms. A study of this system of healing will show how the physical and psychological bodies are linked. During the day the "ETHERIC SHEATH" covers and protects the surface of the skin during sleep this surface energy sinks into the body to clean all the internal surfaces. The Etheric form is what "TRAVELS" when you do ritual work such as the end of the last chapter.

The interaction between the physical and Etheric produces not only Chi, but also the first of the Egg-shaped Aura's, the HEALTH Aura. It is almost colourless (perhaps a faint bluish-white). It radiates stiff fibres about 2-3 feet from the body. These fibres are densest in the 2-3 inches closest to the body, which is what gives the Aura its layered appearance.

In good health these fibres stand out stiffly, showing a strong current of Prana energising the body, if the body is in poor health, the fibres droop and become entangled and matted. This is usually the first or easiest of the Aura's to see (an Aura is created wherever two levels interact). Sometimes the Aura's impression is over-shadowed by the more colourful deeper levels. It is easier to feel than see. Get someone (preferably of the opposite sex) to lie on his or her stomach and give the whole back area a very light skin (not muscle) massage. Keep your hands moving lightly over the whole back for 4-5 minutes. This is to get an increased blood supply to the skin surface, which helps to vitalise the health Aura, and at the same time produces a link between you and your subject.

Then you should walk 4 or 5 meters away (well out of the subjects immediate aura) and shake your hands, flick your fingers and rub your wrists together. Do this until your hands become hot and tingly. Then go back to the subject and put your left hand slightly on the back of the subject's neck. Concentrate on matching your partner's breath. Bring your breath down to your abdomen, at the same time visualise a link or flow between your breaths down to your friends. In this way you can help the other person's breathing become deep and rhythmical. Then move your right hand over the back, about 1/4 to 1/2 an inch off the surface of the skin. You will feel areas of increased pressure (strong fibres) and areas of decreased pressure (weak fibres). Where there are weak fibres you can visualise a return of strength, by pulling and combing these fibres out. Remember that you do not have to force this to happen. Relax and breathe properly, then all you need is practice. Once you've gone over the entire back, swap places with your "patient" and feel what it's like from the other side.

The next level of the aura uses the other Auras as a screen to project its impressions upon. Anything you touch or the places you stand in, whatever you meet exerts a pressure, through its links, and particles detached from your health aura remain on or around the spot. The strength of the subsequent link depends upon the amount of Zen (Prana) you vitalise it with. The Prana and the Zen (the in-breath and the out-breath) cause the intensity of the colours in the aura. It is the level you "work" with pain control and visualisation. It looks/feels like a vaporous cloud of electricity. When it's in the body, its colour, independent of the Elemental colour it gains because of its action, is peach blossom, as it moves away it becomes a faint rose, then finally loses even this colour a few inches from the body. This means that any colour it shows is the result of its Elemental action at the time. It is the action of your Prana that works on the other person's health aura. It can appear as incredibly tiny and bright sparks (especially when you are healing) or it can look like a heat haze, a sort of colourless vibration.

The Pranic aura is sometimes drawn off by other people, and vice versa without either party giving conscious consent. If your aura remains open to outside influence your own "CURRENT OF LIFE" can be disturbed. Whenever you meet someone who's aura is clouded, your own auric vitality suffers. On the other hand, you gain auric strength from healthy people and environments. This is the mechanism behind the "contact highs" you may have experienced. In your position, you can't afford to have too much of the work you are doing on your aura disturbed. The "SEAL" that you made will stop most of this, but you should be able to protect yourself under any circumstances. The aim of true Magick is to develop your own abilities. We use tools to gain strength, but then we develop our OWN strengths, once they are awakened.

If you find yourself in a situation where you feel your vital energy is being **"VAMPED"** (drawn off), you put your feet together and clasp your hands just below your navel and concentrate on deep rhythmic breathing. This closes the circuits of energy in your body. If a stronger effect is needed, you deepen your breathing and your relaxation (take your time) visualise your aura around you and feel the link between you and the source (sometimes after a lot of practice, or if the link is particularly strong, you can trace a link back to its source). Then imagine your aura gaining a more definite edge, at first it is soft, and the link passes easily through it; then as the edge becomes hardened, the flow gets gradually shut off, the aura forms a diamond hard edge and becomes perfectly egg-shaped as it contracts, the link is cut off completely. Sometimes you may have to go through this procedure many times. You can further strengthen it by visualising a bright shaft of steel hard light that shines from the Seal and literally cuts the link. Use the method that uses only the necessary energy.

When you're dealing with the aura, always remember that it is not entirely physical and our 'NORMAL' senses are. So, if you want to see the aura you have to either modify your existing sight, your physical eyes (which is obviously too dangerous to do) or modify the light the aura gives off (remember we don't see objects, only the light they reflect). This you can do to a certain extent by using screens designed to cut out normal light. Or you can develop or re-develop auric sensitivity. I say re-develop because you will find yourself remembering to have this sensitivity as a very young child.

There are four main auric "EYES", or points of perception. Two of which you have been exercising by doing "FLOWS" during ritual. These first two "eyes" are in the centre of the palms of your hands. The right-hand eye is FIRE-action, projection, and the left-hand eye is WATER-reaction, absorption. These two are opened first because they do the giving and taking of energy. Later you will be doing work on the Sacral Chakra, the EARTH-pattern forming and fixing eye. The last of these eyes is the famous THIRD EYE, in the centre of the forehead; it is the AIR-form perceiving eye. These two will be first dealt with a little before Initiation and fully opened after Initiation because their action is disturbing to the formation of the Tree. It is very difficult to do both things at the same time, because sensitivity without control results in pain. It is true that you can and will gain some degree of auric perception, but it will be proportionate to the amount of auric control you have. It GROWS it doesn't just happen!

The colours of the aura are the result of the "INTERNAL" flow of force that radiates from the Astral Centre (the Sun) and is reflected by the Etheric Double and the physical form. These colours can tell you all what is happening in the other person, mentally, physically and even spiritually. The full aura appears to be a luminous cloud (I'm using physical terms to describe a non-physical entity, so please take that into account when reading this). It is a play of constantly shifting colours; certain colours are predominant in different people. These are directly EVOKED by the person's state of being. To strengthen and exercise this type of auric Sight, you can set up a flow of polarities with the person you did the healing work on. It is a good idea to get to work on and with each person in your Coven. It's easier with a person of an opposite polarity, so do it FIRST with a person of the opposite sex. It is important at this stage that you don't concentrate too much on the meaning of the colours; don't try to get too deep into the other person. If you relax, a gradual understanding of the meaning will develop with the unfolding of your intuition. Patience and perseverance are essential, as it takes years to develop and refine auric perception to its full potential.

This ritual is very similar to the mirror flow, except it is done on a Sunday, because the Sun is harmony and sharing. You go through the normal procedure of calling down the Sun, and then you sit facing each other, Inside a Circle of Four Etheric Candles. In the centre of your Magick Circle you burn some Frankincense and Myrrh (this acts in the same way as the screens talked about earlier). The flow should go out of your right hand as you breathe out, through the Frankincense and Myrrh, and the left hand of your partner as she/he breathes in.

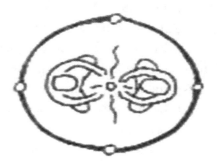

You "work" on the other person just as you work your cards. Then you "PULL BACK" to yourself but maintain the link and OBSERVE. Again, I stress the need to do this in a relaxed and FRIENDLY way. You are trying to see hidden secrets, you are trying to develop a most difficult sort of TRUST, and it requires a great deal of patience and gentleness. When you can discern a pattern of colours (this does not always happen visually; all of your senses are developed aurically) you should then practice evoking (bring out from yourselves) the Four Elements. When you can do that to some degree, practice evoking the YIN and YANG aspects of the Elements. THIS REQUIRES A GREAT DEAL OF PRACTICE. Remember to trust your INTUITION because it is THIS that is your sixth sense. The whole Planet is developing auric communication.

The Magick Circle that we use in the Temple is what is called in acupuncture the reverse KO cycles.

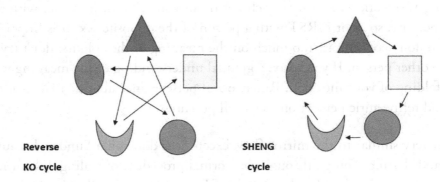

Reverse
KO cycle

SHENG
cycle

This helps to break down our old patterns and ways of dealing with energy. It also helps train your sensitivity by using the most potentially developing energy, learning to flow with and through it to create SPACE for new development. You can also arrange the circle as a five-pointed star (the Pentagram)-the generative SHENG cycle in acupuncture. Fire is to the south expansive pole, the same as before. Air and Water are the receptive north polarity. Earth, the Yin energy is at sunset. The Etheric energy, the life force, is the beginning, the east. Arrange yourself so that there is a group for each Element. The five group can use UPWARD movement and irregular sharp clicking sounds visualising red triangular shapes. The type of voice you use is a sort of chatter. It's best to just let the upward movement pull the sounds out of you, try not to use actual words. When the five is evoked (drawn out from you) it is passed on (use mime etc.) to the earth group. Fire burns and leaves ashes, the Earth.

The earth motion is HORIZONTAL, while the sound of a dull drumming with a constant beat. Visualise yellow squares and the voice is singing. Again, no words, just allow the Earth Element to become your entire energy, you are the ashes left after Fire, and your mass attracts to it an atmosphere-Air. The energy is passed on to the Air group. This movement is ZIGZAG, like a wind through the trees, sighs and joyful weeping. Visualise white or blue circles. Air circulates the moisture from sea to mountain and the flow is passed to the Water group. The movement is DOWNWARD and contracting. Visualise black Watery crescent shapes. Water's voice groans (like in sleep) and yawns. Water nourishes the growth of Wood. The flow is passed to the Wood group. Here the movement is SPIRALED OR EGG-SHAPED. Visualise green or dark blue egg shapes. Woods voice is shouting. Wood burns and the flow is passed back to fire and so on. Find different ways to throw and catch this energy both inside and outside circles.

"May the energy of the work just done,
Aid in the development of Love and Understanding in all things".

IX
The Hermit

IX The Hermit — Merlin & Draco

Building the Basis of the Tree of Knowledge-Key of Time

*"I will generate the Enlightenment thought
that I attain success for all others and myself".*

The aura of an undeveloped person (by that I don't mean inferior) is not polarised, it doesn't "flow" with the rhythms around it. It uses most of its energy defending or attacking something either inside or outside itself. At sometimes, agitated or near psychotic states, it "FLASHES" and vibrates with 10s or even 1000s of links draining and changing it constantly. The work you've been doing will initially "SETTLE DOWN" your aura. Each time you work with it, after that, it will clean out and strengthen itself. If you don't use the energy evoked to heal and develop you, it will build up and begin its own cleansing process. This is sometimes difficult to handle, both for the person and those around, so it is better to avoid the situation by always using what you evoke. Cleaning on the more fluid Etheric level is often easier than on the seemingly fixed physical level, but a combination of both is best. There are many ways to do this that we've already covered, BUT the best way is to use your increased auric Fire - evoke the Fire, if it needs to be softer and receptive - evoke Water. If you have the necessary Elements evoked in your aura, this will change the quality of your links; give you GREATER control over yourself and greater scope of the development of your Art.

We have worked so far on the development of sensitivity and intuition, then protection and some control. Now we need to call on more specific forces to do the next stage in the Alchemising of the aura.

The KABBALISTIC CROSS (which was adopted from the Egyptian Isian Cross Ritual) is one of the most powerful and most effective rituals you'll be using. It's a deeper form of the Cross ritual mentioned previously. This version uses the Hebrew and/or Egyptian language, because that language was designed as a Magickal Weapon. The words not only have a symbolic meaning, but when you INTONE them they have a specific vibration, that invokes a specific Elemental quality. This is simply an extension of the use of colours. Before you use these

"WORDS OF POWER" you prepare the body by relaxation and the deep complete breathing described before. You can further develop the evoking power of your voice by occasionally (once a week) practicing this exercise.

"Inhale a complete breath very slowly but very smoothly take as much time as possible but remain relaxed then retain the breath for a few seconds then expel the air with one GREAT BREATH through your mouth which should be opened as wide as possible.

Always finish the vocal breath with a cleansing breath and inhale a complete breath, hold for a few seconds pucker your lips as if you were about to whistle (don't let the cheeks puff out) push the air out in short, hard puffs until there is absolutely no air left in the lungs, relaxing this breath can be used whenever you do any sort of cleansing especially after treatments (either giving or taking)."

The Isian Cross should take the place of your daily salutations (the cross you've been doing three times a day) and it is done when you first get out of bed.

Do it FIRST on a Sunday morning, just before a Full Moon. Stand with a straight back facing the East. Relax your body. Uncurl your fingers breathe deeply and evenly deepen your relaxation concentrate on your breathing, and visualise tension draining off your fingertips draining into the Earth with each out breath. Each time you breathe in visualise pure, natural living energy, energy from the Earth itself flowing up your legs and into your entire form, vitalising and renewing, pushing any unwanted tension out the fingertips. Relax.

"Visualise the floor or ground beneath you beginning to breathe, ever so slightly but in unison with you Spend some time feeling this harmonious breath then visualise the whole room doing the same thing. Breathing deeply in unison with your breath then the whole house, then the street, the suburb, the city, the country, the whole world, even the entire solar system, the galaxy, everything. The whole UNIVERSE breathing gently and in harmony, then visualise the individual parts of your body each part of each part breathing separately. Yet in unison visualise the centre of your solar plexus the single atom that is at the exact centre. Visualise the particles of that atom. All breathing in unison Look deeper into the core of the atom see the flows of energy that make up each particle Then visualise the "MIND MATTER" that makes up the energy then the potential that forms the mind, and finally dissolve the entire visualisation into the void that contains everything.

Form your right hand into a Wand, and then raise your Wand to your forehead. Visualise a point of white light (Prana) about 6" above the Crown of the Head, use your breath to direct an increasing flow of energy to the spot. See it grow and shine a sphere of brilliant electrical energy. Take a full breath and INTONE/VIBRATE with a deep resonant voice, Vital rather loud, Rich in tone and limber. Rather forceful; the word;

ATOH: (I AM) or in Egyptian AYASHU (eye a Shu). Visualise the ball of light responding to the vibrations of your voice, as if you were exciting and enticing it. Relax and be gentle, true power is not force. Bring your Wand down to your Solar Plexus at the same time visualise pulling a shaft of brilliant silver light down through the top of your head and then down to the feet, just below the ankles. Direct the flow with your Wand. Bring your left hand and place it palm down on your chest just below your Wand. This hand "holds" the Solar Plexus, the centre of the first line of the Cross. Visualise a second sphere of light forming below and between the ankles, then expanding as you "feel" the Prana with your breath Then intone;

MALKUTH: (MAHL KUUT) - (THE KINGDOM) or in Egyptian ATUM; (Ah Toom) which vibrates and vitalises this Sphere, then take your Wand to the left shoulder and visualise a third ball of light forming a small bright spark. You vitalise (evoke) this Sphere with the words;

VE GEBURAH: (VAY GOO VORAAH) - (THE POWER) or in Egyptian EM THOTH; Take your Wand, which draws a second shaft of silver light through the body from that shoulder across to the right shoulder. Visualise a fourth ball of light, that grows as the others did and intone;

VE GEDULAH: (VAY GOO DULAAH) - (AND THE GLORY) or in Egyptian EM AUSET (em-aw-set); Then bring both hands up together in the middle of the chest in the prayer position, feeling the balance of the forces evoked, the God ATOH; the man MALKUTH, the destructive force VE GEBURAH; and the constructive force VE GEDULAH. Visualise the Solar Plexus sending a spark of peach blossom coloured Prana to the midpoint between your palms. Visualise the spark growing right through your hands. Through your chest to cover the whole body, as it touches the four other spheres, its colour changes to gold and this gold goes out to fill the entire aura, then intone;

LE OLAM: — AMEN (LAY OLAHM AMEN) (FOREVER, SO IT IS) or in Egyptian EM TET A AB; Set up the same healing flows as you used in the Jupiter ritual.

Slowly let yourself "come back", you should never end these rituals abruptly; the end should be a gentle "merging of levels". Be sure to write down in your diary what you experience from this ritual. Practice it and perfect it. The work up to now will have taken about 6 months. If you started in the AUTUMN, it should now be SPRING. Your Aura has undergone three separate stages of development

A) **Underdeveloped**   B) **Polarised—given direction and selective Sensitivities.**

The first stage of re-arrangement—the Cross; the Four Spheres are;

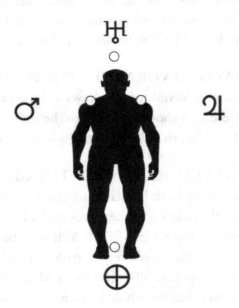

You now need to set up a test of your progress so that you don't waste your time and energy getting too far ahead of yourself. Magickal/auric strength must grow, it's not just a matter of understanding, it's also doing the necessary amount of development exercises and the amount needed differs from person to person. You set up a Tuesday Ritual (Mars is the Sphere of Judgment - not MORAL judgment, but judgment or assessment of a situation - because it is the storehouse of experience, it is the source of meaning we give in things). In this ritual, Four Wicces (the Wardens of the Magick Circle) go into the Temple and decide on a specific Element to Evoke, from themselves, into a flow.

Draws In

Pushes Out

Each of the fingertips has an Elemental quality. To evoke a specified Element, the appropriate finger is held out straight, so the Chi can flow easily. The other fingers are curled to inhibit their flow. At the same time, you concentrate upon the appropriate shape at the point of origin of the breath (where your fingers touched during the breath control exercise). You do the circulation of light in the appropriate Elemental colour.

To make the flow YIN, you concentrate on your in-breath and you do eight breaths, then rest, and repeat. Use your left hand.

To make the flow YANG you concentrate on your out-breath for seven breaths, then rest, and repeat. You use your right hand.

Once the Wardens have established a flow and are satisfied with its quality, they call in the High Priest or High Priestess to test the flow. It doesn't matter what you do to test the flow, but you need to distinguish the Elements and learn whether they are Yin or Yang. This ritual is a test of BOTH sides and each of you should have a go at doing each thing (each of the Quarter's is "different" to work). You know enough ways of sensitising yourself by now, so this ritual should be no real trouble. Once the High Priest/ess has decided what the quality of the flow is, she/he tells her/his decision to the Wardens and they discuss the result. THERE ARE NO RIGHT ANSWERS. This is not only a test it is an exercise. If the answer is different, find out why. Each of us colours what we perceive, because of our own Elemental make up and this ritual helps you work out how to translate your methods of auric sensitivity. Once you are satisfied with your ability to evoke and discern WHAT you've evoked, we began to build the Tree of Life (this will make up a major part of the rest of the Wicces work). The first part of the Tree we work on is the PRESENT, the Middle Pillar.

THURSDAY - JUPITER - EXPANSION

Relax yourself as much as possible use the circulation of Light, tell yourself that you are about to take a new step, you are going to try to consciously shape part of your body, if you succeed you will have taken control of your aura, you will have begun to take hold of an amazingly gentle strength that you will use in the future to make your life as interesting and fulfilling as possible.

Relax yourself even more, feel your body sinking gently down let the power of the Planet fill your aura (pull it through with its colour and its symbol Jupiter). Then let your mind empty. Visualise a black screen falling gently down over everything. If things "shine through" the screen, repeat with another screen Don't force this, take your time, relax Until everything is emptied out and there is nothing but a blank screen.

Let your Zen (your point of concentration) drift lightly up to a point 6" above the Crown of the head you should recognise this point but look at it again, as if it were the first time you had ever seriously decided to actually GO there. Feel this point breathing gently as you breathe, relax. Slowly watch it grow with Prana that your Zen attracts, this part of you is and always has been, outside the confines of the physical body. At the same time, it is the source of everything and as it grows your entire body feels the effect as a faint prickling sensation. Your voice, when you intone the name of power for this Sphere should be gently sensual as you get better with a couple of weeks practice you can say the word with your Zen, in the Sphere itself and not with your physical voice If your mind wanders, use the intonation of the name to call it back. The name means I SHALL BE (forever), it is EH-HE-YE (Pronounced AY-HAY-YAY). This name will "wake up" the Sphere, listen to it and watch it, feel it, smell and taste it for at least five minutes before visualising a shaft of silver Light coming from beneath this Sphere to penetrate the top of the skull through the brain down to the larynx (the voice box) in the throat. Stop and watch your Zen attract a spark of Prana from your breath, then another and another till a second ball of light lights up the neck and lower part of the head

This is DAAT the Sphere of the Abyss it is the empty room, the Prism, the space before and after death in a lot of ways it is the Air principle with the Spirit being the Wood Element the point of interaction with everything. Let yourself intone, vibrate the name YE-HO-VAH ELOHEEM (YA HO VA E LO KHEEM), which means (the Four Elements in all Nature). Intone it a number of times until you can clearly feel a definite awakening of the area and the Sphere is coloured by the name to become violet. Don't fool yourself, take as much time as is needed at least five minutes before you visualise the shaft of light coming from the bottom of this Sphere and penetrating down through the lungs to the Heart and Solar Plexus Sphere just below the sternum or breast-bone. Let your Zen (concentration) attract Prana to form a third ball of warm gently pulsing Light. This is the Fire Sphere of the Tree of Life, the Sun Centre/warmth. The diameter of the Sphere should be the thickness of your body.

You visualise and colour this sphere golden yellow with the name YEHOVAH ELOH VE DAAT, (YA HO VAH E LO VAY DART) Tetragrammaton God of Knowledge. The sensation of this Sphere is warmth gently pervading the body radiating from the centre. Spend another five minutes getting the feel of this sphere before continuing the shaft down to a point midway between the anus and the genitals Let your Zen attract another ball of Prana that becomes the Water Sphere of the Middle Pillar the reproductive powers the direction and use of Auric energy. This becomes a purple Sphere whose surface is "marbled" with blue clouds that direct and control the energies of the sphere as you intone SHADDAI EL CHAI (SHOD DOY EL HOY). Use another good five minutes to allow time for your Zen which you keep centered by your intonations and visualisations, to attract the necessary strength of Prana. Then visualise the shaft going down the inside of the legs to a point midway between and just below the ankles. Let your Zen build the bottom Sphere, the Earth, the kingdom which is divided into Four Quarters (like Quarters of an apple that has been cut twice).

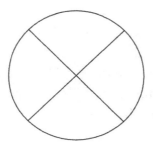

The colours are brought to life by the name ADONAI HA ARETZ (ADOH NAY HA AH RETZ) Lord of the Earth. Allow another five minutes for this sphere to be energized. Then as you breathe very slowly in bring your Zen up the shaft of light (lift it with your breath) as you breathe out imagine it fountaining out the top of KETHER (KETTER) as a brilliant blue shower (blue is another colour of the day) this colour is balanced by red (Mars) to become the finest gold dust that gently falls over the entire body, vibrate the word AUM and circulate the flow of light.

To help create the Middle Pillar, you think of all the things you can attribute to each Sephiroth (the Hebrew name for the spheres) as you vibrate its God name Project a visualised PICTURE of each concept into its appropriate Sphere if you have a tape recorder (or better still, live musicians) find a piece of music for each Sphere (make a tape that will automatically give you the necessary time for each sphere) It will also help if you burn some Frankincense and Myrrh

Once you have a working "feel" for this ritual you can then do it as a Coven. Choose an appropriate day. Arrange yourselves in a circle, feet towards the centre; male, female, male, female etc. the High Priest/ess stands in the middle and begins by taking the Coveners down into a relaxed, hypnotic, trance state.

Then she/he suggests a Deosil flow and intones, WITH the Coven AUM, until there is sufficient energy generated (this is decided by the High Priest/ess) Then she/he intones the God name (the name of power) for KETHER once by her/himself, and then three times with the Coven. The High Priest/ess then builds an image of this Sphere by talking of all she/he can think about the Sephiroth. When you are doing this, it is important to relax and let your intuition paint pictures for you, you are the centre of the flow and your task is to provide a mirror, to reflect back to the group the impressions you receive

The High Priest/ess then verbally sets up a flow from each KETHER to the next ... around the Circle, until there is a "spinning wheel" of KETHER, to form a CONE PYRAMID This process is repeated with each sphere down to MALKUTH (pronounced Mahl Khoot) which is visualised as a ball slowly rotating around the High Priest/esses feet in the centre During this spinning the most complete number of times to say the Mantra—the God name of the Sphere—is 108, the same number as the Moon.

In this way the entire Aura's in the Circle become one and you share your strengths a true act of love.

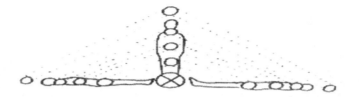

The High Priest/ess then gets the Coven to intone A-U-M (each syllable is one of the three breaths) and suggests that the Cone is spinning faster and faster till at the peak of the power, she very strongly intones A-U-M three times in unison and the wheel is slowed until it stops The High Priest/ess then does a KABBALISTIC CROSS and tells the Coven to slowly awaken and to come around feeling fresh healthy and at peace. You use this ritual as the basis of your weekly meetings until you have all been the Principal Ritualist at least once.

"May the energy of the work just done,
Aid in the development of Love and Understanding in all things".

The High Priestess has gone into the dream to summon A-UaM-Uaa. A variable is one of the three "Mothers" and she goes into it... but... splitting faster will take all of it... the peak of the secret... she goes out by means A-U-M there are two's of main and... the wheel is slowed until it stops. The High Priestess then does "KARMA IS THE CAUSES" to light the Cause to death and...

X
WHEEL OF
FORTUNE

No. X The Wheel of Fortune
The Maiden Goddess Fortuna

Tools & Subjects-Key to Above and Below

"I will generate the Enlightenment thought
So, I attain success for all others and myself".

Magickal strength and understanding is the result of increased communication and awareness between the different levels of the mind. This gives the Wicce a greater freedom of action. Some things that are difficult on this physical level are very easy on the more fluid Etheric levels. Each of us has confined our Self, our level of action, to this physical level by different means, so each of us needs tools that approach our common problem of gaining freedom from an angle that will use the "NATURAL STRENGTHS" our experiences have given us. We need tools that will use and develop the strengths we've already awakened and prepare the mind and the body for new strengths. Some of the most basic Magickal tools have already been incorporated in your Magick Circle work and more will be included in the rest of your common work, but it is helpful to develop the adaptability of our approach. We have, as a group, the ability to cover an immense amount of ground and there is a lot to be learnt. Magick is an immense subject. There are literally thousands of "PATHS" and each has its own merits and uses its own ways to improve the growth of the traveler.

The only way to see the COMMON truth is if each of you selects at least 2 (not too many more) of the many tools available and develops them by applying your basic understanding of the Natural Laws. You select 2 tools that are wide apart in their approaches. One aimed at increasing your health and your chances of survival, such as healing or martial arts. The other aimed at developing your artistic expression, such as music or theatre. This will then develop the two directions of YESOD (The Moon/personality) down to MALKUTH (The Earth/ survival) and up to TIPHARETH (The Sun/art). The "TOOLS" you use as a Wicce are MACHINES, which are designed to enable you to develop and use auric strengths and sensitivities. You will find that the use or control you have over the Tool will be an accurate reflection of the amount of auric and Magickal strength you've developed.

Only when your aura is strong and relaxed can the Tools act effectively. This use and development of individual Tools is equally as important as the rest of the Magick Circle work, and you REALLY TRY to harmonise the two.

Because you have "LINKED AURA'S", the group will begin in some ways, to act as one mind. It will "act out" the conflict between the personal and the social aspects of your personalities. If you learn the art of harmonising without cutting off or denial here, at this stage, you will make it easier to allow each other to develop auric vision later. The Moon level of the mind needs to be a constantly changing level of personal and social (Yin and Yang) priorities. Each has its importance, and each has its time. The two are not separate; they are two sides of the one coin. The group situation is an externalisation of the internal environment of separate levels.

The invasion you fear from the people around you is the same fear you have for the so-called sub (pushed under/out/away) conscious levels of your own mind. You cannot afford to relax and "flow" with your own inner strengths until you learn to TRUST. (Perfect Love and Perfect Trust is what we aspire towards).

To develop auric sensitivity means developing honesty and understanding, together. YESOD is the only level of your mind that feels fear about its mortality. This is because we have used conflict and competitions as the basis of our development ever since the male began to dominate culture. The LEMURIAN and ATLANTIAN cultures were Matriarchal. We have now developed to a stage where we have to recognise within ourselves not only polarity; the opposite sexes, but gender, the fact that each sex contains the other within itself. This is again the harmonising of internal and external relationships and objects, personal and group work.

The thing to remember is that no Tool is an end. The "powers" they seem to generate come from you. All the Tool does is amplify, and call your attention to, different functions that are natural (not supernatural) to your development. As these Tools develop your auric strength you will need to be more careful of your use of it. The annoyance you normally *"vibe out"* at people without really meaning anything, can and does cause real pain when it is done from a Polarised and strengthened Aura. After *"Initiation"* which is the culmination of the work covered in this series of books, you will have a working Tree of Life in your aura, so you need to be able to control your vibe BEFORE you even think about getting it that sort of strength.

The only real power is one you don't have to use. For example, a person who can't fight has no choice but to be passive. But a martial artist can choose to be a pacifist, as he has learnt to yield and flow with the strength of his opponent. This is the attitude you develop towards an apparent opponent, internal or external.

Much of what we see as disease is in fact the processes of the body cleaning out our systems. They all have psychological counterparts and sociological counterparts as well. You can learn to flow with them; all it requires is the decision to TRUST yourself and others.

Power in itself isn't bad, but it can be used in destructive ways. If you look for control, make it self-control, then you won't need to control others and if you use Magick for gain, make sure you pay the society that you've gained from. This payment has to be REAL to you, and worth what you gain. For example, if I make a talisman or do a power Ritual to get a job, then I have to do the job well, otherwise I turn positive Karma – using my full potential in my everyday life – into negative Karma, stopping someone who would have done the job as best they could from getting it. We can see enough of the pattern of Nature's development to be able to see that it is the development of experience that we are involved in. The payment Nature demands is that you use your conscious understanding and awareness to make that development harmonious. The reward for this is pleasure, not momentary pleasure, but the real pleasure of flowing with all the parts of you.

All the tools are focuses that enable channels of communication between levels. We have seen how the Earth/physical level is developed by the other levels. If you look again at the Mandala in the beginning of chapter six, you will see that a small movement on the Water level produces a larger movement on the Earth level. The matter of the Etheric level is not as fixed as the physical levels and the Laws governing it are more fluid. Our point of contact between levels is the Aura, so all your Tools must be linked to it. We use symbolic languages (form, colour, vibration of sounds etc.) to direct where we want to go and what we want to do.

For instance, you could have decided to work your aura with a crystal, to develop clairvoyance. You would use a Natural crystal that you go out and find for yourself (Australian Aboriginal Magicians use quartz) on a Tuesday (clairvoyance is the use of memory, past and future, which is one of the Martian functions). Or you could purchase a crystal that had been shaped and polished into a Sphere. You then do a flow with your crystal (as you did with the cards) and cut off any links that it may have (if you are working with Initiates get one of them to "Banish" it, if you are not working with Initiates you keep cutting the links until you can banish it yourself). Put it into a Sandalwood box that is lined with jet-black silk, felt or velvet. These two *"walls"* stop any outside Aura touching the crystal.

It is kept above shoulder height when not in use (also to protect it). You handle it every day (after doing a Kabbalistic Cross) in a quiet room or Temple/Magick Circle, without strong or direct sunlight (non-polarised Light). A Magick Circle is always the best place. If it is possible, you should set up a personal Shrine in your own home, apart from the Covens Magick Circle Temple. You don't try to do anything just to get to know the *"feel"* of the crystal and let it get to know you. Don't let anyone else (apart from your guide, if you have one) come within the Aura of that crystal whilst you are doing this preparatory work. After 2 continuous weeks, you can start to *"build the crystal into polarity"*. Set the crystal up about 2 to 3 feet away from you in the EAST. You set up a flow with the crystal in three stages.

1. In a sitting position extend your palms toward the crystal sending your energy out through the right hand around the outside of the crystal and into your left hand.

2. Sitting in the same position extending your palms crossing the grid flow of energy sending it out through the right across the flow of energy around the back-left side of the crystal down and around crossing the flow of energy again into the left hand.

3. Sitting in the same position now draw the energy up through the earth up through your spine, out through your Third Eye, out into the top of the crystal and down through it and back into the earth coming back and flowing back into you through your spine.

When you have done this, and then change its Elemental value (as you did in the flow tests in the previous chapter). Get to know how the crystal reacts to each of the different viewpoints of the Elements. Remember the crystal reflects you. This is the same basic procedure used with every Tool, from the I CHING to the TAROT cards, even if you were developing the art of painting Mandala's, you would do the same thing with your brushes to make them Magickal weapons. If you are working within a Circle of Initiates, you can choose a couple of the *"subjects"* that are available. Any person in the Circle who has an expertise can help by sharing their knowledge with the rest. If you work together, you will find that you can cover a lot more ground.

Ideas such as Natural Therapies, growing and caring for crops, pottery, crafts, etc., should be shared and developed. Communal ventures such as food co-ops can help with learning to use the advantages of good strength. This is the same sort of pooling of resources that we practice in our group rituals. You have four great enemies (the negative aspects of your drives).

- The first is **FEAR**. If you approach new experiences from an entirely intellectual or emotional viewpoint, you can only assess them by PAST experiences. The more *"new"* the experience is, the greater will be the gaps in your assessment. These gaps become manifested as uncertainty and that uncertainty becomes FEAR. The only remedy for FEAR is knowledge, which comes from experiencing the Trust that we have been talking about.

- The second enemy is **APPARENT KNOWLEDGE**. This is the "result" of fear. Instead of allowing ourselves to experience fully, we pull back and take second hand knowledge. No matter how well the experience is conveyed you can only really KNOW what you experience. You can see how these two of your enemies work upon each other, till finally the need to experience, becomes greater than the willingness to participate, and it becomes necessary to gain POWER (the third enemy) over outside sources of experiences (other people).

- The **POWER** is false because it does not increase development of you or the person you have POWER over (each side restricts the other). This slowly turns your social environment into a battlefield and this is reflected internally. The constant waging of war drains the vital energy of our systems and we develop all the negative qualities of **OLD AGE**, our fourth enemy.

- If the battle is converted/transmuted into the Natural cycles of change that make up our biological rhythms, AGE becomes development. Once the Geburatic (Mars) levels of your memory are touched, the concept of reincarnation becomes a realised experience and youth and age become repeated cycles.

"May this energy of the work just done
Aid in the development of Love and Understanding in all things and myself".

XI

JUSTICE

No. XI Judgment – The Goddess Amaltheia/Justicia

Ritual and Banishment-Key to Cause and Effect and Prophecy

By this stage I feel that we should change the generation Mantra from a PISCEAN viewpoint of asking permission into an AQUARIAN statement that accepts our own Divinity.

"I generate Love and Understanding for all others and myself".

You already have experience of Ritual, enough to realise that it can be either a wonderful or a meaningless jumble of words and gestures. The deciding factor is how you "set your mind" beforehand. It isn't always easy to do this, but relaxation and emptying can help. Once you have decided to do a Ritual put your heart, soul and body into it. The E-MOTIONS gives the energy for motion. The emotions energise the thoughtform your intellect evokes when you visualise. It's a good idea to "set a pattern" for the beginnings of your Magick Circle work.

- **Ritual wash or shower** - this should be done in silence - only speaking when necessary from now till the end of the Ritual. When you wash the body, try to visualise your whole being becoming clean, healthy and very alive. Start the shower hot but always end it with cool water.

- **As you walk, slowly, from the shower to your Temple** - skyclad, unafraid, a WHOLE person, needing no justification, not judging or being judged - think first of the idea of TOTALLY loving and accepting your SELF - physically and mentally, then extend this LOVE to the others in the Circle - visualise that you are walking in a ball of Light, your aura, that is the colour of the Planet of the Day. Visualise this Light shining *"out"* to the other members.

- **Before you enter the Temple** - stop at the portal entrance of the Circle - and contemplate this room as a NEW WORLD - then do the Egyptian Kabbalistic Cross.

- **Enter, then turn and acknowledge the Air Quarter** - The beginning of your journey. Visualise your body ascending a spiral staircase around three circles of the Temple - as you ascend from Earth to Water (1st circle) the *"Spirit Fire"* (The spark of KETHER) descends from Air to Fire. The 2nd circle takes you up to FIRE and the Spirit Fire (your own DIVINITY) descends to WATER. The 3rd and last circle takes you up to AIR and the Spirit down to EARTH.

- **Sit quietly in front of the AIR (Entrance) facing the centre of the Magick Circle.** The next person sits on the person's left side (Deosil) use the emptying and relaxation. Then visualise (make pictures of) your purpose for being there. Watch your breathing. Say Aum once, then the generation Mantra at least 9 times, 108 is better. You do this before every Ritual.

- When everybody is in place and has time to Relax and gather their energy (remember Ritual is a discipline and a Magick Circle is very sensitive to every movement and sound), the HPs/HP, if there is one, enters last. After the Ritual proper you again set a pattern, this time to bring you back to the everyday world.

- Once finished the Ritual proper, allow 4 or 5 minutes for everything to settle. The motive is fixed (The energy contained) with the Mantra Aum.

"The energy of the work just done,
aid in the development of Love and Understanding in all things and myself".

Then the High Priest/ess declares the Ritual ended.

Step 2) Any entity, real or imaginary (they are just different of the same reality) must be THANKED by the HIGH PRIEST/ESS, then each of the other participants as they do 3 circles around still Deosil visualising the "Spirit Force" and the body changing places again.

Step 3) Stop at the exit and contemplate the outside world – do an Egyptian Kabbalistic Cross and leave.

This routine will become automatic but keep it flexible to suit different occasions. It will prepare your mind/body/Aura so that you receive and retain the maximum benefit from each Ritual.

It is important that each person knows their role and carries it out without faltering, but this takes practice.

The Ritual you are going to do now is called the Lesser Banishing Ritual of the Pentagram, this is a little different from the one in my last book, Complete Teachings of Wicca – Book Two-The Wicce. This will be your introduction to so-called HIGH RITUAL. You visualise the Ritual as a full life cycle. You can create a total environment through this ritual if you use everything there. The colours and set out of your Magick Circle and the acts performed by the group are both symbolic and actual at the same time, they are designed to be understood by all levels including the SUPERNALS – the incense burnt is Frankincense or Myrrh – the sound of the vibrated NAMES OF POWER – in fact the whole thing from the *"Wash"* to your exit is a *"theatrical play"* with symbolic and actual meaning and force, it tells of the Universe cleaning itself of all imbalance.

This Ritual creates a link (if your aura is strong/clear enough to hold it) from your KETHER to the MACROCOSMIC KETHER (the Four *"Gods"* that are called by name). It also links the Fire level (CHOKMAH and BINAH) to the macrocosmic Fire Level – the four SHINING ONES (the actions of the four Watchtowers personified).

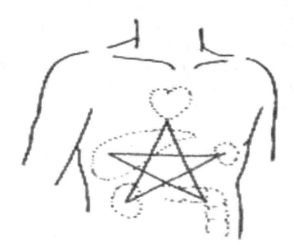

It is done firstly on a WEDNESDAY, the day of MERCURY, the base of the right-hand Pillar of Action. This Ritual will manifest externally the cleansing and generative action of the Five Elements that take place around your Solar Plexus.

The Colon is the Yang AIR organ in the body; its function at this point (*"the Splenic flexure"* of the COLON) is essentially getting rid of waste matter. So, when you evoke (using an Athame or Wand as you do with the Cross) a Banishing Pentagram, you start from the point just above and 30 cm in front of the left hip, and visualise your Aura at this point linking to the *"Splenic Flexure"* with a line of White Force, the perfect energy to use to begin with.

Next you need the Zen, to give your action the energy needed to form its Magickal task, so you raise your Wand, visualise a line of blue flame to the level of the Auric Eye at your forehead and visualise a (red) link from your heart. Then you need to focus that energy, so you extend your line of force down to the right hip. Visualise a black line of force from the right kidney. In Chinese Medicine the right kidney is the MING MEN MO, the "PUSHING POWER" of the body, so it is perfect energy for our task. Next, we need to filter what we have worked so the next energy is the Spleen. You take the Wand to a point in front of the left shoulder and visualise a yellow link from the Spleen. This energy does 2 things. First it takes back out anything that is useful to the body. The Alchemising action has already gone through revitalises some of the Colonic *"waste"* in the same way as recycling through what the plant world does.

The Spleen then encapsulates and rejects what it doesn't want. Finally, we need to externalise the waste, so take the Wand to a point in front of the right shoulder and visualise a green link from the liver. This is the physical Yin Wood organ in Chinese Medicine, it has 3 types of functions, over 200 of which are concerned with cleansing blood, it also secretes bile (which assists digestion) and regulates metabolic processes. Then you take your visualised line of force (an auric link seen as a line of blue flame which connects in sequence these energies) back to the **AIR** point above the left hip to complete the circuit.

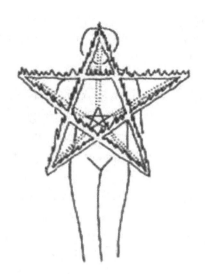 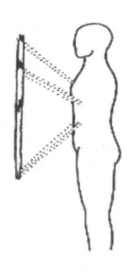

The lines of the Pentagram of blue flames are excited and energised (as they are electric wires receiving a boost of energy) as you vibrate the God - names of the appropriate Watchtower. Each of these names has four letters (the Four Elements) and is pronounced as 3 syllables, (the 3 breaths, a syllable with each).

Element	Quarter	Shining One	Lord	God	Pronunciation
Air	East	Raphael	Euras	YHVH	YE-HO-VAH
Fire	South	Michael	Notas	Adonai	AH-DOH-NAI
Water	West	Gabriel	Zephyrus	AHIH	EH-HE-YE
Earth	North	Auriel	Boreas	AGLA	AH-GE-LAH

When you breathe in at each point make the link between the organ and the Aura in the diagnostic colours (the Yin colours) of the Elements.

- CIRCLE   WHITE
- TRIANGLE   RED
- CRESCENT   BLACK
- SQUARE   YELLOW
- OVOID   GREEN

As you breathe out, use the Prana projected through your Wand to create the connecting lines of blue fire. To help with this visualisation, burn some alcohol; Methylated Spirits has the same affect, because the colour of that flame is the colour needed.

Once the Pentagram has been traced, you bring the Wand back to the Solar Plexus (just below the sternum) and feel the aura of Power around your hand grow stronger, hold the breath in and visualise the contained breath generating a golden glow around your hand, when the strength has built as far as it can, you then push the Wand out through the centre of the Pentagram (breathing out in a strong even flow) and vibrate the name for that Quarter. You then draw a Quarter of your Circle, from the centre of the Pentagram you have just done to where the centre of the next Pentagram will be, in the South. Then bring your Wand back to the Solar Plexus – generate more power (evoke the hands Aura) then do the Pentagram of that Quarter and so on till you have completed the Magick Circle and you have linked the Earth Pentagram to the Air Pentagram. Then you go to the centre of the Magick Circle, face east and assume the pain control stance to form the Earth Cross with your body. This part of the Ritual demands the most complicated form of visualisation so far, the visualisation of the manifestation of the Shining Ones. To bring in the Shining Ones (or anything else) through the Pentagram, visualise an upright Triangle of Red flame and the desired form coming through this portal.

In the East (Air) is the Shining One RAPHAEL. He's seen first as a Pillar of blue flame just outside the Magick Circle (through the Pentagram). This changes to become the Traditional Shining form. The colours of this Shining One are a vibrating yellow with Airy touches of Mauve and blue that gives the whole figure the impression of shot silk. There is a gentle breeze blowing from behind the figure, through the Pentagram to you. This becomes more *"vital"* as you call it by vibrating the name RAPH-A-EL.

The Fire Shining One (in the South – Fire) on your right side is at first a blazing pillar of flame. Then this becomes a Shining form as well. The colours are a bright red, highlighted by touches of vivid green. The name you intone/call is MICHAEL. This name will bring gusts of heat through the Pentagram. (MICH-A-EL).

The Water Shining One (West – Behind you) appears first as a Pillar of silver and green flame. This becomes a Shining form whose colours are blue offset by orange. The name GABRIEL

will bring a flow of watery mist from the figure to you. GAB-RI-EL.

The Earth Shining One (North – your left side) manifests as a golden yellow pillar of flame, which becomes a Shining form whose colours are citrine, olive, russet and a little black. The name is AURIEL. The final visualisation of this ritual is of a flaming golden Pentagram in front of your chest and a shining silver hexagram with triangles interlaced in the corresponding position on the back. The ascending triangle has a faint red hue and the descending triangle has faint blue tones.

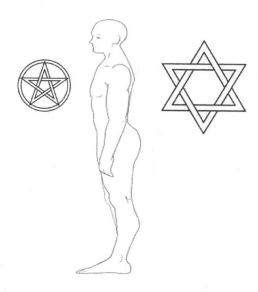

The Banishing Ritual should be done on the third circumference of the Magick Circle, you begin by evoking the Pentagram in the East and vitalising it with the God-name, and then the South, West and North, finally link the Four Pentagrams, by completing the Magick Circle. Then go to the centre, assume the Cross position, facing East, visualise the forming Shining One and say:

"BEFORE ME – RAPHAEL SHINING ONE OF LIGHT

Visualize the Water Shining One forming behind you just outside the Magick Circle and say:

BEHIND ME – GABRIEL HEALING SHINING ONE OF THE WEST.

Visualise the Fire Shining One just outside the Fire Pentagram and say:

ON MY RIGHT HAND – MICHAEL SHINING ONE OF STRENGTH

Visualise the Earth Shining One outside the Earth Pentagram and say:

ON MY LEFT HAND – AURIEL THRONAL SHINING ONE OF THE NORTH.

Visualise the Flaming Pentagram about 3 feet in front of your chest and say:

BEFORE ME FLAME THE PENTAGRAM S OF FIRE

Visualise the shining silver Hexagram behind and say:

BEHIND ME AND ABOVE ME SHINES THE SIX RAYED STAR."

Then go and sit in the East, in the Magick Circle. The next person does the same Ritual, then sits on your left and so on, till everyone has done it and your Magick Circle is complete. Then set up a flow Deosil and vibrate in unison or sing (with correct breath and posture) **"LOVE IS ALL WE NEED, TRUTH IS ALL WE SEEK, LIGHT IS ALL AROUND!"** Visualise the groups aura becoming stronger and more vital as you do this. Keep it up for 5 to 10 minutes. Then slowly stop, allow a short time for everything to settle and leave as described before.

Individual members outside the coven can do the actual BANISHING part. It's a good idea to banish your Bed for instance, because this means that as you sleep your aura will be protected and strengthened. Once you have all done this Ritual 8 to 10 times and are familiar with it, you can change its nature. Each person enters, does 3 circles, then lies with their feet towards the centre of the Circle (size permitting). The PR enters last and goes to the centre of the Magick Circle, goes through relaxation and creates a flow, then ACTS out PHYSICALLY the whole Ritual from the centre (turning to face the appropriate Watchtower) as the rest of the group (goes with her/him) and visualises their energy being with the PR doing the Ritual.

Once again, set up a Chant flow and spin the Circle (as in the Middle Pillar Ritual in Book Two), then leave as normal. When you are all out of the Magick Circle have a general discussion about it and write down (in a coven Book of Shadows) the results. To solidify or set the Banishing you need 2 more steps.

1. Unite the two methods (physical and mental; do them both at once).

2. Make and wear for the rest of your Wiccan Seeker stage 2 stars, one Pentagram of woven gold wire (with the break on the lower left point) to be worn below the sternum on

the front and the other star, a Hexagram of silver wire (with the breaks at the top and bottom) to be hung on a leather strap and worn on the back at the same level. Make your own, or they don't work for you otherwise. Once this Ritual is mastered, which if it's done regularly and in depth, with full attention to visualisation and evocation, will take about 3 months, and then you can extend it into the Agape, "FEAST OF LIFE AND LOVE".

This Ritual can be strengthened by a morning of intense physical action, which should be kept as pleasurable as possible, you should work up a sweat a couple of times that morning. Get into your body and push it a bit, stretch as much as you can. The Ritual should be done outdoors in a beautiful place or Magick Circle, where you are not likely to be disturbed by curious onlookers. You get to know the land by walking very slowly and noticing everything, but very relaxed – do *"flows"* with the ground at different places. You all must agree upon the strongest, most beautiful spot. Try to find where the energy of the land has created a Natural Magick Circle. Ask it, the living force of the land, to show you where the best place is.

The form of this Ritual is basically the same as the Banishing Ritual except in this Ritual you select four Wardens who play the part of the Quarters dressed in robes of appropriate colours and they carry in offerings and Tools of that Quarter. The Air Warden takes in the music (special Magickal instruments such as Didgeridoo's AIR, Drums EARTH, Sticks FIRE, Bells WATER, whatever you can think of, can be made and kept for ritual use). The Fire Warden takes in the Fire and incense (Sandalwood). The Water Warden takes in the drink – pure fruit juices or pure grape wine; the containers are important. The Earth Warden takes in the food. This food is for a feast, but it must be pure energy, i.e. food as on the earth week of a fast.

The High Priest symbolises becomes RA the Bringer of Light and Life. Above the heart paint Sun symbol in gold. Once the PR has evoked the Shining Ones, he then lifts his face to the Sun and reaches with his whole being to the source of life and says:

PR:	All hail Ra – the God of Life.
Coven:	responds Atum Ra (distillation).
M:	All hail Ra Hail Ra – the Centre of Love.
G.	Atum Ra.
M:	All hail Ra – The Resurrected Phoenix.
G.	Atum Ra
M.	All hail Ra – The Source of Light.

G.	Atum Ra.
M.	All hail Ra – The Zen within.
G.	Atum Ra

PR directs a flow towards the Air Warden.

M.	All hail Ra – The centre of Art.
AIR	All Hail Ra. (offering the music)
G.	Atum Ra.

PR turns and directs the flow towards the Fire Warden.

M.	All hail Ra – The Torch of Love.
FIRE	All hail Ra. (offering the incense)
G.	Atum Ra

PR turns and directs the flow towards the Water Warden.

M.	All hail Ra. – THE FLOW OF THOUGHT.
WATER	All Hail Ra. (offering the drink)
G.	Atum Ra.

PR turns and directs the flow towards the Earth Warden.

M.	All Hail Ra. – THE FOOD OF LIFE.
EARTH	All Hail Ra. (offering the food).
G.	Atum Ra.
M.	You are Four Times Blessed.
G.	Ra is Four Times Blessed.
G. & M.	Atum Ra, Atum Ra, Atum Ra.

Coven: The Coveners then call down the Sun in the normal way.

M.	Feast with Me in Love and Peace by the names Atum Amon Ra.

Then the feast and dancing begin. Remember ALWAYS move Deosil even in this Ritual

The next part of your work which is a follow up from our last lesson you will do individually in your own home Temple, or out in the country but not in the group Temple. This is the first stage of building of the right and left Pillars of the Tree of Life, in your aura. It is your past and future, the lessons you've learnt and the ones to come. It is the unique way that you balance these flows that develop your individuality, and this is why it's done alone.

Know this Ritual well before you do it the first time, which will be a Monday, just before a Full Moon (the aura is the Moon's level of action) make a salt Water Magick Circle (use a wet white rope or your Magick Cords soaked in consecrated water if you like) - Banish it – draw a white Pentagram inside with the upper point towards the East – light an Etheric Consecrated Watchtower Candle at each Cardinal point then take out the matches/lighter etc. through the West, Banish the Magick Circle again – Evoke the Shining Ones and ask each for their help – then lie down in the centre on your back, with your head towards the East. (The candles contain the force generated by the shape of the Pentagram so that the Magick Circle remains complete.)

Relax yourself as much as you can use the Emptying technique relax your body again lightly cross your ankles and then cross your wrists just below your navel this closes the circuits of Chi in your body and if you concentrate on rhythmic breathing for 4 to 5 minutes you will increase the working strength of your aura. Get the Magick Circle to breath with you then do a Kabbalistic Cross uncross your legs and hands and resume your first position then do the Middle Pillar (from top to bottom, control always comes from above).

Then visualise the flow of the aura coming up MALKUTH through the Middle Pillar and out in a Silver (The Moon) shower through your whole aura. Slowly move your arms out to form a Cross and visualise (with your breath) a line of red energy from each Sphere out to the right (Yang) hand. They meet and form into a red triangle with the point out on the palm of the hand (the Fire "eye" of the aura). Then visualise blue links from each of the Spheres to the palm of the left hand they form a crescent on the palm, whose "horns" point out from the body. The Water "eye" of the aura."

Visualise the *"pull"* from the two palms spreading your legs apart and splitting the MALKUTH in two.

This new shape (the Pentagram) will cause two new "flows" to form and the energy to be concentrated on the other two of your Four auric *"eyes"*. The *"eyes"* are the Etheric forms "points of contact" or perception the palms of the hands are Fire and Water. The Earth *"eye"* is just below the navel and the Air "eye" is the so-called Third Eye in the forehead These last two are excited by the Pentagram shape.

The flow comes in the two halves of MALKUTH up the inside of the leg and enters the body midway between the genitals and the anus travels up the body till it reaches the forehead (the Pineal Body) and there it splits into three directions. One goes straight up to KETHER and the other two break off to either side. These two flows fall back down through the aura till the action of the auric eye that is 1 inch below the navel pulls the flows back to the central core of energy. The "capsule" to the left side is visualised becoming darker and darker till it becomes black. The "capsule" to the right becomes correspondingly lighter till it becomes white.

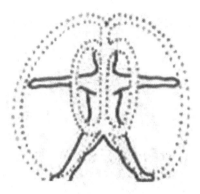

Visualise the TAI-CHI symbol, (Great Wheel) high above you and you can just see it and it is so high it is spinning very slowly at first.

As it descends (its central axis is your Sun Sphere) its spinning becomes faster and faster until the spinning releases the colours of the Six Spheres of the Two Pillars. These then become united with the Black and white capsules the black and white Spheres from outside the body. At the top of their appropriate Pillars the BLUE SPHERE is at the right shoulder The RED is at the left shoulder ORANGE below the BLUE on the right and GREEN below the RED on the left side

The Aura flows Blue as it enters in the bottom of the Triangle in the palm and red as it leaves the top.

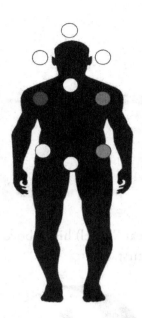

The Flow is Red as it enters the Crescent in the left palm and blue as it leaves the Horns of the Circle.

Slowly bring your hands to your sides and your feet together then take your Zen up to KETHER – vitalise it with the word EH-HEY–YEH - (I shall be forever) spend 4 to 5 minutes feeding this Sphere pure Ether slowly visualise a shaft of silver Light come from KETHER to the white Sphere at the top of the Right-Hand Pillar the Sphere CHOKMAH. The God-name for this Sphere is YEH - GOD IN ALL. Spend the same amount of time 4 to 5 minutes fill it with Light and Strength and all that you know about this level of action … keep your mind centred upon the Sphere (practice) then visualise the silver shaft going across to the black Sphere BINAH visualise and vibrate the power name YEHOVAH ELOHIM Tetragrammaton in all Nature fill this Sphere with all you know of it make its colour the richest, softest black. Then after 4 to 5 minutes take the silver shaft down to DAAT at the throat use the God-name YEHOVAH ELOHIM think of this as the combination of YEH and YEHOVAH ELOHIM – CHOKMAH and BINAH. The next Sphere CHESED is linked by the same silver shaft its God-name is EL – GOD – after the appropriate time take this lightning flash of silver Light across to GEBURAH - vibrate the name GIBELOHIM or almighty God then take the Lightning flash down to TIPHARETH – vibrate YEHOVAH ELOH VEDA-AT which means Tetragrammaton God of Knowledge. The next Sphere is HOD (the right hip) vibrate ELOHIM TSA-VA-OT Lord of Hosts. Then NETZACH vibrate YEHOVAH TSAVAOT. The next Sphere is YESOD. The name vibrated is CHADDAI EL CHAI (The CH is a hard guttural as in loch). The final Sphere is MALKUTH and is vitalised with the name ADONAI HA ARETZ this means Lord of The Earth. Here again the best number of times to intone each Mantra is either 9 or 108, you can use your MALA or PRAYER beads to keep count.

THE LIGHTNING FLASH

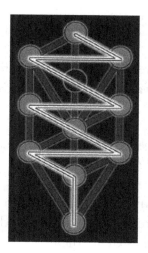

Once the Tree is complete, you circulate energy through it. Up with the in breath and down with the out breath. Remember to thank the land, the Moon and every entity and force that assisted you during this Ritual.

Practice the Tree Ritual often. Watch what different effect the different days you do it on, cause. Get to know which Spheres are weak (Spend extra time on them). Practice using the appropriate Sphere as a filter (as you'll find that the Spheres react to their own situations, in their own ways). But remember you are building the Tree. Don't take things "out" of the Spheres, except what comes as a Natural reaction to the work you are doing. The Tree won't be "solid" in your Aura until you are an Initiated Wicce and on the path of the Priestess or Priest of Wiccecraft. In these early stages you must keep reminding yourself to be gentle and kind.

Be content to feel your strength building. Use the increased energy inside your own systems; you have to learn to control it there first. If you take the time to feel for this growth, it will save you the necessity to push yourself later.

To fully charge the Eight Spheres in the body you can combine physical exercise and visualisation with breath direction and Chants.

DAAT: Stand erect and relaxed inhale a full breath then as you exhale allow the neck to drop forward vertebrae by vertebrae, starting from the top. Use the Chant - YEHOVAH ELOHIM (Yehowah el kheem). Breath in and straighten the neck from the bottom up. Breath out using the Chant. And let your head drop as before but this time to the back Repeat to the right and then to the left.

CHESED: Inhale a full breath make a circular action with your right shoulder twice backwards twice forwards. Exhale and fill the Sphere with the Chant - EL (Ell).

GEBURAH: Repeat the same procedure with the left shoulder intoning the Chant - ELOHIM GIBOR (Elo kheem ga boor).

TIPHARETH: Inhale and retain your breath. Lightly clench your fists and raise your arms forward till they are level with your shoulders Pull your arms back to the shoulders extend them out then pull them back again. Relax and let your arms drop to your sides as you inhale using YEHO-VAH ELOH VE DAAT (Yehowah eho vay dart). And sending the Prana to the Solar Plexus.

HOD: Inhale and retain raise your arms above your head interlock your fingers and twist your body to the right middle right and middle again exhale sending Prana to the right hip With the Chant - ELO-HIM TSA VA OT (Elo kheem sah vay oat).

NETZACH: Same as above but to the left using YEHOVAH TSA VA OT (Yehowah sah vay oat).

YESOD: Inhale and retain raise your arms above your head Clasp your hands ... and concentrating on the base of your spine Pull up the front of your abdomen and bend forward To the right back then left front left back Right and front again Straighten up and exhale using **CHADDAI EL CHAI** (Choddoy el hoy). Sending Prana down to fill this Sphere.

MALKUTH: Inhale and retain with your whole body straight Lean forward from your ankles circle to the right then to the left Come erect and exhale intoning ADONAI HA ARETZ (Adoh nay ha aretz). To vitalise this Sphere don't forget to visualise the four sections Separate parts of the whole.

Then take your concentration above the crown of your head and vibrate the name EH-HEH-YEH (Aye hay yay) to fill KETHER then fill CHOKMAH with YEH and finally BINAH with YEHOVAH ELOHIM (yehowah elo kheem). When you do this in the morning it evokes your energies and fits you into the day. At night it harmonises the days experiences and loosens any blocked or sluggish energies.

To deepen the effect begin with the Kabbalistic Cross and say the Enlightenment Chant at least 8 times. Sit in a semi-lotus (or whatever is comfortable) with your left leg over the right and your left-hand palm on top of your right, in your lap. Let your thumbs touch so that your fingers and thumbs form an oval that circulates your energy. The left side is the receptive fixing side that helps you "focus" the day. Your hands, the Fire and Water "EYES", recycle energy into the Earth "EYE" at the navel.

Keep your back straight by visualising a shaft of pure white light coming from the centre of the Earth and entering your body at the base of the spine. Relax the area and vitalise it opening to receive the energy as it travels up through you it stretches your spine making it incredibly long. Before it radiates the Crown of your head out into the infinite depths of space. Let your head fall slightly forward, your tongue rests on the roof of your mouth, your face is relaxed and there is a slight smile formed by your lips

All you do for the next 10 to 20 minutes (longer if you like) is watch passively as your body breaths. If your mind wanders which it does a lot at first. Gently bring it back with a Chant (make one up if you like or use your favourite). Don't get hassled about it. Relax and enjoy the peace and calm. Don't control, just watch. Stretch and yawn (yawning activates the kidneys) then sigh and hum to complete the distillation before doing the physical exercises. After preparing a space in your aura like this. The exercises then make the Tree of Life strong Clear and easily accessible to you. Finish with the Chant for fixing your energies and the Kabbalistic Cross Consistent relaxed work will give you much better results than spasmodic effort".

Once you've perfected these techniques you can increase the effect yet again by including in your visualisations of the Spheres the ARCHETYPAL IMAGES. These are the race memories of the functions of the Spheres.

KETHER: Is a Crowned King seen in profile?

CHOKMAH: Is the Archetypal Father, let your own ideas develop this.

BINAH: Is the Archetypal Mother. These Spheres are your Mother and Father, the Earth's Mother and Father, and every single entity's Mother and Father all at once.

DAAT: Is the Empty Room, but to work it you can use the image of JANUS, The Giant with two faces, one looking up and on the other side of the head one looks down.

CHESED: Is the Sphere of the Masters, and the Archetype is the Benevolent Ruler who rules not with power but with Charity.

GEBURAH: Is the Sphere of Clarity, and to help with understanding this you can use the image of ARJUNA being taught by KRISHNA, the need for power and strength as well as Judgment, the warrior in a Chariot.

TIPHARETH: Is the Phoenix Rising from its own ashes. The Archetype is a baby, but the baby is a God.

HOD: Is the Sphere of Intellect and Comparisons and in here is the Hermaphrodite. You are both sexes always, the most sacred and Magickal of all creation.

NETZACH: Is Intuition and Sensuality and in here is the most beautiful, naked woman you can imagine. This is, as are ALL these images, your SELF.

YESOD: Visualise a still place in the centre that radiates a gentle, clear, violet Light that gradually expands to fill the Sphere. As it expands it pushes pieces of blue (repressed) energy in front of it until the Sphere is fully expanded and the blue becomes storm clouds that rumble and flash. This stage represents your

Cosmic Personality in its normal state of Conflict. As you keep intoning the God - name for the Sphere, the storm subsides and becomes the most beautiful, naked man. This is ATLAS and he is holding up the Earth. This changes as you continue the Chant till he becomes aware that he is not holding the world up, he is instead gently caressing it. This is your Magickal Personality, your "body of Light".

MALKUTH: Is the Four Basic Drives, the Archetype sits in a throne that is a growing Tree and She is young, beautiful and Crowned with Laurel leaves. Mastery of this Ritual marks the end of the second six months of work and the completion of the first yearly cycle. It is autumn again; the next six months will be spent incubating the Seed we have just planted. This is the Post-Initiate stage. You need to assess your development with another Mars Ritual as you did at the end of the first six months. This time the test subject is the PR's ability to evoke to each of the Wardens, the appropriate aspect of TIPHARETH, the form of the Ritual, once the principles are in position is entirely up to the PR. But you need to be able, under any conditions, to evoke the Sphere of Harmony and Understanding, Sharing and Love, BEFORE you go on with the Pre-Initiate work.

You can do a "Macrocosmic Tree of Life Ritual" which is similar to the Middle Pillar, except that each layer of the cone is one of the Spheres on the Sacred Lightning Flash. Everybody should get to be PR at one of these Rituals.

"The Energy of the work just done
Aids the development of Love and Understanding in all things".

XII
THE HANGED MAN

No. 12 The Hanged Man —
Cernunnos The Horned God

Levels of Reality-Keys to Reality and Ritual

"I generate Love and Understanding,
to all others and I".

When matter finally *"fell together"* from the clouds of colour (transition from Fire to Water), the two basic directions of awareness were established. The FIRE (The Zen) became wider and lighter, the WATER (The Perceptions) became stiller and more immense. One side of this development used matter as its medium or agent of action, the other developed the Spirit.

The Australian Aborigines say that BIAME, the Great Spirit, Mother/Father and the KETHER that we are all part of had a dream (the Zen/The Dreamtime) and the action of the Zen's penetration caused his body to tremble (the Perceptions), each of these ideas of Nature works upon the other. The Sun is the source of energy in our Solar System and matter that has arranged itself into a form that can *"Work"* that energy becomes the focus of power, this developed the Light into the colours and the metals were precipitated out of matter. At the same time, the Spirit of BIAME became aware of the metals as a vortex or spiral of forces. It is this level of being that we call on when we invoke the Gods and Goddesses of the Quarters. Its basic nature is of the AIR Element, so it must be given energy, focus and result. As BIAME developed, he/she became aware of the directions and became fixed by them. The four directions plus up and down make up the six flows from the body of BIAME.

The level of action is the Shining Ones, the Fire Elements. Physically, the matter that had evolved enough receptive power to hold that energy was "Crystallised" and made into definite forms by the flow of energy through it and the first growth happened.

The Solar System provides matter with an ever changing, repeated, but developing pattern, that causes energy to be transferred back and forth. This enabled matter to form cycles and rhythms. The Shining Ones developed with this new movement to become the Winds – the focusing force of the Universe. The Spirit/Winds became increasingly aware of matter (the source or anchor of their development). This concentration allows Nature to build plant life. Plants have their Astral self, their source of rhythms "OUTSIDE" the confines of one plant. These same-fixed souls are called Elementals; they are the Faeries, the Fae of legend, the Fawns and Satyrs, the Sylphs, Undines and Salamanders.

There are as many types and varieties of Elementals as there are plants. Some Elementals developed the desire for movement and matter was "pulled" into animated life forms. Animals have Elementals just as plants do. The human mind/body system developed so far that a permanent link was established between matter and Spirit. BIAME finally got to see. Every Elemental, even Akashic (aware) such as a human, is the focus of the Shining Ones (the Winds) force and knowledge, this in turn is the developed expression of the Shining Ones who are the curiosity and first created of BIAME.

There are thousands of apparently different ways or viewpoints that you could look from to see this two-fold development and it takes some of us many lifetimes to learn to use, instead of fighting our strengths. The two contradictory directions are the two ends of the same pole, there is no conflict. You can develop the Mars Ritual earlier by invoking the strongest of your past life images and using it as you use the cards, to create a portal/doorway. Go "THROUGH" it – to find your own animal totem – the Path that you took through that stage of development. Then use that as a door to get back to your plant totem, and then your minerals totem. These are your greatest strengths; you will find it useful to know them.

We have divided matter into Four Planes or levels of existence. We have also talked about two Akashic points – the Veil between Earth and Water - the Aura; and the Abyss between Water and Fire, colours and black/white. There is also a Veil between Fire and Air, but it is very different, yet the same. These Akashic points are levels of action and remain empty until our Zen (concentration) fills them. But we can ask the Elementals to assist our mutual development – the more aware we become of each other the more we can work together. This is the real task of the Aquarian Age and of the true Wicce. First to develop our Awareness of the Unity of our own internal functions, then after learning how to work the denser levels of matter, we can extend that awareness to the rest of our developing selves. That hard part is seeing things that seem to be different and learning to recognise the basic Element, rather than its complicated and infinitely varied surfaces.

In the rituals in the last lesson we created links to the GOD/DESS forces and the SHINING ONES forces, these two levels of action are above the Abyss (outside the Magick Circle) and before you call on the forces that can come through the Pentagrams (Invocation) you must become aware of the internal and microcosmic equivalents. The microcosmic GOD/DESSES are the Air Elements of our minds, the part of Biame that is concentrating in this direction, and God/dess is not looking at you, as you are GOD/DESS looking. The four ways we look (action and reaction, source and result - are the Four Elements.

Balancing the Four Elements creates the Tai Chi flow. This Circle is used when you want to "*fix*" something. Learning to flow with a Spiral Magick Circle (The Temple) will help your ability to "CHOOSE" which way you create your links.

The Gods are named:

Yehovah	air of AIR
Adonai	air of FIRE
Eheyeh	air of WATER
Agla	air of EARTH

The Goddesses are:

Asherah	air of AIR
Sekhmet	air of FIRE
Aphrodite	air of WATER
Rhiannon	air of EARTH

The Shining Ones are named:

Raphael	fire of AIR
Michael	fire of FIRE
Gabriel	fire of WATER
Auriel	fire of EARTH

The WINDS or Lords and Ladies are the flowing forces of our minds and bodies, personifications of the movements of the planets and the four Watchtowers or directions divide them. Their names are:

EURUS	water of AIR
NOTUS	water of FIRE
ZEPHYRUS	water of WATER
BOREAUS	water of EARTH

The beings that evolve to touch the material level the most are the ELEMENTALS. Their names are:

Sylphides	earth of AIR
Salamander's	earth of FIRE
Undine's	earth of WATER
Gnome's	earth of EARTH

To direct your internal traveling, you need to be able to create an Aura that *"matches"* the Aura of the level you wish to work. You use solid versions of the cards you have already made. These are the Tattwa's.

The Earth card has the same dimensions (4x5) and the yellow square is 3x3. To limit its action, you put a black border around the card.

The Water card has the same dimensions as before. The Crescent is black. All the cards are *"bound"* by a black border.

The Fire card is Red:

The Air card is Blue:

The Wood card is Green:

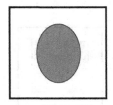

On a Sunday, the day of balance the most important point of control for this Ritual, you work these cards as you did the ones before. They are the basic directions, and you need to become familiar with them before you use the more specific cards. The ones you used before you invoked the action or effect; these invoke and hold a field or Aura of pure Elemental form. They should be banished collectively and individually during their first working. Once they and the Magick Circle have been Banished and the Shining Ones are holding the direction of their flows, outside the Magick Circle, you arrange your cards in their appropriate Quarters so that you can work them from the centre – you are the Wood Element – the Akashic point – so the Wood Card goes in the centre (under the meditation cushion you use to help you hold your body straight and still.) These cards each have their own black bag that you can keep them in when they are not in use (you arrange them in the Banished Magick Circle first and then take them out as you work them).

Sit in the breath control posture facing East. Take yourself into a very relaxed trance state and then while keeping the quality of that state, take the AIR card out of its bag and lay it down in front of you use the rolled-up bag to prop the card up to see it better Set up a flow in three stages let your eyes explore the card, then slowly bring them to the centre and hold them there not stiffly, an even gaze is better than staring, let your eyes blink now and then but do not let them wander. After about 4 – 5 minutes you will begin to see the complimentary colour a wonderful glowing orange appears to be superimposed over the blue Let the strength of the colour build to its full capacity then slowly close your eyes, keeping the after-image of the disk.

Hold the image and focus on it as you did the card with a flow of Prana. Once you have linked the symbol you can control its size because the Prana you breathe into it, gives substance. It is no longer just an after image it is a created thought form and you use this as a lens to focus the Etheric counterparts of the AIR Element. Enlarge a door in front of you then visualise and vibrate the name AIR into it. Let the evoked forces wash over and envelope you when you feel you have been there long enough thank the forces and flows you have met remind yourself to "FEEL" and remember that feeling then let yourself "**COME BACK**". Turn to the South and work the Fire card in the same way. Do not try to interpret what is happening, the experience of the different qualities will explain themselves all you have to do is develop the sensitivity.

After you have worked the Fire card you do the same with Water and Earth. After Earth you turn again to face the East to complete the circle. Stand and spread your arms into the Cross evoke and thank the Shining Ones. Finally put all the cards back in their bags (the Akashic card is worked by and through your every action, so don't work it directly, at this stage). Do the Kabbalistic Cross and leave.

Once you have practiced this ritual and can flow easily with each idea you can begin to create the internal links you will use for your Zen to travel on. The entities you are about to meet are aspects of yourself, your own body. When you learn from them you are listening to your own body thinking (not your head, your body). It is difficult at first to see this apparent division, we fear "FALLING APART". This is why it has been so important to learn to evoke/control the forces of balance (TIPHARETH – and to test that ability).

If you always penetrate from the centre, the penetration will always be balanced. Later you can experiment, but first become familiar with the workings of each of the ideas. The cards will provide a specific destination by generating a specific type of field, but you must use them. The insight of Tiphareth is to see the Solar System as the one action, each part independently harmonious, and this allows you to "SPLIT" your mind/body and yet remain the wholeness and harmony of Union.

The next ritual is the actual evocation of the specific parts of us. It is done in much the same way, except that there are symbols within the symbols on the cards. Put the names in a circle on the back

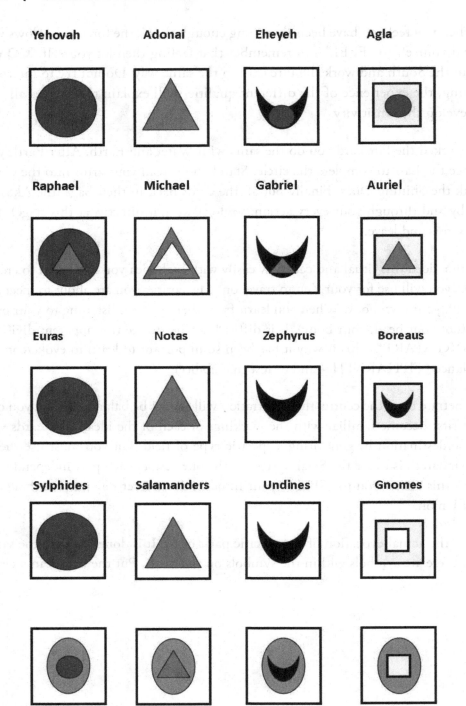

Make a set of Wood cards to be put around the basic Wood card in the centre of the Magick Circle

Put all the Air cards in order in the basic Air Cards bag with it on top. Do the same for the other quarters, and once using the basic cards has evoked the elemental fields, you turn this card over to reveal YEHOVAH card beneath. You flow into this card in the same way as you did the basic card. When the doorway has enveloped you, or you have stepped through the doorway (the key to the door is the name vibrated through TIPHARETH), gently call YEHOVAH asking it to work with you in peace and love. When you feel ready, thank the God and return through the door. In your Magickal Diary that you have taken in with you (along with coloured pencils or crayons) do a full-page sketch of the impression you just received. Then turn that card over and repeat the procedure with the RAPHAEL card. Sketch it on the next page in your book.

Work the EURAS and the SYLPHIDES in the same way. Then turn to the South and work through the Fire pack. Then turn and work Water, and finally Earth. When you finish, take the link around to Air to complete the Circle, stand in the Cross position facing East – evoke and thank the Shining Ones – evoke the Pentagram and the Hexagram – say the Chant – do a Kabbalistic Cross and leave. These forces, like every force can be either constructive or destructive; they have potential for both, so you must build your knowledge of them before you try to direct them. Get to know how they act in your body. Each Element has a Yin organ, which is the internal focus of the Elements "ETHERS", the internal focus for AIR is the LUNGS, the Prana that you breathe in is the intrinsic factor of all your experiences.

If the lungs function correctly each part of the mind/body is "FILLED" with Prana. If the lungs are not functioning properly, the body feels "EMPTY" and so does the mind, a feeling of grief and negativity gradually fills the personality.

The internal organ of WATER is the KIDNEYS, and if they function correctly the right kidney (the Will – directs the flow of Prana). It has three *LEVELS* or directions, ways of modifying the Prana, just as the lungs have three breaths or three ways of stretching. These are the three Alchemical Principles, Mercury, Sulphur, and Salt. The left kidney focuses/screens the more physical energy that is supplied by the Spleen (the blood), it directs the food to where it's needed as a basic nutriment. The left kidney uses the pushing power of the right kidney to get the nutriment to the organs.

If this system of focusing is not "FLOWING" the menstrual cycles are disturbed and as this flow is disturbed the psychological flows become disturbed. Fear results as you become pushed further out of your Natural flow. In the Ritual you are the Wood Element, your actions are personifications of the Elements. The Wood internal organ is the Liver and because of its Elemental Nature (Wood is the Element of interaction between the microcosm and the macrocosm) it has the most intimate relationship with its Yang organ, the Gall bladder. (The Liver secretes Bile, a pure essence of the body, which is not excreted out of the body system, but which the gall bladder stores, and is later used by the Spleen in digestion, and then the kidneys pass it back to the liver). This internal circulation is the way the Liver gradually "DEVELOPS" the internal organs so that they fit in with the external cycles. The mind uses this organ to direct the construction of the links the organism uses to fit in with the other organisms around it. If the internal flow is relaxed, the external links are strong, but easy to manipulate, if the flow is weak or blocked the links become tense and brittle and the personality becomes anxious and agitated.

The prime penetration of the Zen, the internal Fire organ is of course the HEART. Its shape and pumping action not only pushes blood around, but also provides the energy necessary to pull the surrounding circle of Prana (the lungs) through to the physical level, to cause the vitalisation (marriage of physical blood and metaphysical Prana) of the whole body. The feeling of vitalised involvement is translated by the mind as joy.

The Yin Earth organ is the SPLEEN, which handles the YIN digestion after the mechanical (YANG) digestion in the stomach. This organ supplies the basic picture or pattern of the centre of the organism, so not only does it inject the food (superimpose the body's aura by shaping the foods) but it also produces white blood cells, the warriors of the blood. They are armed with this central "key" and anything that is foreign is filtered out of the body. If this function is inhibited or dampened the body loses its ability to hold or fix the Zen and this causes the mind to over-concentrate in an effort to "hold-on". This is the creation of obsessions.

If you ask the microcosmic Elemental forces you evoke with the cards to help, they will work on their respective levels of each Element's action. The Elementals will help with the condition of the physical organs. The Winds will help with the mental processes associated with that organ or Element.

The Shining Ones can channel the Spirit Fire necessary for Creative Expansion and linking to the God/desses inside yourself fulfills your Spiritual need. Remember they are personifications (visualised and animated thought forms) of your own separate internal functions. You will see how they carry out their separate functions, which express their individuality, but they also (usually without knowing it) work in harmony with each other as one unit, a person.

Each function in the cycle affects the next. The negative feeling of the Air Element develops into the fear of Water, which causes the anxiety of Wood. This tension restricts the flow of the Zen, the joy of Fire and this in turn leads to obsessions – which completes the cycle and causes a rigidity, which restricts the breath and this, causes the deepening of the negativity. This cycle can be broken where your strength is greatest and then used in a positive fashion.

For instance, when you find yourself feeling anger you can "TRANSMUTE" this excessive Fire by visualising the angry vibrations in your Aura collecting and forming a RED TRIANGLE. Once you have successfully "DETACHED" the energy from its object (or source if someone is vibing anger at you), and controlled it by containing it with your visualisation, you are free to express it as any of the more positive Fire actions, such as joy, creativity, warmth and affection, or you could use it to tone up your blood, heart or small intestines, etc.

The Air feeling of wholeness cause the Water focusing to produce relaxation, this enables the Will (Wood) to form strong and flexible links which channel a strong flow of Zen/Fire (involvement/joy) to produce a secure self-image, the EARTH pattern, which draws to it a strong flow of Prana, AIR.

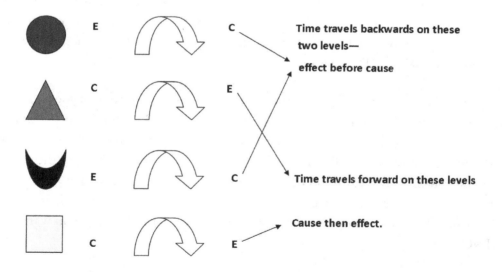

After you have used your cards to become internally aware on this level, you use them to "GO THROUGH" to deeper, internal, less physical levels. As matter changes levels (to your Zen penetrates) the Laws of Nature that affect it, change as well. As your awareness of these different levels increases you will find you will have stages where things seem to stop. If you look around the cycle, you will find that it has rather changed Nature. Some of the differences are startling.

One is called the Law of Reverse Effect. The AIR principle is the primal effect, which by its presence causes the FIRE level, the effect BEFORE the cause. The FIRE level is the primal cause that affects the WATER level. The WATER level is an effect that focuses on a cause (physical matter). The EARTH level is a cause that creates effect. This direction of flows is the basic direction of change, or time, for that level.

The Moon (our present Akashic point or level of interaction) is the pivot between the past and the future. It is the meeting of flows that captures and holds the Zen. Physically, Light comes from the Sun and is reflected from the surfaces of the object. Etheric matter is Astral matter "CLOSE" to the physical level and it is made up of luminous points of matter. True Astral matter is pure Light.

You will find that Etheric matter is much easier to mold and shape than physical matter (especially if you use a physically invoked or held field of energy – a Talisman). Not only can you change its shape in the normal four dimensions; position, length, breadth and depth, but in Time as well. Time is change and if you perceive it "OUTSIDE" physical change you go above the confines of time. Sometimes the totems you find in the mirror flows are FUTURE INCARNATIONS (to investigate this, use the same Ritual as the Mars Ritual, but this time use Jupiter, Thursday). You can also change the "DENSITY" of Time as you change levels by using hypnotic suggestions, to have perhaps a week's experience in the Trance state while only fifteen minutes of "REAL" Time passes.

If you run into anything that is frightening or if anything gives you trouble, you simply Banish it gently (you are moving your own internal energies) with a Pentagram in the appropriate Quarter and vibrating the appropriate name of power. Take your time and get to know what you are doing. You must always "BIND THE NEGATIVE" of your actions, or the movements of energy you cause. This means you must put a definite limit on the actions and result that you want; for example, the border of the cards limits or contains their field. If you ask for something from the microcosmic entities, you must be careful to say that you want that and NOTHING ELSE.

You will find that you need to build your control slowly at first, later when the basic movements are learnt and mastered, you will build and use strength with greater flexibility.

There are Seven HERMETIC AXIOMS that will help you work your internal levels of awareness.

1. The Principle of **MENTALISM**:

   "The ALL is MIND; the Universe is MENTAL". – The Kybalion.

   Everything is a different expression of the same thing. The infinite potential, the original AIR factor contained potential ideas, we are aware because of those ideas, every development came from ideas, mentality, so this is the underlying key to control.

2. The Principle of **CORRESPONDENCE:**

   "As above so below, as within so without". - The Kybalion.

   The same Laws that govern the development of the Planets, govern the development of your mind and vice versa, in fact the same elements are present on all levels of reality and if you understand their relationship in one level you can apply that understanding to other levels.

3. The Principle of **VIBRATION:**

   "Nothing rests, everything moves, everything vibrates". – The Kybalion

   Matter is Bounded Energy, but it also constantly uses (Gives off) energy on all levels.

4. The Principle of **POLARITY** –

   "Everything is dual, everything has poles, everything has its pair of opposites, like and unlike are the same, opposites are identical in nature, extremes meet, and all paradoxes may be reconciled". – The Kybalion.

   This means that what we call opposite is in fact the same thing. If you compare WHITE and BLACK paper what you see is either total REFLECTION - WHITE, or total ABSORPTION – BLACK. Both are relationships between paper and light. Once something acts it creates polarity.

5. The Principle of **RHYTHM:**

"Everything flows, out and in, everything has its tides, all things rise and fall, the pendulum swing manifests in everything; the measure of the swing to the right is the measure of the swing to the left, rhythm compensates". The Kybalion.

This is the basis of Karma day becomes night. You can control Karma by controlling the way we create the opposite of what we do. For example, if we say love is the good things, the happy times etc. we "create" an unbounded opposite, yet to come, sadness, discontentment etc. If, on the other hand, we see love as sharing based upon understanding, then its negative is the time before the love becomes all that comes later, so you never "*lose*" love.

6. The Principle of **CAUSE AND EFFECT** –

"Every cause has its effect; every effect has its cause; everything happens according to Law; chance is just a name for a Law that is not recognised, there are many Planes of causation, but nothing escapes the Law". The Kybalion.

There are no accidents. The things that come to you come because of the links you send out, another aspect of Karma. This principle also incorporates the Law of reverse effect. Mastery of this principle changes the WICCE from one who is affected to one who can choose to be the cause.

7. The Principle of **GENDER** –

"Gender is in everything; everything has its masculine and feminine principles; gender manifests on all planes". The Kybalion.

This principle completes the complex and subtly varying picture of the interactions of **POLARITY**. Behind each male action, is always a feminine reaction? This is important to remember when you are looking at your own sexual identity. As we are both and have been both in different incarnations.

By now you will find that there will be other people who want to join your Magick Circle. One of the best ways to learn is to teach, so each person in the Coven should guide at least one other person, through the Wicce Training stage. This is really a two-way relationship and in trying to give the benefit of your experience, you crystallise your own knowledge.

We have talked about making the edge of your Aura hard when we talked about protection. You should devise Coven Rituals to exercise your control of the edge. The easiest form for this Ritual uses a **PR** in the centre doing the active part, taking the others, who lie with their feet towards the centre through the visualisations.

Start with the general flow up the centre of the body then down the outside, as an egg shape feeling for parts that are too soft and sluggish and parts that are too hard and brittle. Take your time, slowly bring the Aura to a uniform relaxed state. Then go through the hardening start with a picture of a cloud condensing to water, then to ice, then becoming crystal then diamond.

Alternately you could use flowers becoming soft wood, hard wood, coal, then diamond. Or some other picture like that once you feel you can put an edge on your aura it is equally important that you practice the reverse of this procedure and take it through similar stages so that it can become soft and totally receptive with no edge at all.

Practice this at different stages of your work as a group and individually.

"May the energy of the work just done,
aid in the development of Love and Understanding in all things".

XIII
DEATH

No. XIII Death – The Goddess Hecate Invocation and Evocation-Key to Life, Death and Rebirth.

"I generate Love and Understanding
For all others and I".

As soon as you feel that you can effectively Banish or Properly cleanse an area, thing, or yourself properly, you are ready to invoke the Force of the Sun and the Moon. These Rituals are based upon Egyptian God-forms, rather as the original Egyptian Kabbalah. The Egyptian God-forms are far older than the newer Kabbalistic ones, but not as old as the Australian Aboriginal Dreamtime, and all are the same thing, seen from different angles (therefore useful for different purposes) They represent the Celestial and the Primordial, The Angelic and the Primitive dancing together in a cosmic movement as one. These Rituals can take a form that provides a link between you and Egyptian Magick (So you can use the results of the Work some of you did at that time) and the three aspects of RA. The first Ritual is begun just before the Sun appears above the horizon – the God-form is KHOPERI, (Cairpra) the God of human intelligence becoming Divine. He is visualised as a man with a Scarab beetle as his head. The direction you work is the East. The midday form of the God is RA – the Lord of Rays and the direction you work in is the South. The setting Sun is TUM, who is a King wearing a crown and carrying the sceptre and the Ankh. The direction is west.

These Rituals should be done on a Sunday in the country, in a Magick Circle of power (that Aborigines call the INMA – meeting places), which you and in the same way as in Chapter XI.

The Magick Circle is drawn in white (chalk) or yellow (Sulphur) and an Altar (a rock or log) is set up in the appropriate Quarter and covered with a white and gold (the colours of the Sun) Altar cloth. You find eight *"Sun"* flowers (white or yellow) from the surrounding bush and ASK their Elementals (do a flow with the flowers) if you can take and use these flowers to *"HOLD"* the four Quarters of the Magick Circle, one goes to each direction and four go in a vase on the Altar.

On the Altar is a white candle, an Ivory Wand, or a White one, cut from a Tree, with the Elementals permission tipped with gold, and a small bowl of milk (preferably milked that morning) in which is a teaspoon of honey.

Place another small bowl with clear local water and a spray of Mint, Eucalyptus and/or Rosemary, and a third bowl containing the Consecration Oil for anointing. This has an Almond oil base and contains Wild Celery, Wolfs bane, Damiana, and Wild Mistletoe. There is also on the Altar a Thurible with incense that is appropriate for the Sun; such as WOOD ALOES, SAFFRON, CLOVES, but the best is OLIBANUM. A pyramid is made to the same proportions as the Cheops Pyramid (which was given to you during the first book, "Complete Teachings of Wicca Book One – The Seeker", of this series of books on Wiccecraft) out of golden cardboard with the symbol of the Sun painted in white on the sides, to be placed at either end of the Altar and aligned so that the faces are orientated to the poles.

The Pyramids focus the forces of the day and Time because of their shape; they are like three-dimensional cards. The sides are based upon the ratio of PHI Ø and PI π. PI can be stated in terms PHI, the mystical SACRED CUT. It is an unending ratio that governs growth processes from leaf distribution to the proportions of your body. It is easiest to see by the fact that it is the ratio you can divide a line AC by, at point B. Where the relative size of AC to AB is the same relative size as AB to BC.

A   B   C

This is the proportions produced by the Pentagram as well.

A   B   C

The shape of the Pyramid, square bottom, Earth fixes the pattern (therefore the points must be orientated, the pattern fixed is that of the Earth's Aura) and the Fire triangular sides clear and vitalise the flow by invoking Fire – Zen, especially at this time of day, in this Ritual. The colours and the Sun symbol further set this field, so that twin points of concentration of the Sun's consciousness are present in the Altar.

Ether flows in the base points and become condensed and balanced in the Kings Chamber, and finally spray out of the top.

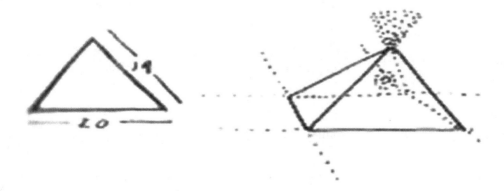

Once everything is set up, you use the Wand to reconsecrate the Magick Circle, beginning and ending in the East. As you do this you evoke the Ring of Fire that you used in the Banishing rituals – just the ring, not the stars. Its flame is the golden flame of the Sun and you concentrate upon it protecting you. Then you go back to the Altar and dip your finger in the water and touch your forehead to purify yourself. You then clear the flow in your hands by putting water on the middle of the inside of your left wrist and rubbing your two wrists together. You then purify your navel with the water. Once the channels have been cleared with the water their action can be "held" by anointing the four areas (visualising them becoming stronger and clearer) with the oil. You then light the incense. Then take four of the flowers and beginning with the East, place one at each Quarter, asking each of the Elements to work with you in love and peace.

Then return to the Altar and call upon OSIRIS – ASAR KHENTA MENTIU, twelve times. You are to *"TAKE ON THE ASPECT"* of this God for the rest of the ritual. Now you wait for the Sun to Rise (or reach its Zenith or set) keep your mind centred upon RA by repeating "TUA RA" (Ra, I adore thee!) or some appropriate Chant. When the God arrives (the time comes) you say whichever of these is appropriate:

A	Khepra	a	hen	Neter	pen seps
Hail	Cairpra	who now approaches in		Divine splendor
A Ra		eb satetu		Neter ankh
Hail Ra		Lord of Rays		you who are the God of Life
Neb Mert		hra-Nebu		ankh pest - k
Lord of Love		All people live (when)		you shine
A Tem		ta-K	Chu	em	pet
Hail Tum		you give splendour		in Heaven
Em Bennu		aq		per
As a Phoenix		going in and coming forth		

You then replenish the incense and prepare to evoke the Shining Ones – Chu (the Ch is guttural as in the Scottish loch) that are the Archangels. To do this you dip the herbal spray in the water and bless each Quarter in turn visualising the appropriate shaft of Light. Go back to the Altar and this time dip the spray in the milk then bless each Quarter again. The Water holds the aura of the plants to call the Elementals. The milk supplies the denser animal aura needed to attract the Shining Ones. When you return to the Altar this time you sprinkle a final blessing to the Right, then the left, then finally to the centre and the front of the Altar.

The next stage of this Ritual needs you to generate a lot of Fire (Penetration) energy. Using a Chant can do this, singing, dancing, sex can be used if you like. When you feel the climax approaching, you visualise yourself being filled with the Sun and shout joyously inwardly, not aloud:

| Nuk | neb | esep |
| I become | One with the | Lord of Light. |

When you have allowed the experience of the ritual to settle down, turn and thank each of the Watchtowers. Then you knock strongly ten times on the Altar to declare the Ritual ended. The flowers are then burnt (or placed in a stream or river) and their ashes scattered to the four winds. You direct the strength evoked by this Ritual towards holding and building the Sun Sphere of your Tree of Life. You practice this Ritual in a Coven, with a PR and individually — for each of the three aspects of the Sun. You could also do it in your head, at work or on the bus or wherever you are at sunrise, midday or sunset.

Once you've mastered this Ritual you have sufficiently built your auric strength to be able to INVOKE - bring in from the MACROCOSM some of the forces you have worked microcosmically with. Remember control always comes from above; use the Elementals to work the physical, the winds to direct the Elementals, the Shining Ones to direct the God-forms of your mind to direct the Shining Ones. You need not only do your previous work as a basis, you need an environment that will support and sustain your actions, a shape that will help the generation and concentration of your Auric strengths. The FIRE generative Temple is a double cube built on a "power spot".

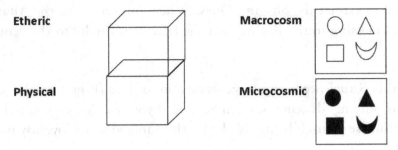

That has been brought together to form the eight pointed star, the Hexagram.

In this shape each of the points, as you go around, has an alternating charge or polarity that keeps the flow of the Zen going from physical to Etheric, this in turn sets up a counter flow of forces "down", to the physical from the Etheric. There are two groups of Circles, one on the ground and one above your head.

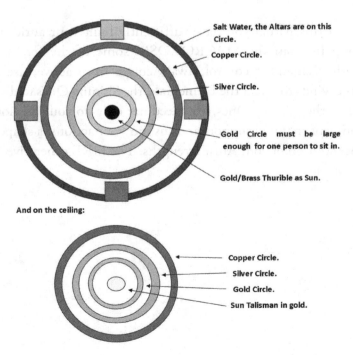

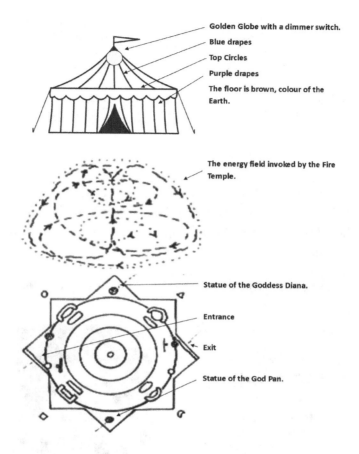

Golden Globe with a dimmer switch.

Blue drapes

Top Circles

Purple drapes

The floor is brown, colour of the Earth.

The energy field invoked by the Fire Temple.

Statue of the Goddess Diana.

Entrance

Exit

Statue of the God Pan.

As much as possible should be made fire proof and adequate fire precautions always taken. The colours blue and purple should be used respectively as drapes around the Magick Circle area; the Altar and the AIR Quarter should be all in blue. The Altar is best as a slab of uncut rock or wood on which you put whatever you feel is appropriate as well as your two Altar candles. The red objects are found for the FIRE throne and Altar in the South, the green is water in the West, and the yellow is Earth in the North. Just inside the main drapes at the entrance and exit of your Temple is hung a white semi-transparent VEIL. Which symbolises the Veil between the Earth and Water levels?

Once through the veil you will find yourself in between two Pillars, one on the left is Black and the name BOAZ is written on the side of the Pillar that faces into the Temple. The one on the right side is White and called JOACHIN. They are both about shoulder height and are topped by equilateral triangular pyramids of the appropriate colour with their name written in English, Hebrew, and Magickal script.

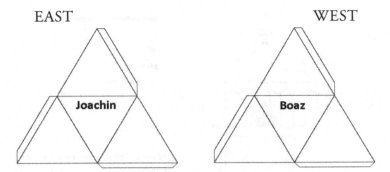

EAST   WEST

Joachin   Boaz

Just in front of the white Pillar at the entrance facing inward, the "Banner" of the **EAST** hangs on its own stand. The "Banner" of the West, hangs on its own stand in front of the black Pillar at the exit. They are made of silk.

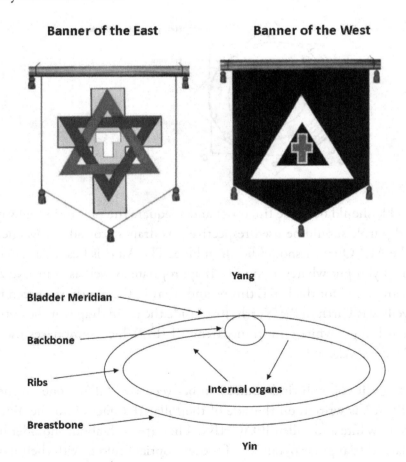

Banner of the East   **Banner of the West**

Yang

Bladder Meridian

Backbone

Ribs

Internal organs

Breastbone

Yin

Behind the main body of this series of writings there are many *"extra chapters"*, one of them deals with the making of the Four Elemental Weapons that go in this Temple. The Wand is the Air Weapon, the Athame the Fire, the Chalice is Water, and the Pentacle is Earth. But there are also Higher Tools that are used in High Magick.

Once built, your Temple should be properly banished by each member of the Coven. Each member must ask the Shining Ones to link and hold the flows of energy in the Temple so that they are continually purified and strengthened. The Magick Circle should be invoked in the name of RA, so that it will be anchored to the centre of the TREE. If you are working with Initiates, there will be in the Temple *"Elemental Lords and Ladies"* or Winds. They are not Lords/Ladies in the sense of being rulers over others. They are Elementals that have learnt through working with an Initiate how to change states and become Winds. They learn this, as the Initiate becomes a Priest or Priestess. The Initiates will tell you their names (or the Lords/Ladies themselves might, if you ask them). They are not as fixed in their appearance as we are, but they sometimes take on definite sexual characteristics and as Wicces create links to ask Four Elementals to work with them, there are usually two male and two females, or all are androgynous with no sexual organs, or they can all be hermaphroditic (for balancing energy).

If you are not working with Initiated Wicces, ask the Shining Ones to ask the Winds to work with you, but NOT outside the Magick Circle. Elementals will not intentionally harm you, but they are playful and sometimes get stuck in your web of links. This frightens them and, in their efforts, to get free, they can hurt both themselves and you.

If someone has an Elemental entangled in his or her aura, there will be purple colouration around the Iris of the eye – the edge is used in Iridology as the diagnostic area for the skin. The purple colour will be just out from there – the Etheric sheath.

They will also feel a tendency or pull to the left shoulder. This doesn't happen very often, but if it does, you put Sandalwood Oil on the bottom of the neck between the neck vertebrae and the back vertebrae and at the very base of the spine. The YIN action of the herb contains the flow of the Governor Vessel, the great YANG vessel of the body. Then use St. John's Wort Oil (Hypericum) down either side of the spine (the bladder meridian). This part of the meridian can be understood if you look at the shape of the body.

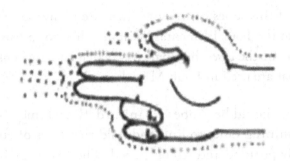

Hypericum is a Yang action so the points on the bladder meridian (that are the natural clearing points for the internal organs) are all smoothly discharged (the Sandalwood on the Governor Vessel ensures that not too much is given off) and this frees the Elemental. If you do this in the Temple, the Shining Ones will take the Elemental and heal it.

No one who has not reached this stage of the work is to enter the Magick Circle alone. Even when you clean the Temple, you will treat it as a Temple - the cleaning implements must be Banished/Consecrated, and you must be skyclad or robed and always moving in a Deosil direction. The Kabbalistic Cross must always be done when entering or leaving the Temple.

The Magick Circle works as your HEART and the condition it is kept in will determine its level of function. The main function is the bringing through of the necessary healing strength of the land you live on, so that the group can work with the living soul of the land. The Magick Circle acts on the land as an acupuncture point would on you and the more you heal the land, the more the land will heal you. The Four Winds each have their own "pictures" or lands of action – as a Wicce you are trying to create a BASE for your relationship to the non-physical Universe, both inside and outside your body. The wind you will be particularly working with to begin with is BOREAUS, the North Wind of the Earth.

There are two ways to do the invocation Pentagram, both starts from the top – the Fire penetration – you use an Athame mudra (hand symbol).

That is with your little finger and ring finger both bent in and the others pointing outward with the thumb. From here you can go either to the left hip with an Earth Invoking Pentagram, this is a "sedating" invocation, what is invoked is first expanded then fixed and cooled.

The other way the invoked energy is brought through cooled, Fire Invoking Pentagram, fixed and then it is expanded to have a stimulating effect. The first brings things through to you and the second raises you to them. Work with the first and understand it before you work with the second. Always work in a Magick Circle.

The ritual begins by first Banishing the Circle with the LBRP, then when you return to the East draw the first Invoking Pentagram. As you fill the Eastern Pentagram with the name JEHOVAH visualise a scene slowly forming through the Pentagram (as if it's a window). It is a beautiful dawn over the ocean. There are pinkish and yellow clouds floating gently in the breeze, this breeze comes gently through the Pentagram to you as you call EURAS – visualise the appropriate card and through it visualise a small cloud being blown gently through the Pentagram to you. Go with EURAS on the cloud … into his domain for a short while (4-5 minutes). Ask the wind to work with you in PEACE and LOVE, and then gently "come back".

Take a line of blue flame from the EAST to the SOUTH, draw another INVOCATION PENTAGRAM and as you fill it with the name ADONAI – visualise a tropical beach scene. Warm blue sea waters, surf on coral reefs inside the reef is a lagoon of relatively calm water, small waves lap the long golden beach. Beyond the beach grow palm trees swaying gently in a hot tropical wind. Feel this wonderfully warm wind come out from the Pentagram as you call to NOTAS. When you feel the wind blowing playfully through you warming you through and through you go with him onto the beach. Feel the hot sand on your toes the sea spray. Listen to the sounds around you. Ask NOTAS to work with you in PEACE and LOVE, then gently come back to the Temple.

Then take the circle to the WEST and draw the Invocation Pentagram for Water – fill it with the name EH-HE-YEH – through the Pentagram you see a waterfall, tumbling down over a cliff and dashing on the rocks – about halfway down there are three rocks that jut through the water flow in a triangular formation. From these and the bottom of the waterfall there is a cloud of mist and spray that is gently blown out of the Pentagram to you as you vibrate ZEPHYRUS … When you feel the wind go through with it into the Water Quarter ask ZEPHYRUS to work with you in PEACE and LOVE then gently come back.

Take your Circle to the North and draw your fourth invocation Pentagram – fill it with the name AGLA. As the vista of this Quarter becomes slowly clearer you will see that just in front of you is a wonderful field with flowers here and there. On your right is a wide and deep river there is a shallow crossing just ahead where a herd of animals are crossing.

On the other side of the river are great fields of wheat and grain. Back on this side on your left are orchards with trees of every kind full of ripe fruit. Beyond these are herds of animals grazing peacefully together. Behind them starts the forests. These are at the foot of the mountains and one rises majestically above the rest. This is "The Mountain of All Things" the mountain that Moses received the Law on Olympus. The mountain that BIAME became manifest upon the top of the World. The closest point on Earth to the ice capped mountains and heaven. When it melts it flows down to give ample water to the valley below. Call out to BOREAUS and once you've felt the wind come through the Pentagram you go with it into the North Quarter feel the grass and do a flow with the first flower you come across. Go over the river to the fields, come back and go to the orchards, all the time you will feel as if there are layers of burdens that fall away from you the deeper you go into the scene you will become stronger and happier, healthier and more sensitive to the forces around you. Reach up and pull a piece of fruit from one of the Trees and eat it. Feel the incredible energy and vitality that this Etheric food has. Then go to the beginning of the forest and look up at the mountain feel how it loves you and you love it, evoke and share your Sun centre with the mountain and BOREAUS.

You are ALIVE as you have never been before, there is no feeling of fatigue or cold as you climb up through the forest, watch the animals then up to the snowline. The snow is crisp but although you are skyclad you are not cold, and it is easy to keep climbing till you reach the top of the mountain. Orient yourself look back towards the East assume the pain control position and evoke the Shining Ones. Ask them and BOREAUS to work with you in PEACE and LOVE. Sit on top of the mountain and begin the Chant "Love is all we need, Truth is all we seek, Light is all around" and feel it vibrate through the whole scene watch how the countryside reacts to the sounding of your note the way you vibrate AUM, get it so that your note and the countries note are mutually supporting each other.

When you feel you are ready to retrace your steps thank each entity as you pass it until you are back in the Temple. Take the Circle to the East. Go to the centre, stand in the Cross position and evoke and invoke the Shining Ones, this Ritual is done with a Moderator first then practiced individually then combine the physical and Etheric forms of it.

Then the Coven records and discusses the Ritual; finally, you develop the "HABIT" of invoking in the morning and Banishing at night. Physically every now and then, but always at least go through the Ritual mentally (Ethereally). This will greatly strengthen your "PERSONAL WICCE POWER" because amongst other things the Ritual increases the flow of Prana to the Solar Plexus. This will become obvious to you when using your "Tools".

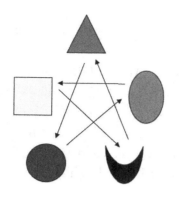 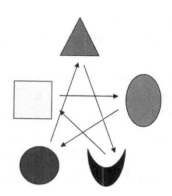

It is here that you will probably encounter THE WATCHER AT THE THRESHOLD, (The Dread Lord of the Shadows). This is the personification of all the things your conscious mind "suppresses or buries". To do this the Watcher needs to keep the other levels of your mind sub-conscious.

The Watcher can be a frightening figure and you will find that it will sometimes stop you from getting through. This entity MUST be faced! You must realise that it is YOU – the part of you that you don't want to look at.

Once it is faced, it ceases to be a problem; you will find that the terrible hidden part of you is not terrible at all. Once you learn to understand - not easy at first, but keep trying, you will find that it is never impossible to get past. Some people I am told, don't encounter the Watcher at all, they have no suppressed side to them. These people are also EXTREMELY rare. Some will be easier to handle than others, but you never give yourself too much to handle. Try to see why it is there, what caused it in the first place and try to LOVE it. Hidden in this form are your greatest strengths. Once you have learnt to handle your Watcher (Lord of Shadows), you have overcome your most dangerous fear. Your fear of accepting yourself as you are without the forced or imposed morality and fear that your links with society give you. BOREAUS can help you with this. This wind can also be used to "bring through" virtually ANYTHING.

If, for instance, you are about to buy a car, you enter the North Quarter, take some "Offering" to BOREAUS (LOVE is the greatest gift anyone can give) and ASK (not ORDER or DEMAND) him to help you. Because of the strength of your Aura the part of you that is BOREAUS can create a strong link between YOU and A GOOD CAR that is within your ability to pay for. You bind the negative of this operation by drawing a Banishing Pentagram (once you come back OUT of the invoking Pentagram) and forming an image of you NOT getting the desired effect and BANISH it strongly using the God-name AGLA, then the God-name EL (strength) and finally balancing everything with the words "I.O.EVO.HE. BLESSED BE."

Be sure to place a LIMIT on what you ask for from BOREAUS (THIS is what I want and NO MORE). Also work within a reasonable SPHERE of INFLUENCE. Some Wicces have been known to ask for castles in Spain, or physical immortality as their first request. Magick may well be able to pull these things into your Sphere of conscience (eventually) but you must start at the beginning and SLOWLY and CAREFULLY build your "Sphere of Influence", until it does encompass all that you want, but remember ONE STEP AT A TIME.

Never use Magick for destruction or in anger! You will find that these forces cannot be mishandled without hurting the person who is doing the mishandling. Your Karma is hard enough; don't make it harder for yourself and the people you work with. Words are the most dangerous part of a Wicce, as they are directed with their word to the person intended, but if not in balance with harmony and peace, they will rebound as quickly as possible with a vengeance and bite you in the Karmic arse.

XIV
TEMPERANCE

No. XIV Temperance
The Goddess Rhiannon

Preparation for Power-Key to Becoming Thrice Great

"I generate Love and Understanding
For all others and for myself".

Your mind is learning how to change from Earth to the Moon (The level of Wicce). Mankind is becoming aware of its aura, becoming aware of its links and the way the shape can mould our World. We need to be able to direct these energies and forces, but not in direction that create warring pressures as does the selective training of intellect OR emotions as in sexual conditioning. We must learn to adjust to our own internal cycles. The changes you go through are RHYTHMIC and returning, nothing is ever lost, we are both male and female, intellect and emotion. Each of us expresses that rhythm in our own individual way; as a Wicce you aim at adaptability so that you can have the freedom of a greater number of choices and wider experiences.

MALKUTH (The Earth) is self-aware. YESOD (The Moon) is externally aware. NETZACH (Venus) is aware of itself, MALKUTH and to a certain extent, YESOD. HOD (Mercury) is aware of itself, YESOD and to a certain extent MALKUTH. TIPHARETH (The Sun) is aware of all the Spheres below the Abyss and to a certain extent those above the Abyss. From this level you can use the strength of the Tree to KNOW that what you are doing is in harmony with the things around you, this is the goal of the Wicce to be in total harmony.

The next set of Rituals is designed to bring through and solidify the lower spheres of the Tree in your Aura, so that the rest of your Work has a firm basis. They prepare your Aura for Initiation into the Priesthood, which is the fixing of TIPHARETH, the Sun. The first SEPHIRAH (Sphere) RITUAL deals, naturally with MALKUTH and is done on SATURDAY. Each member of the group will be the subject of a ritual. You take turns being the PR as well. Take part as the Wardens also strengthens your Work.

Step 1: The PR prepares the Magick Circle, checks the incense on the Air Altar, for MALKUTH the incense is Dittany of Crete or Sandalwood. On the FIRE Altar, there is the burning oil. For MALKUTH the oils are Willow, Lily or Ivy. On the WATER Altar there is water-containing soil.

On the **EARTH** Altar, is an **UNCUT** Rock Crystal? The most effective gems would be four garnets, one of each colour – yellow, red, green, and brown. Light the Altar candles (2 on each Altar), leave. (If there are to be extra people to help build the flow, they should enter now.)

Step 2: The four Wardens (A balance of people) each wear a cloak of the Elemental colour as in the Temple, with the appropriate shape in the complimentary colour on the back.

AIR does a full BANISHING Ritual as he/she enters.
FIRE does a full INVOCATION Ritual as he/she enters.
WATER does a full BANISHING Ritual as he/she enters.
EARTH does a full INVOCATION Ritual as he/she enters.

They sit on their appropriate cushions, each holding the Wicces Elemental Tools. The High Priestess enters carrying the Tools of Malkuth; a golden RING and a golden TRIANGLE. She walks Deosil three times around the Magick Circle and then stands in the centre facing the entrance.

Step 4: The HIGH PRIEST/ESS says, *"ENTER"* and the *"subject"* enters and goes around the Magick Circle till she/he comes to the Earth point – the statue of PAN and she/he lies down with her/his feet towards the middle.

Step 5: The HIGH PRIEST/ESS goes through a "Macrocosmic Tree" Ritual (As before) with the subject and the "Extra" people. The four principles set up a flow, which is generated by vibrating and visualising AUM in unison. This flow passes from AIR to FIRE, WATER then EARTH who directs it then to both AIR and the HIGH PRIEST/ESS – the HIGH PRIEST/ESS should let these rhythmic pulses of auric strength build in her/his own MALKUTH.

When the strength is sufficient direct it at the MALKUTH of the subject and call upon the GOD, SHINING ONE, WIND, and ELEMENTALS of each Quarter to build in peace and Love the Sphere of MALKUTH in the subject. Everybody visualises this happening. Each of the entities works in turn upon the Sphere of the subject's feet.

Step 6: Once each Quarter has been called and has done its work, the Wardens set up the same flow as before and as the HPs feels the strength building this time, she visualises a perfect MALKUTH forming between her hands, which are held out towards the subject, with the Circle in the RIGHT hand and the Triangle in the LEFT. The PR intones ADONAI HA ARETZ and *"sends"* the Sphere of vitalised Prana to the subject's MALKUTH.

Step 7: When the subject "feels" MALKUTH vibrating at her feet she sends her consciousness down to it, intoning the God-name internally and visualising the name pulling the Zen down to it in the Sphere. When she has entered the Sphere, she visualises the Garden of Eden in which a Tree grows that is a living throne, and in its sits Lilith, the Earth Queen, the true Judaic Goddess. The subject can call upon SANDALPHION who is the Sphere's Shining One. She can also call on the GNOMES, the SPHINX and BOREAUS. Once she has spent long enough to introduce her to the entities she climbs back up her body and slowly *"comes back"* to the Temple. Thank each of the entities you used. RISE – thank the **PR** and take the weapons – then the Wardens – say the Chant – and do three circles and leave.

Step 8: The extra people leave – thank the forces EARTH, WATER, FIRE then AIR, leave. The PR puts out the candles and the flame and leaves.

The Rituals for YESOD, then NETZACH and finally HOD are basically the same.

YESOD – MONDAY:

Air Altar	Jasmine
Fire Altar	Jasmine Scented oil
Water Altar -	Salt Water
Earth Altar	Quartz or Moonstone

Weapons	Perfumes and silver sandals
Scene -	"The Machinery of the Universe"
Archetype	A beautiful naked man (Atlas)
Guides	GABRIEL, BOREAUS, DIANA (as the Moon Goddess)

NETZACH – FRIDAY:

Air Altar	Red Sandalwood or Rose
Fire Altar	Rose Oil
Water Altar	Green Water and one red rose petal
Earth Altar	Emerald or green colored Earth
Weapons	Green Oil Lamp and a green Singulum around waist
Scene	Classical Mythology – A lush garden
Archetype	A beautiful naked woman (Yourself)
Guides	VENUS, UNDINES, and HANIEL – the Shining One of this Sphere who is coloured lush green.

HOD – WEDNESDAY:

Air Altar	Storax
Fire Altar	Storax scented oil
Water Altar	Purple coloured water
Earth Altar	Opal
Weapons	The **APRON** – to conceal the splendour of the Wicce, a square of purple cloth 10 x 10 with a gold colored Caduceus.
Scene	Desert, Ancient Egyptian. Through a purple haze comes a chariot pulled by two lions. The other animals here are twin serpents and the twin jackals.
Archetype	The Hermaphrodite
Guides	MICHAEL, HERMES, ZEPHYRUS.

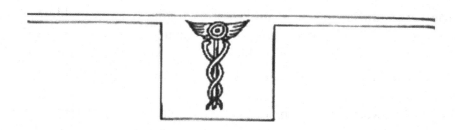

The intellect (Mercury) and the emotions (Venus) cannot coexist at the same time on the personality (Moon) level, because of the Moon's action of polarisation. Yet we are "made up" of both aspects. To satisfy all the parts of our mind/body we fit them into a cyclic pattern. This is the reason the week (7 days – 7 colours – 7 planets – 7 Chakras) was fitted to the Moon (the months). The pattern used is derived from an arrangement of the metals illustrating an awareness that we must have had and lost. Just as a child has the ability, and uses it, to see Faeries, not some children, most children.

When you were born your ability to communicate directly/Aurically is what enabled you to learn to use your body. You learn the "IDEA" of movement from the flow between you and your mother in the womb, through the umbilical, your navel. After you were born, this remains your way of manipulating Etheric energy (your links). The two functions "SWAP OVER". During the pregnancy the WILL – your Etheric counterpart – your Elemental Self, is slowly assimilated through the Mother's navel into the Fetus.

This is what the Saturn Ritual (chapter 7) is about. The memory of the Abyss is the memory of conception, the Lights are *"penetrations"* that happen when the sperm and ovum become vitalised by being concentrated upon and fed amounts of Prana by the orgasm. The blue/white colour is the Yin action of sharing, while the red Lights are the result of an aggression-based orgasm. You are attracted to the one you feel most comfortable with. The moment of birth, which fixes the basic pattern of the Jupiter forces, (the birth chart) should be made as pleasant and relaxed as possible. If you are pregnant you can extend the Saturn Ritual, by taking yourself down (or up?) to the Saturn "level" (as in the Ritual) cross your arms and legs and practice deep rhythmic breathing to revitalise your Prana. Do a flow **VERY** gently with your child through your navel and **ASK** it what sort of environment it wants to be born in.

The room for birth should be Banished and invoked. Both Mother and Father should be *"in contact"* flowing with, their child. There should be quiet and soft lighting. The child should be laid on the Mother's stomach and softly stroked. The umbilical cord should be cut only when the pulse beat stops. Once the initial change over happens the child can be washed in blood temperature water and dried gently. The Father should make an accurate recording of the time and a birth chart should be done and kept.

The next part of your work involves the invocation of four God-forms that represent the five water Spheres; Jupiter, Mars, Mercury, Venus, and they will help you build TIPHARETH, the Sun.

The Jupiter Sphere is personified as DIANA, the Goddess of Nature, and the unreachable and untouchable Virgin Huntress. Closely in contact with the Spiritual side of Her being, but out of touch with Her physical evolutionary drives. The great God PAN, the lusty God of Spring, represents the Martian Sphere. He is closely in contact with his physical drives, but out of contact with the Spirit. He sees DIANA and wants her. He chases Her for ages until finally they touch. This touch generates through their orgasm, the Sun, APOLLO their child – you. It also changes the reckless PAN into the reflective HERMES TRISMEGASTOS – the Father of Magick – the Three Times Wise – Mercury, and the aloof DIANA becomes the sensuous APHRODITE – the Sphere of Venus. The legend was the play enacted during classical Grecian times in the Eleusian Mystery School's Initiation Ceremony. PAN and DIANA as the two polarities in Nature are an even older concept than that; they go back to anti-diluvium (before the great flood) times, to LEMURIA. Here again, we are personifying actual forces inside you. The personification is a conscious arranging of that force, so that you can communicate with it easier.

The four Rituals are macrocosmic Tree rituals, like the one before, done one week apart, starting on a Sunday just after the New Moon, so that two are done as the Moon grows and two as the Moon Wanes. It is necessary to hold the God-forms for a week each and the Sun level is the "real" intention of the Rituals. In the first, after the full Cone of Power has been built, the PR brings the Covens attention back to the Jupiter level. The blue of this level is visualised growing and shining out to fill the whole Cone as the PR calls to DIANA and the group intones EL alternatively. The PR visualises the form of DIANA taking shape behind Her. The Coven (with eyes closed) concentrates on invoking the Sphere. When the flow reaches its peak, the PR intones EL very strongly, and then draws out of herself the form of the Goddess. She then *"takes on"* the part of the Goddess and tells the group all she knows about DIANA and Her relationship to the Sphere of Jupiter. The PR/DIANA then tells the Coveners that she will cause them each to experience themselves as Her – DIANA

– expanding to fill the Universe over the next week. Then She slowly brings the Coveners back – every now and then re-asserting the idea of "becoming" DIANA for the next week.

The second Ritual follows the same pattern. The level "brought out" is the Martian level. The PR calls PAN and the group vibrates ELOHIM GIBOR. The colour is red. The post hypnotic suggestion and the evoked God-form are given PAN'S characteristics, the feeling is of everything "coming in" to the Spheres of awareness, all the senses become sharp and clear, EVERYTHING is important to PAN. On the days either side of the Full Moon you should pay special attention to the midday Sun and invoke the Full Tree – concentrating on the Sun Sphere.

The Third Ritual is for the Mercury Sphere. The colour is orange, the God-name ELOHIM TZAVAOT and the God-form is HERMES – the messenger of the Gods – the giver of knowledge. The week's meditation is the intellectual reality of our existence.

The last Ritual in this series is in the Venus Sphere of action. The colour is green, and the God-name for the Sphere is YEHOVAH TZAVAOT and the God form is APHRODITE – the Goddess of sensuality and love. The attribution to be stressed for the week is the emotion reality of the love of the Universe and the growth of INTUITION – the sense we are "developing".

These Rituals where you take on the form of a God or Goddess must be approached without FEAR and with LOVE your aim. The way you create the initial links sets the pattern for your relationships until you gain enough experience to be able to cut the links easily. For the same sort of reason, it is not advisable to do "work" with people outside the group that is linked to your Temple during this stage of the work.

By now your Tree will be "CONDENSING" in your Aura. The four lower Spheres are still not fully formed, but at least you have a firm basis on which to build the rest of the Tree. It is necessary to work MALKUTH frequently because it is the "roots" of the Tree – the way you "link in" to the Earth's energy. Try to get the four "divisions" as clear as possible, especially when you are doing the MIDDLE PILLAR and TREE Rituals. Centre the four auric eyes on it.

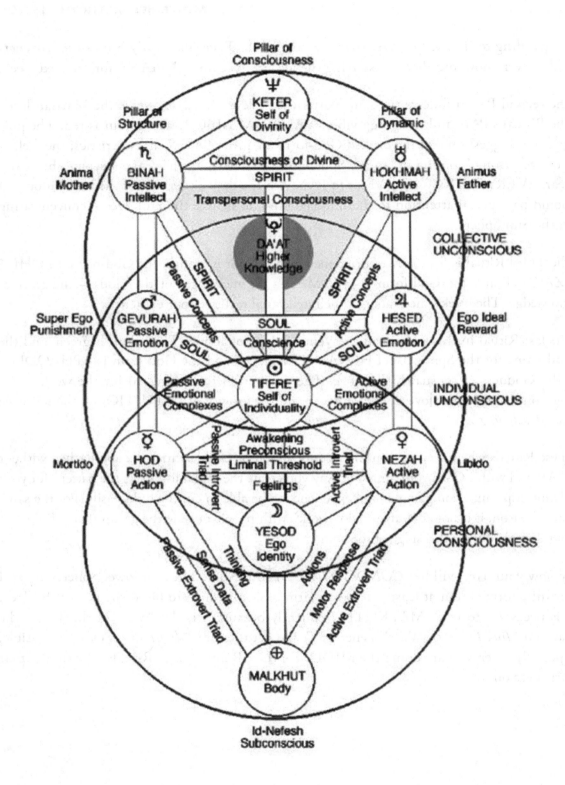

The next step is the reorganisation of the MOON level. At present this Sphere is the point of contact between you and your environment. The blue "marbling" is the "shielding" of the Sphere; it is the defenses we have learnt.

We are now going to lay the foundations for you to be able to use a "body" that you will manufacture from your Aura, and which will be directed from this Sphere. This body is called the "BODY OF LIGHT" or as within Wicca we call it the FAMILIAR. It is the Etheric double, but charged, freed of the body except for a fine, strong thread of "Will" from the navel. Its main use at first is an extension of your physical senses, (you are already working on the Four Eyes). Once you gain the INITIATED level as a Wicce (control of Jupiter) you will be able to direct this "FAMILIAR" to work ASTRALLY while you go about your daily routine, or you can get it to "take over" the body, while you go "adventuring". This means that you get to function consciously on more than ONE level, independently AT THE SAME TIME.

The first step in creating this body is to work out a TOTAL picture of it, so that both Earth and the Sun levels can direct the formation of it. Make a list of the attributions you would like it to have (remember it IS you) such as GENTLENESS, BEAUTY, CLEAR PERCEPTIONS, FREEDOM FROM FEAR, NON-JUDGING etc. It can have any quality you wish – BUT - these qualities will affect you – they will BE YOU. You must "feel right" being called by that name. To give you an example, the name SHILBA is a cryptogram derived from the first letters of Strength, Health, Intelligence, Love, Beauty, and Advancement. Another example is BRAVE EAGLE, which symbolizes valor, freedom, keen perceptions, wisdom and flight. It's YOUR name – YOU choose it! This name is used as a TALISMAN to give the links you create a different sort of strength. You use it during group functions; the more it's used the better it works, but only with people you have worked Magickal links to. The people you share your name with should understand what it means. My first Magickal name was Avena (grain of wheat), to me symbolizing from a seed I will grow.

Do a Ritual to call down the Powers of the Full Moon, then have each person explain their Magickal name to the others.

You also construct an IMAGE of what you want this body to look like. Here again, it's up to you. It can be anything living, an animal or a Shining One. You create this drawing or model as if it was your most important Magickal Tool. BANISH it – protect it in black silk – it is linked to your aura and kept covered outside the Magick Circle. Work it until you get a clear mental image of it whenever your Magickal NAME is used. Then do another Ritual. This time is the day of the New Moon and show and explain your image to the group.

This "BODY OF LIGHT" is what you will use as your point of action once you banish your "WATCHER". In fact, it is your WATCHER transmuted and restored to be your strength rather than your restrictions.

The sensitivity you have to auric flows can be worked by practicing with paper models of the crystal structures associated with the various Spheres. Crystals focus the Fire Element, the Shining Ones, so they typify the ACTION of the energy the Spheres express. Make paper models (heavy paper is more sensitive than cardboard) of each of the structures and hang each on a piece of cotton inside a glass case. If you don't have a glass case you can hang them in a room with soft lighting and NO wind, Temples are good for this.

The structure of the TIPHARETH, DAATH, and KETHER crystals, all show the living pyramid. The perimeter of the base divided by twice the height equal's pi, or as we have seen, the sides of the Triangles are 19 and the base is 20. You will find that the paper structures spin when you watch them. The positive Ethers that flow through a relaxed EYE are collected by the field that the pyramid invokes in a spiral that comes down over the structure – if the structure is aligned to the poles, the spiral enters the base of the Northern side after making this spiral is reflected/concentrated at the King's Chamber and the interaction produces movement. The other structures vary in their actions/reactions, play with them and see how to get the most from them; use what you know about the Spheres to put you in harmony with each of these generators or accumulators.

For DAATH you can make a pyramid lined with crinkled reflective foil with the top cut off and holes in the sides at the height of the King's Chamber (one third of the way up) to let Light in.

Align it on a Banished and Invoked mirror. This can be used for Scrying, and after Initiation you will find that you can "*fix*" an Etheric image onto a Talisman by using this Talisman of the DAATH crystal – the Diamond. The HOD structure is a series of concentric Spheres hung inside each other with large and small circular holes in each so that you can see right into the centre – the arrangement that works best is Seven layers, each one, one of the colours of the spectrum.

For YESOD, which is our present point of action, we use a cone structure with a spiral of silver wire that circles three times from base to tip and are worn on your head with the end of the wire at your forehead – the "*Air EYE*". This "DANCE HAT" or "*WICCES HAT*" can greatly enhance your work with the other structures.

"The energy of the work just done
aids the development of Love and Understanding in all things".

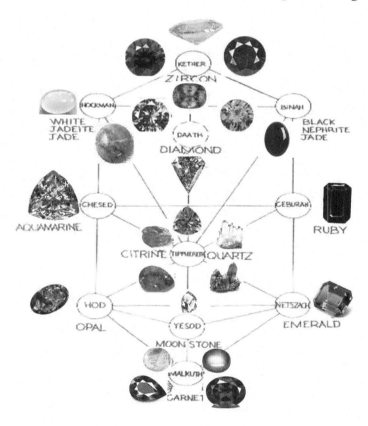

THE ENERGY OF THIS WORK JUST DONE

AIDS THE DEVELOPMENT OF LOVE AND UNDERSTANDING

IN ALL THINGS.

XV
THE HORNED GOD

No. XV The Horned God - Pan

The Lord of Shadows-Key to the Shadows and Demons Within

"I Generate Love and Understanding for All Others".

The word DEMON has been used by Wicces and Magicians for centuries and it's been misinterpreted because of ignorance and fear for the same length of time. Originally the spelling was the reverse of the word 'named' = DEMAN. When a Magician talks about a Demon, he is talking about some form of pressure between the levels of the mind, what is today called a neurosis. Just as there are individual and group or social neurosis, there are microcosmic and macrocosmic demons. They represent the parts of our self that we flow against. We try to push these so called "bad" ideas away from us because of conditioned prejudice and the fact that we trust the picture that our social environment presents us with as real and complete.

The pressure we exert against these energies (original normal healthy drives) distorts them so that they appear grotesque and horrible. In fact, your Etheric form takes on whatever attributes are contained in its name.

To help you bring this apparently self-destructive side of your nature "in to line", your work group needs to find and work its group totem. This is done just as finding your own totem is, except that you all do it together, as one unit. Sometimes the group totem and the personal totem seem to be in conflict, it is up to everyone individually to work through this apparent conflict (remembering that it is only apparent). The totem gives you a strong link to the positive side of the Mars sphere of influence and this will increase your ability to see what the group Demon really is.

Even the most terrible Demon is simply the result of faulty communication between levels. Once you understand the functioning of the tree you can see that if the pressure between any two levels can build too far then their normally beneficial influence can be cut off. This results in what psychiatry calls a PSYCHOSIS or a "breaking off" from reality (?).

We've already talked about ways to divert or even totally alleviate pressures that build, but you have spent YEARS living in a neurotic society and each day you ADD to the strength of your "suppressed side". These suppressed fears, biases, frustrations etc. must be faced sooner or later and finally overcome so that part of your mind/body can work in harmony with the rest of itself. First you must LOCATE your WATCHER or Demon. If there is a malfunction in your mind/body system there will be a corresponding malfunction in your Tree, you know how to test the strength of each Sphere with the Lightning Flash, now you should extend that knowledge to check the Paths of Communication BETWEEN levels.

The group should do a macrocosmic Tree Ritual – begin the Lightning Flash as usual – go from KETHER (Uranus) to CHOKMAH (Neptune) to BINAH (Pluto) to DAAT (Saturn). Then at this stage visualise a faint (trace Paths) that radiate from DAAT.

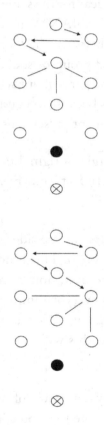

Then allow the flow to choose the strongest. The Wicces Path is to CHESED (Jupiter). Note any difference. From Jupiter allow trace Paths to form, then follow the same procedure.

Here the Wicces Path is to GEBURAH, note any difference. Do the same sort of thing with the rest of the Tree as you go down the Lightning Flash. This way you can build a "map" on the way the group functions with the Tree at this moment. It will show you where the most work is needed, it gives you a vantage point to see how you have been shaped by society and what you need to gain in a balanced union of love

Another way to "fix" or find the WATCHER is the use of the pendulum. Take a piece of cotton about ten inches long and tie a ring, or something you have worn constantly for some time, to one end. Draw a Circle approximately 9 to 10 inches in diameter and divide it into four (the points of the compass) with two straight lines. Now hold the string so that the ring hangs at the middle of the circle and your elbow rests on something solid.

Make yourself as relaxed as possible then ask aloud a question that you KNOW the answer to. In this way you will find out which of the five possible movements means YES and NO, and PERHAPS and I DON'T KNOW. The five movements are around the Magick Circle; Deosil, Widdershins, or along either of the 2 lines, or an erratic movement (which usually means I DON'T WANT TO ANSWER – you must use tact and gentle persuasion). By careful questioning you can uncover the time and place and the circumstances surrounding any suppressed incident, by this means by confronting yourself with yourself, you can get rid of a lot of neurotic pressure.

If you use your Pendulum on your Elemental cards, you will find that each Element produces a characteristic movement. You can then use this for all sorts of dowsing and diagnosis.

You check the validity of your positioning of the WATCHER, by discussion and the use of all the Tools the group is developing. The functions of the Tree have a POSITIVE or NEGATIVE (QLIPHOTH – to use the Kabbalistic term) side to them:

SPHERE	POSITIVE	NEGATIVE

♅ ♆ ♀ the Abyss – There NON-EXISTENCE

There is no QLIPHOTH in the normal sense.

DAAT   Knowledge Ignorance.

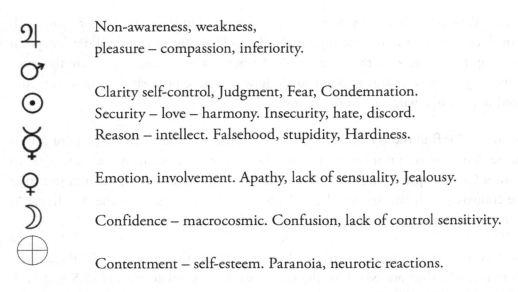

♃ Non-awareness, weakness,
pleasure – compassion, inferiority.

♂

☉ Clarity self-control, Judgment, Fear, Condemnation.
Security – love – harmony. Insecurity, hate, discord.
☿ Reason – intellect. Falsehood, stupidity, Hardiness.

♀ Emotion, involvement. Apathy, lack of sensuality, Jealousy.

☽ Confidence – macrocosmic. Confusion, lack of control sensitivity.

⊕ Contentment – self-esteem. Paranoia, neurotic reactions.

Now that you've located your WATCHER (personal as well as the group WATCHER), you are ready to BANISH it. To help the evocation you call on the God/dess, Shining One, Wind, and Elemental of the appropriate level. You BANISH the group WATCHER first. Your own personal WATCHER is done later. You need the group's love and understanding because you are about to bare your souls to each other and this can sometimes make you feel terribly alone and vulnerable.

Make a copy of this Magick Circle on a large Banished ground sheet. The TRIANGLE OF ART, which is in the NORTH QUARTER, is done separately for each Ritual, but the groundsheet is kept and used by the whole group – the more it is used – the stronger it becomes. The Tripod in the centre of the Triangle burns Frankincense, Myrrh, and Dittany of Crete (if not Dittany, local Mistletoe or Sandalwood). The Triangle itself can be the colour of the level concerned and/or covered with local Mistletoe. The name (what you describe it as) is written along the base of the Triangle. The lines in both the Circles are white. The Circle for the Triangle is the same circumference as the inside Circle in a large Square.

The 21 gold crosses (Tao) are made separately and placed on the Circle when it is in use. This Circle has been used for the same purpose – evocation – for centuries and is a particularly strong Etheric machine that will help you to "bring through" the form of the WATCHER in the Triangle of Art. If the /Ritual is done in the Temple, the main body of the group forms a circle around BOTH the ground sheet and the Triangle of the Art. They set up a clockwise flow with the Chant "AUSET". The person closest to the Triangle should make certain there is always sufficient incense burning.

The Four Wardens enter the main Circle in the East – go around Deosil 3 times.

AIR – Banishes; FIRE – Invokes; WATER – Banishes; EARTH – Invokes; then they take up their appropriate positions in the arms of the Cross in the centre of the Circle the Chant to generate the enlightenment thought (the clear perceptions that sees the true essence of things) is started with AUM then said 36 times. The Principle (combination of Moderator and subject) enters the Magick Circle carrying the appropriate Weapons for the Spheres involved. The purpose for the operation is stated in a clear, strong voice;

Principle:	(Magickal Name) HAVE COME
Wardens:	BY THE NAME YEHOVAH
Principle:	TO EVOKE AND COMMAND FROM THEE
Wardens:	BY THE NAME ADONAI
Principle:	(The name of the Sphere) IN ITS NEGATION.
Wardens:	BY THE NAME EH HEH YEH
Principle:	O APPEAR IN THE TRIANGLE OF ART
Wardens:	BY THE NAME AGLA
Principle:	O THAT I MAY BANISH IT FOREVER
Wardens:	AUM
Principle:	IN ALL PEACE AND LOVE, I CLAIM PROTECTION FOR MYSELF AND ALL WITHIN THIS TEMPLE (OR MAGICK CIRCLE) BY THE NAMES, YEHOVAH EL YEHOVAH ELOHIM

You need a LOT of incense in the tripod and a beeswax candle at each of the triangle points.

A beeswax candle is placed in each of the four Pentagrams.
The writing in the outside square is in gold; the word
In the centre is as well-the rest is in white.

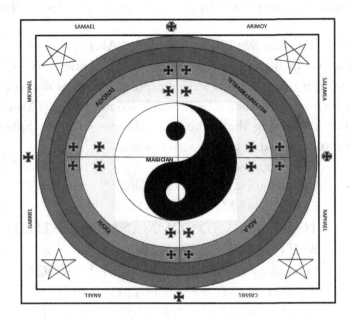

The Wardens set up a Deosil flow using AUM while the Principle visualises and directs this energy to build up in the Triangle. When the Principal feels the flow, she should raise her hands in front of herself palms down pointing directly at the Triangle and vibrate the appropriate Sphere's God name.

> "By this holy name do I command you Demon,
> to show yourself in your true form.
> So that I may see and understand you,
> For what you really are".

If the WATCHER doesn't appear, you go through the same procedure from, I (Magickal name) HAVE COME; right up to this stage again. Then take the Magickal Weapons and thrust them towards the Triangle saying;

> "By these Magickal Weapons I do call thee forth,
> So that I can see and understand you,
> For what you truly are."

The Wardens and the Principle vibrate AUM in unison three times and then the Demons name. You can repeat this up to 7 times. If you are still unsuccessful, Banish the Circle and try another day. Just because you cannot see the Demon, doesn't mean he isn't there. The evoked Demon may take the form of a vision for the Principal or any of the Wardens, or for that matter anyone inside the Temple if that happens the person concerned should direct the Demon to the Principal and then the Triangle of Art. Once the WATCHER is evoked the group can question it through the Principal you must NOT allow fear to fill your Aura when you finish with the WATCHER the Principal says:

> "Depart and leave this place as you are not of me or mine.
> Though once you were, go now in peace and love.
> By the Name (the Spheres God name)".

When it has gone the group intones the Mantra to fix the motive 36 times, each participant thanks all the entities (including the other participants) and leaves in the order they came in. Each person BANISHES the Temple. Record and discuss this Ritual and its effects. You will find the results differ from time to time. This is due to a lot of things, ranging from the Principle's Auric and visualising strength to the time the Ritual is done. You can evoke and banish the demon, as many times as you think is necessary. The personal WATCHER should not be banished until one week before Initiation. The Ritual is done alone and can be done in the group's Temple, your own home Temple, or a place of power in the country.

"The energy of the work just done
aids in the development of love and understanding in all things".

XVI
THE TOWER

No. XVI The Tower — Temple of Saiss

Power-Key to the Power of the Isarum Wicce

"I generate Love and Understanding for Myself and all others".

Your development of your auric strength brings with it its own responsibility you must realise that the thought forms or visualisations that you have been working with have caused your WILL, the strength of your "links", to increase. This means that you are exerting more auric "pressure" on the people around you than you were before you started this work. You must learn new ways to control or direct your energies because what WAS a natural reaction, such as so-called "healthy anger" can now no longer be entertained, because of the auric violence that accompanies such states of mind. At the same time, you can't deny power, because you need it to develop first yourself, and then your environment. Every time you use your full potential to develop or express something, you widen your scope of reality. As your REALITY is widened, then everyone you meet meets a wider scope of experience and both sides benefit.

Your work has brought you to a stage where you need to go very carefully through the 4 Laws. The First 2 deal with the generation of power, "MAN KNOW THYSELF" and "BE IN ALL THINGS". The latter two deals with control and direction of power. "DO WHAT THOU WILT" is the correct use of power, if you remember that you are always shaping and moulding yourself when you use power. True power doesn't HAVE to be used, this is the power of LOVE when it is SHARED rather than given or taken. LOVE (sharing) is always dependent upon the WILL (the Links) you've been developing. To share, your "links" must be able to give AND receive. Power should always be used to fit in and develop the flows around you. The more you use your "power" to help other people's fears, in healing etc. the more you learn about your own. It is sometimes necessary to see the problem EXTERNALLY so that the intellect can perceive and understand it.

You already know of two of your levels of action. The first is what we call Physical (and Magick is not anti-materialism, simply anti-restriction). It is important that you use the everyday world in the BEST way that you can. PHYSICAL well-being should never be unimportant to you.

You ARE Physical, you need comfort, food, pleasure and all the other good things that the physical world has. All that Magick says, is that this isn't all there is! There are whole worlds waiting to be explored and used; all you must do is clean and sensitise your physical body, so that you demonstrate your self-awareness to yourself and THEN you will allow yourself to use other "levels of action".

The second "level of action" we touch is the aura. You've learnt how to strengthen and protect this part of your being and you are learning to use its perceptions. You should be beginning to realise just how much of your interaction with your environment depends upon it. Every communication you have with other people is influenced by BOTH your aura and theirs. If both auras are in harmony, we talk about a *"rapport"* or intuitive understanding. On the other hand, if the auras of two people are in opposition or discord, then no matter how clear their speech is, neither party can see the others point of view. If you are arguing with someone and you want to stop, relax physically as much as possible (use your breathing) and THEN watch your friend's breath and MATCH IT with your own, at the same time fill your aura with the Sun. You will be surprised how effective this little exercise is, use it and develop it and remember to be GENTLE, with yourself and others.

Both "the body of Light" and "the WATCHER" is aspects of this level of action. The Moon is either your strength or your weakness depending upon your attitude towards it.

The "Etheric" is the next level of action it is the level of the Spheres below the Sun, the transition or meeting point between the Yin forces of physical incarnation and the Yang forces of Solar development. Everything here is in a state of constant "flux" and it takes some practice to familiarise yourself with the apparently impossible job of accepting the intellect, the five Elements and the emotions, the four elements, BOTH acting in you at the same time. It is on these lower Astral Planes that the average person tries to create and maintain their centre. Because of the nature of this level, they wind up being caught between two extremes, which they translate as Heaven and Hell. Some people see one thing as Heaven, while others see the same thing as Hell. You are learning to "flow" with both sides of your nature. Time also shows this two-sided characteristic on this level. Depending upon the circumstances, you may have to consider the Law of Reverse Effect or you may not, time may flow forward or backward. The situation may even change halfway through the experience.

The ASTRAL Plane, the next level of action, is composed of matter that is light (this level is the Sun) - not the same "sort" of light as on a physical level – but light all the same. Your

Astral "body" is usually a ball-shape and its auric field appears to be much "denser" than your physical aura.

When you do Rituals, you produce a "finger" of Astral Matter, which attracts other matter to it, to "construct" the required object or symbol.

This is how you create an external polarity for your projected energies, your Prana, to flow to.

The planets above the Sun, which make up the next level of action, are the forces you will learn to control as you reach the "Adept" stage of your Magickal development. This level is sometimes seen as the Sphere of the Masters (there are Martian and Jupiterian Masters). These Masters are people who have reached beyond the Abyss and this gives them the choice of going on with their own development or resting to enjoy their present state. Some of the Masters can be "linked" by you after your Initiation. They enjoy sharing your learning with you. There are two stages above the Abyss – the Magus can reach above the Abyss to Neptune and Pluto, the primal male/female source inside everything. A Master can touch every part of every part of everything; She/he is consciously **BIAME**, the Great Spirit. These are the six "dreamtime" bodies we each possess.

We are acting consciously on each of these levels at this moment; we don't "see" it because on different levels we act through different mediums. Magick is learning to act on many levels in harmony and that means increased communication. For example, if you make a Talisman to heal the KIDNEYS, the act of making the Talisman, which could be a "picture" of a healthy set of kidneys and/or a Black Crescent, will cause the Astral body to send out "fingers" to construct an EFFECT – healthy kidneys. As you fill this with Prana (work the Talisman with your breath) you give the EFFECT the energy that it needs to draw to it the necessary things to CAUSE it to happen physically. If you work out the appropriate day (the kidneys are ruled by Mercury, there's a list of CONCORDANCES behind the main body of this study.) You can construct a pyramid as before mentioned, except that the colour is orange and the symbol is Mercury. You make a stand for the middle so that you can put your Talisman at the "Kings Chamber" which is a third of the way up from the base level.

The Kings chamber is the exact centre of the bisection of the five corners.

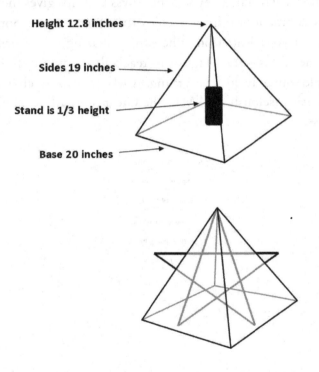

Height 12.8 inches

Sides 19 inches

Stand is 1/3 height

Base 20 inches

Representing the Pentagram of Isis. This space is the *"Fire within"* - PYRA-MID, and if it is aligned to the Earth's field (through North) it will concentrate the "energy of the day". This will "charge" your Talisman with The EARTH'S BREATHE, as it channels the effect of the day's planet. A Pyramid frame can be used to meditate in because its constant flow will help you to centre. Don't stay in for longer than 1½ hours – if you balance things too much, they stop. You can also use an open pyramid (just a frame) to charge water with the Sun's Prana.

This purified water can be drunk and/or used to clean the four Auric Eyes (hands, forehead and navel) especially after healing, and during fasts.

You know that BOREAUS can be asked for anything you need. He (or you, because the microscopic entities are you) can usually deliver what you ask. A refinement of this as a Ritual is called the "TREASURE MAP", a sort of Talisman that can be very effective for personal and group development. It is a way to concentrate the attention of more than one level on a single focus or set of focuses. If you use it in harmony with what is flowing around you, you can gain access to different levels and talents within yourself. All you need do to acquire the necessary talent, which is Natural to us all, is to tell your inner source what you want.

Remember to balance what you take from the macrocosm with what you give back. Often simply developing what you get to its full capacity best does this. For example, evoking and using your artistic vision is GOOD KARMA, but simply evoking and then not using/ expressing what you've evoked can cause pressures to build internally and this can cause disease. Think carefully about what you have and how this can be developed. You must expand your SPHERE OF INFLUENCE slowly and steadily. Take a DESIRE to play music and use the desire to form an image of the type of music you want and put that into your TREASURE MAP.

Every time you use any Talisman you must build a positive Etheric form into it, by first linking to it (as usual) and then "fixing" your gaze on it until its complimentary image is formed, then slowly close your eyes, but keep the Talisman in focus. Fix the after image in one spot. This makes the image a focus, which receives a flow of the appropriate complimentary colour. If your treating the liver for example, and your Talisman is green, you fill the Etheric Talisman with a flow of RED PRANA.

The different directions of TIME on the different levels and the mechanism that causes the eye to create the "afterimage", both follow the same Law of Reverse Effect. You vitalize the afterimage Talisman as you exhale, into it. As you breathe in you take the impure distracting energies out of it and then you "BIND" them, by visualising them being tied in a bundle. Finally, you Banish the bound negative form. The more clearly this is done, the stronger will be the Aura that you give back to the physical Talisman, then the easier it will be to use. Be very clear and definite in your own mind about where the LIMITS of your Talisman's actions are. It is easy to get caught at this stage, you must be careful not to BIND this positive side as well.

You must always allow the "effect" you create with your ASTRAL FINGERS or CHORDS, room to grow and develop internally, so the Etheric and auric levels of your action can "fit" the Talisman to the physical form and vice versa.

Finally, you must select the time considered as much as is convenient or you think is necessary. As the Moon is building and the physical form is expanding, if you charge a Talisman now, that expansion causes the "vibe" given off to increase. As the Moon shrinks the Talisman draws into itself, so a Talisman made at this time usually has a sedative action. Both can be useful at times.

If you call on a Planet or Zodiac sign, it should be an appropriate time. For instance, if I want to invoke the forces of Venus on Tuesday (Mars) in early October and the Planet weren't in the sky. I could still call on the Planet through Libra, because Venus is the ruling Planet of day. If you can't find some external link, then you must evoke the Planets influence from your own Tree. This is one of the reason's you've taken so much trouble to build it, but because it won't "be set" until after Initiation, it's not a very profitable source of energy for you at this moment, because it is easy to drain what little amount of the Planets Vibe you have worked or fixed in your aura.

On a Thursday in a Banished and invoked Magick Circle at home or in a workroom make a folder out of BLACK PAPER 22 x 21 units – seal it. Inside put two pieces of white paper 20 x 19 on the first sheet draw the card Air of Water, but instead of the name EH HEH YEH, the God of Water, vibrate the name EL – because Jupiter is AIR – the first Sphere – of the WATER level of the Tree. You draw your map on the second sheet.

First set the limits of the Talisman by fixing the field with a black, totally absorbing border quarter of a unit wide. Then divide the Talisman into four segments with 2 diagonal lines, because the object or "receiver" of this Talisman is the Earth Sphere at the base of the Tree. In the top quarter you put something that depicts, for you, your aims of self-knowledge. In the right-hand quarter depict the fulfillment of your self-esteem needs. Concentrate on the sexual/social drives in the left (your left, not the pages) quarter. Finally, in the bottom place the physical things you need for survival.

Keep the pictures/sketches/Diagrams/symbols – NOT WORDS, very clear and simple.

The Ritual to charge the Talisman can be done immediately after the folder is made or you can wait til Saturday, so that you work both "ends" of the Talisman's action. Sit facing NORTH in a Banished and Invoked Magick Circle with the folder in front of you. Take yourself into a deeply relaxed state and activate the full Tree in your Aura. Open the folder and concentrate on the symbol until the afterimage occurs. Slowly close your eyes and work the image, turn the page over once your eyes are closed. Visualise the symbol as a door and go through it. Then open your eyes and concentrate on your map. Fix a picture of each Quarter firmly. Not stiffly in your mind. Become totally familiar with it. As if you've never seen it before then let your gaze become fixed on the centre, keep it there and count slowly up to sixty. This should be long enough for the afterimage to be clear. Close your eyes slowly and work this image with a flow of Prana. Use each Quarter starting with Earth as a door to the four rooms in the house, that is your map. Visualise going through each room and do a flow with each object, you have placed inside the rooms. Sit very still in the centre of the house on the *"cross"* and feel the links you have made to each thing. Contemplate already having each item. When you feel it is time slowly and gently come back to your body. Thank all the entities concerned, BOREAUS especially (as you used the North Quarter) then leave in the normal fashion.

There are thousands of adaptations of the basic form of that Ritual. For example, you can use it to aid your work on your body of Light. The level of action you are directly working on is the auric level of the Moon. You can use a Silver Crescent as your door, or as this level represents the Air and Fire actions of the Earth level you can use;

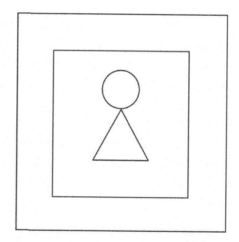

On your second sheet you put the image of your Familiar, surrounded by the Serpent of the Macrocosm eating its own tail, (Ouroboros). Around that depict the four "Water" Gods – **PAN** – Upper left (your left); **DIANA** – Upper right; **HERMES** – Lower right; and **VENUS** – Lower left.

Use any colour you want, but the background is purple with blue in it. The Goddesses and Gods are looking in at the image. Start the invocation from the EARTH Quarter and end with WATER, so that you can call on ZEPHYRUS to get the UNDINES to shape the Familiar from the Water levels of Venus and Mercury.

Work out and use other versions of these older Rituals. You can get the whole group to work on some together. For example, to help bring through the group totem so you can use its strength, or to do "distant" healing. In this case you use a picture or photograph of the person, or you could use something that the subject has had on their person for a long time (over a year).

Healing presents a sort of problem. We, as Wicces, tend towards SELF HEALING, but that does not exclude the sharing of your strengths, either as a healer or patient. Ideally, both sides should feel a part of each role and can change from one to the other. The work you have been doing is all this sort of healing. Our aim is not just to relieve symptoms or to cure disease but to develop ourselves and our environment at the same time.

If you use the group to generate energy for distant healing, you spend some time calling RAPHAEL (the Shining One of TIPHARETH for this Ritual). He can take the energy to the subject (bring the subject's aura to the Temple). The Moderator visualises the subject being there (use something that the person has worn for over a year or a photograph), or someone who has a link to the person can "take on" the Aura that RAPHAEL brings. This can be dangerous, but it is a useful training experience, it depends on how well you can flow without holding anything in.

Once you are aware of the health aura and have practiced the auric massage as described earlier, you can extend this treatment to include specific Prana flows to specific organs. This can be done directly by placing your left hand at the back of the patient's neck if they're lying on their stomach and on the forehead if they're on their back, then with the Right hand over the affected area visualising the words "I AM STRONG" vibrating inside the affected organ.

As you breathe in, you draw off, through your left hand, any disorganised or inharmonious energies. You can reinforce this "drawing out" with the command "GET OUT". Again, this is visualised as vibrating inside the organ. As you use these auric commands your breathing and your patient's must match, so that the commands come from your combined flows. Every now and then flick your fingers away from the patient as if you were throwing away the disease. Then put your right hand over the affected region and your left hand pointing behind you and down at the ground. Breathe in through the "EYE" in the left palm and visualise the energy you need from the EARTH being drawn into you. Breath out and project the energy into the organ. Visualise the organ filling with clear strong Prana. Then change hands and use the "CLEANSING BREATH".

Inhale a complete breath, and draw out of the patient, all that must come out, through your left hand. Retain the Air a few seconds and visualise the unwanted energy being encapsulated. Then pucker your lips as if you are going to whistle (but don't let your cheeks swell out). Push a little Air out with a firm even pressure. Stop for a moment retaining the Air, then push out some more. Remember to use considerable force to push out the Air. Visualise it is flowing through your right hand into the EARTH. Make sure all the Air is expelled. This cleansing breath can be used to "take" pain as well. You can also incorporate into your own pain control technique, which can then be extended to your patients. Breath in, inhaling Prana. Then send the Prana to the pain site, to re-establish the circulation and nerve current, as you breathe out. Alternate the 2 ideas for 7 breaths then use the Cleansing Breath.

Different energy is available at different times of the day. In acupuncture, the HORARY CLOCK illustrates this effect. The noon referred to is the Sun in Mid Heaven.

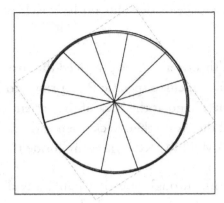

The period from 11 am to 1 pm is when the heart (YIN Fire) meridian is receiving the fullest concentration of energy. You can regulate or help this action by working "doing a flow with" the point on the meridian that is governed by the same Element, in this case the point is HEART 8, which is between the fourth and fifth bones in the palm of the hand on the Heart line.

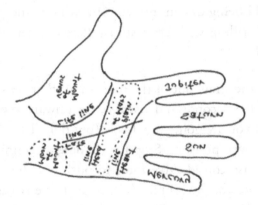

From 1 to 3 is the small intestine (**YANG** Fire) and its point is small intestine 5, at the end of the flexure of the wrist.

From 3 to 5 is the Bladder (Yang Water), its point; Bladder 6 is just above the crease of the little toe.

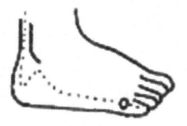

From 5 to 7 is the Kidney (YIN Water) time. The Horary point, Kidney 10 is behind the knee on the inside of the leg.

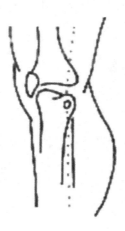

From 7 to 9 is the time of the Sex and Heart governor meridian (Yin Fire, which also corresponds to the right kidney – the pushing power). Its point, Pericardium 8, is on the Headline of the hand, on the third bone of the palm.

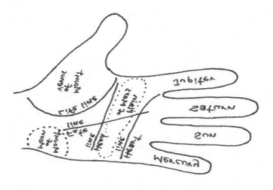

From 9 to 11 is the time when the three-heater (YANG Fire) meridian is *"fueled"*. The three heats are the three breaths, which are controlled from three points on the front of the body that relate to three nerve ganglia (Masses) near the backbone. The three points are:

Dan Chu – midway between the nipples – this relates to the heat generated by the Heart and Lungs.

Chu Kwan – the central point, the duodenum, midway between the bottom of the ribs and the navel. This relates to digestive heat.

In-Ko – one unit below the navel—this relates to the lower heater, Bladder and Kidneys.

The Horary point is Three Heater 6; it is between the two forearm bones, three fingers up from the flexure of the wrist on the outside of the arm.

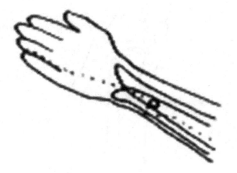

The time between 11 and 1 am is the Gall Bladder (YANG Wood) its Horary point, Gall Bladder 41, is on the top of the foot in the angle between the fourth and fifth bones.

The time after that, 1 to 3am, is the Liver (YIN Wood). Its point, Liver 1, is just off the inside corner of the nail on the big toe.

Between 3 and 5 is the time of the Lungs (YIN Air). Its horary point, Lung 8, is one finger space up from the lump on the end of the bone that is near the base of the thumb.

Between 5 and 7 is the Colon (YANG Air). Its point is Large Intestine 1, which is just off the outside corner of the nail on the index finger.

The next two-hour period between 7 and 9 is for the Stomach (YANG Earth). Its point is Stomach 36; it is on the outside of the leg, three fingers down from the kneecap in the hollow space below the beginning of the bone.

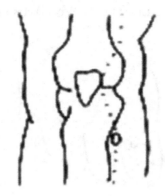

The period between 9 and 11 is the Spleen (YIN Earth) it is on the outside of the first foot bone, just before the joint of the big toe.

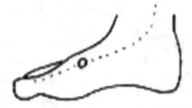

When you are traveling you can keep yourself *"in tune"* with the area you are in by regulating the appropriate point at the correct times. You may have to go through five or six of the points and times, if you hate traveling a long way. If the point is hot, it is excess, so you calm it before starting any work. You do this by gently drawing the energy out of the point with your left hand. If it is cold, it is deficient, so you tonify it by putting the appropriate energy in with your right hand. If there is a surface pain there is excess, if the pain is deep it is deficient. Another way to sedate is to tonify the opposite point (e.g. the Spleen point between 9 and 11 at night). To thoroughly clean the 12 bilateral acupuncture meridians, you can incorporate the circulation of light with rhythmic breathing in yourself and in healing others.

Start at the beginning of the Yin meridian on and under the big toe of both feet visualise the flow of energy-Chi rising the inside of your legs to meet at a point midway between your anus and your genitals. Then take the flow around and over both sides of your genitals then up the front of the body on both sides of the midline until you reach the level of Dan Chu between your nipples.

Here the flowers go out to the nipples then down the inside of your arms, over the palms of your hands then over the tips of the fingers back up the outside of the hand, the outside of the elbow over the shoulder to meet at front in the hollow in the middle of the collarbones above the breastbone. Then the flow goes up the middle of the throat over the chin and mouth along the nose to the middle of the forehead, there it swings around to the right, to circle the head and come back to the middle of the forehead. And then straight over the top of the back of the head then the first neck (cervical) vertebrae.

The seven neck bones express the seven planets. The top one is Saturn. The next Jupiter, then Mars, then the Moon, Venus, Mercury, then the Sun. To protect your aura, you can put Sandalwood oil at this point because every Yang meridian in the body passes through this area. It is the meeting point between the seven planets and the 12 Zodiacal Houses. Here the flow separates to go down both sides of the backbone. The first of the 12 thoracic (chest) vertebrae expresses the force of Aries. The next is Taurus then Gemini etc. until Pisces which is the last of them. Then the flow goes either side of the Five Lumbar vertebrae – the large backbones that have no ribs attached. The first of these is Earth, the next is Fire, then Wood, Water, and finally Air. The flow continues down to meet at the point between the anus and genitals. Then goes out under the cheeks of your buttocks to flow down the outside of your leg and finally join up to complete the circuit.

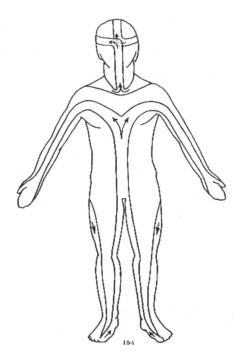

15-1

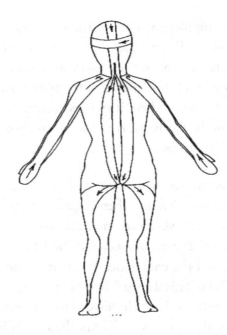

You can use the breath to control this flow breath IN blue energy from the feet up the front and down the inside of the arms to the fingertips. Then OUT red for the rest of the cycle. The YIN part should take slightly longer than the YANG.

Spiritual healing is directing energy from the deepest level of our being; it can be done by anyone who has done enough work on opening the "eyes in the palms". This treatment can clear any blockage or mistake in the formation of the tree in your Aura. In fact, radiating white (purifying) light from the palm of the hand is an effective treatment for any disease, physical, psychological or spiritual for any person, animal, plant or place.

The subject sits, facing East (the new beginning) or North (the source of wealth – BOREUS) with their legs folded under them so that they sit on their heels. The left (receptive) foot is on top of the right. The hands are held in the prayer position so that the light from the Palm Eyes will be circulated rather than lost. The back is held straight, the neck slightly bent forward, and the eyes closed and looking toward the centre of the forehead tell the subject to relax and allow themselves to open to receive universal light the light of spiritual matter (KETHER) is the underlying substance of all else.

That active partner (the one giving light) sits alongside the other person on the right of the Lady and to the left of a man breathing in, you both stretch your hands up and back … separating the palms and turning them towards the front as you breathe out you bring your hands down in front of you as you let all your breath out bend over and put your forehead on the triangle with your thumbs and index finger on the floor in front of you. As you let all your breath out and stay there for as long as you can.

As you begin to breathe in, stretch your hands out in front, then up and back to the same sort of stretch as before. Breathing out bring your hands back to the prayer position this is called the "Salute of the Sun" and it's a good way to begin any sort of harmonising work the active partner then changes their position so that you face each other. Your knees are one "Fist" apart.

Visualise white light building between your palms say the generation mantra and concentrate your eyes on the centre of your forehead (the Air or form perceiving eye) until you become aware of the building up of light (don't force this, just relax and observe for 4–5 minutes, saying the mantra – internally or externally – continuously).

When you feel that there is sufficient build, let your left-hand drop to the level of your navel with the fingers outstretched except for a circle formed with your thumb and index finger. This mantra will cause a flow of Light (Prana) to enter the navel (EARTH) eye from the universal centre (KETHER) you then hold your right palm about 30 cm (level with your partners knee's) from the forehead of the subject.

Visualise the light streaming into the back of your head (the base of the brain) through your Air eye to your hand and from there it flows out to clear and purify the Air eye of the subject. Allow at least 10 minutes and up to 20 minutes for this initial link to form continue the Chant the whole time and try to match your breathing

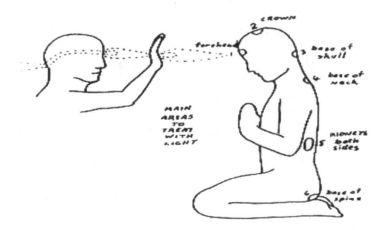

If your arm gets tired you can change hands by bringing the left up behind the right project from the flow of the palm, then lower the right to form the receiving mudra at the level of the navel. Be careful not to break the flow or vary the distance from your palm to the area you're treating. You can repeat the same procedure as often as you need to.

If you are clearing the spheres of the tree you can follow the lightning flash down allowing 5 to 10 minutes for each sphere. Don't be specific just flow white light and trust the life force to sort it out if you are doing a general treatment take the energy up to the top of the head (stay 30cm away) Stay, there for 2-4 minutes come down to the point at the base of the neck.

Spend 4-6 minutes here continue down to the level of the kidneys. Use both hands to radiate both kidneys with light for 6-8 minutes. Then bring your palms and the energy together and direct the flow in to the base of the spine.

Keeping your palms together bring the flow up the centre of the spine separate at the base of the neck and take your palms up either side of the head. Visualise pulling out all the blockages and rubbish up through the spine as you do this it helps if you breathe in as you draw it up. Concentrate on drawing any "External Zen" out of the body then clap your hands directly over the crown of the head and at the same time say **PUM** (like an explosion) visualising the negative energy flying off into space.

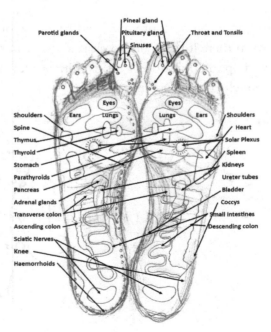

During the flow you can direct the flow to any other part you feel needs treatment. This is a spiritual healing that channels the life force of KETHER and as at this level there is no difference between the life forces, it is one of the most thorough treatments for any form of invasion physical, Auric or spiritual. It is then necessary to evoke Jupiter (HESED) and from there the Goddess of mercy KWAN YIN (use the mantra OM MA NI PAD ME HUM) and ask her to guide any released entity to its own Karmic path.

Thank each other (and KWAN YIN) then say the mantra to fix the energy at least 6 times. Finally do the "SALUTE TO THE SUN" to finish DO THIS OFTEN.

The hands and feet, like the points in any shape, have a stream of energy constantly flowing through them that is a "picture" of the rest of the body. The feet are the lowest points of the body, so if an organ is not functioning properly and its energy is not drawn into the rest of the system, it accumulates in the feet and causes the formation of tiny crystals. These can be worked by massage and the flow of energy resumed. This can also be used to diagnose the state of health of your internal organs. If there is pain when you press firmly on an area, then there is a corresponding "Elemental hunger" in the organ associated with that area.

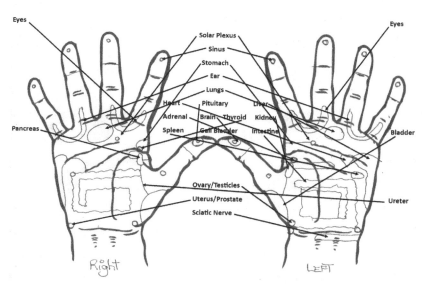

The hands have a similar pattern. This time the pattern expresses the out/flow of waste and the in/flow of sensual experience. These areas can be worked by firm massage.

Your group-work at this stage should become innovative. Design and work your own rituals, to exercise your awareness and put your theoretical knowledge to practical application.

"May the energy of the work just done
Aid in the development of Love and Understanding in all things"

XVII
The Star

XVII The Star
The Celestial Mother Of Time & Space

The Tiphareth Weekend
The Festival of the Sun-Key to the Secret of Secrets-The Light

I Generate Love and Understanding
For Myself and All Others

The invocation of the Sun Centre – TIPHERET – takes a week to prepare for (7 days) and two days to perform. It is done before, or as, the Moon cycle comes up to the Full, on the Saturday and Sunday closest to the Equinox.

The site must be selected one week before on Saturday and the circle worked and the local Nature Spirits (Elementals and Winds) informed about what is to happen the following weekend. A good way to locate the Circle is to use a "Dowsing Rod". You make one out of a Y branch of a Eucalyptus tree the length of your arm. You cut it down with a clean and banished knife after doing a flow with the tree and asking its Elemental which branch you can have. My husband is excellent at dowsing and uses it for looking for gold and water with great success. Tell the Elemental what you want it for and that the Circle will be used to invoke the Sun, to heal the land as well as for your personal work. After the branch has been cut, you "treat" the cut, your saliva can heal a plant, just as they heal us, and thank the Elemental.

It is a good idea to make "tips" out of the metal that is appropriate to the work to be done in that Circle. As this circle is going to be used to invoke the Sun, the tips are gold.

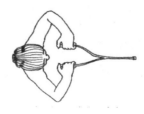

You hold it as shown, do a full tree visualisation, evoke the Sun and set up a flow from your right-hand thumb into the gold tip of the rod and out the other end as you breathe out.

As you breathe in you draw Sun energy back in through your left thumb. The top part of your body must be held very loosely, and you allow the rod to direct or "pull" you to the Circle. These Circles are to the land what an acupuncture point is to the body, or a pore is to the human body, they are the breathing and power points, so when you use them, you treat the land at the same time. This is the reason the Elementals in the area will be willing to help if you let them know what's happening.

To help bring through the Sun, which is needed to "Centre" the act of Initiation, the pre-Initiate robe has a gold Sun Talisman (design your own) added to the back of your usual cloak. You also need a Gold Pentagram (the centre is rock crystal or topaz) worn on a chain around the neck, which is the Priest/esses weapon.

The Wardens cloaks should have complimentary coloured edges and Elemental shapes added to the back. During the week the land should be worked Magickally each day. Do as little or as much as you think necessary, but always keep the coming weekend as the aim. Not everyone is needed yet this preliminary work can be done by one person (you can take turns) but if possible, someone should be there all the time. The whole group prepares as if for a festival. Music, good healthy food, dancing, costumes, and anything else you can think of to add to the enjoyment, should be prepared. Don't include any competitive games because the Auric tone of competition is contrary to your purpose here. You can even "dress up" your tents and camping equipment. The whole TIPHERET WEEKEND is a celebration of the fact that we are alive, it's a time to come together to work and play as friends.

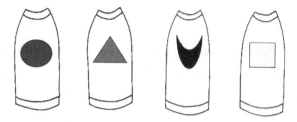

You can increase the strength of your "tuning in" to the Sun level using herbs such as Bay, Acacia, Laurel, Vine, Dandelion, Aloes Wood, Saffron or Cloves. If possible, burn some Olibanum by your bed at night. Include in your preparation a short period every day meditating on **LOVE**. You may be surprised how little or how much you know about love.

The food you take should be as near as possible to organically grown. There must be NO preservatives or synthetic substances. NO white sugar, meat or salt, NO alcohol, apart from grape wine, NO coffee or tea. You should take fruit, vegetables, good breads, milk, eggs, cheese, ghee, yogurt, nuts and any other healthy festive foods. Natural milk and honey is the traditional "Sun drink" of the Wicces; it is especially effective if you include some DAMIANA or HYDROCOLYTE (two herbs for Auric sensitivity). You can "charge" this drink by holding it in your left hand and gently shaking the finger of the right hand over the bowl, at the same time visualising "drops" of Prana falling from your fingers into the bowl. (Water can also be charged this way and used for healing).

You will need to take from the Temple, the Four Lesser Wiccetools of the Quarters, the banners of the EAST and WEST and the four Pyramids from the tops of the pillars. These are wrapped in BLACK SILK that has been Banished, before they are taken out of the Temple and not uncovered until they are inside the banished Magick Circle. You can increase the efficiency of the ritual by using "fasts" as you did for the Saturn ritual referred to earlier. Everyone must arrive early at the ritual site before 9 am Saturday. This gives you essential time to settle and relax before the ritual work begins. The person chosen to moderate the first ritual begins setting up at 10 am.

The Magick Circle is drawn with Sulphur, because its action is needed all the way around the only edge, the weakest point of the invoked auric field. The moderator uses a Chant that is felt to be appropriate to the Quarters of the Magick Circle being drawn. Then the Banner poles are driven firmly but gently into the ground in their appropriate places in front of the Pyramids (which take the part of the pillars) and the banners hung in their place. You could make an appropriate Altar sheet for each Element and cover a local rock or something to make an Altar for each Quarter. Keep these simple so that you can keep them to use at other times as well. The food for the feast can then be passed in to the moderator. It should not be in plastic or metal containers. Four large bowls are placed at the four Quarters for any leftovers or skins and the food arranged in a circle. Leave a clear space in the middle to conduct the ritual from.

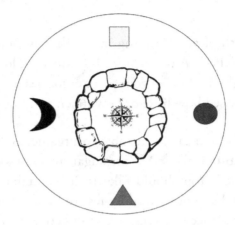

Once all this is finished the moderator leaves, if there is time, before coming back for the main part of the ritual, which begins at 11.30am. The moderator enters and does three circulations' acknowledging the Elements and taking from each an "aspect" of the Sun (which can be visualised as a garment to be worn or energy to be used). Once this is done he goes and stands in the centre, facing the East, with arms spread to form a cross and says to the macrocosm:

> "Come, everyone who wishes to work with us,
> in peace and in love, as sisters and brothers.
> For this is "MAGNUM OPUS"
> In the divine names of Atum, Amon and Ra".

The Four Wardens carry an appropriate "offering" (as in the feast) in the left hand and the covered Elemental Wiccetool in the right. They all enter together and move clockwise to their Quarter then turn together, walk directly to the moderator inside the circle of food and lay their offering at his feet. (The moderator is now **RA** personified). He thanks Air first.

The Warden then goes to the East, uncovers the Wand and begins to do the LBRP (Lesser Banishing Ritual of the Pentagram) of the circle with it. Once the Circle is complete the Wand is then placed on the Air Altar and the Warden stands behind it, but inside the

Magick Circle. The moderator then accepts the gift from Fire, who turns and goes to the Fire Altar, uncovers the Athame and does an invocation that starts from Fire and goes around to Air. The Athame is then placed on the Fire Altar and the Warden takes up the place behind the Altar.

The Water gift is then accepted, and a banishing is done, by Water, using the Chalice that begins with Water and ends with Fire. Then taking the Chalice back to the Water Altar completes the Magick Circle. The Earth gift is then accepted and the invocation using the Pentagram is begun in the North.

Then the rest of the group enter and as each person steps in the Magick Circle, the moderator performs the Sun Mudra. This is a movement of the hands that "Draws Out" the energy of the solar plexus, the Sun centre. Place your hands in the prayer position with your thumbs vertical and resting on your breastbone. Breathe in and visualise "roots" growing from the eyes in the palms, into the chest. As you breathe out visualise/vibrate the name;

YE-HO-VA EL-OH-VE-DA-AT

Between the palms, breathe in visualising a golden sphere of life forming between your palms, breathe out intoning **AUM**, and at the same time you can bring your hands up to your throat in this position, an unfolding flower. Keep the two little fingers, the heel of the palms and the thumbs touching the index fingers are about three inches apart from each other. Still breathing out separating the thumbs and the heel but still touching your little fingers, until finally you bring your hands to the lotus mudra. The tips of the four outside fingers touch. The four inside fingers lay against each other and you complete the **AUM.**

 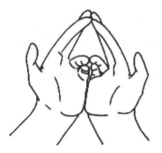

Visualise a sphere of golden light around the tips of the inside fingers, as the moderator says:

"You are welcome to join with us in Peace and love.
For this is our MAGNUM OPUS,
In the divine names Atum, Amon and Ra".

Both people visualise a flow of light between the Mudra of the High Priest/esses hands and the Solar Plexus of the person entering the Magick Circle. The person then enters, goes around three times and sits outside the Circle of food, then begins the Chant to generate the motive. Once everyone is in, RA (the High Priest/ess) invokes the four Shining Ones, the Pentagram and the Hexagram, and then begins the Feast of Life Liturgy (chapter XI).

Then the Feast! Dancing and music as well! You leave the Magick Circle in the usual manner, but the Magick Circle is NOT banished. This Ritual is the beginning of the invocation of the Sun Sphere; it is called the FEAST OF THE SUN.

Everybody must consciously try to open him or herself to the nature that surrounds them. Visualise your Aura becoming progressively more golden over the whole afternoon, except when Mars and Jupiter are called out of each of you in the mid-afternoon Ritual. This Ritual is the first part of the Eleusian Mystery School Initiation Play.

A new Priest/ess and new Wardens are chosen or changed. Then Air Warden wears a mask that depicts DIANA, the huntress. She, or He goes into the Circle to put it on, about half an hour before the main Ritual. She does a full Tree Ritual and asks each of the Quarters to "bring through" the Goddess. At the same time, she visualises the Goddess forming just behind her. She lets the feeling build as she asks each Quarter, then as she invokes the Shining Ones and the Pentagram and Hexagram, she visualises "taking on" the Goddess' life force, evoking from inside the "memory" of DIANA.

PAN is "taken on" by the Fire Warden and the MODERATOR "takes on" RA. Both use masks and go through the same preparatory Ritual.

The Ritual begins with the WARDENS entering the Circle:

AIR does a normal banishing,
FIRE does a normal invocation,
WATER does a normal banishing,
EARTH does a normal invocation.

The generative body, the rest of the people in the group enters, goes around three times and sits down. Finally, the MODERATOR enters, does three circles, and then goes to the centre and stands facing the SUN. The whole group sets up a flow using AUM. When the MODERATOR feels the flow is strong enough he turns to the EAST and stretches his hands, palm upwards and the Air Warden says:

PRIEST/ESS:

In the names of Yehovah, Raphael, Euras and the Sylphides.

GROUP:

Atum

PRIEST/ESS:

I call on Diana, Goddess Queen of Nature.

GROUP:

Atum

PRIEST/ESS:

To work and play in Peace and Love.

GROUP:

Atum

PRIEST/ESS:

Through (Wardens Magickal name) Your present form.

GROUP:

Atum

PRIEST/ESS:

In the Divine Name of Apollo, the Lord of Light.

DIANA:

Who calls my name.

PRIES/ESS:

I (Moderators Magickal name) the Voice of the Sun.

DIANA:

Who seeks to see me?

PRIEST/ESS:

I, the Eye of the Sun.

DIANA:

Who seeks to hear?

PRIEST/ESS:

I, the ears of the Sun.

DIANA:

Who seeks to feel?

PRIEST/ESS:

I, the body of the Sun.

GROUP:

Atum

DIANA:

Call Him!

RA turns to the FIRE WARDEN, stretches his hands out palm up and says:

PRIEST/ESS:

In the Divine names Adonai, Michael, Notas and Salamanders.

GROUP:

Atum

PRIEST/ESS:

I call upon the God Pan, our Lord of Nature.

GROUP:

Atum

PRIEST/ESS:

To work and play in peace and Love.

GROUP:

Atum

PRIEST/ESS:

Through (Wardens Magickal Name) in your present Form.

GROUP:

Atum

PRIEST/ESS:

In the Divine name of Apollo, the Lord of Light.

PAN:

Who is it that calls my name?

PRIEST/ESS:

I (Moderators Magickal name) the voice of the Sun!

PAN:

Who is it that seeks to see?

PRIEST/ESS:

I, the Eyes of the Sun!

PAN:

Who is it that seeks to hear?

PRIEST/ESS:

I, the Ears of the Sun!

PAN:

Who is it that seeks to Feel?

PRIEST/ESS:

I, the Body of the Sun!

GROUP:

Atum

PAN:

I will come!

The Goddess and God then rise and walk towards the PRIEST/ESS who takes their hands and joins them saying:

Let this union be known by the sacred and divine name LOVE!

All three invoke the Sun with the name:

Yehovah Eloh Ve Daat!

Then visualise the golden Sun Sphere filling the whole Magick Circle. The three then go to each of the people in the Magick Circle and touch them lightly just below the breastbone. They then return to the centre. The MODERATOR silently sends PAN and DIANA back to the Quarter after thanking them. The whole group spends 5 to 10 minutes meditation on the Ritual – FEEL don't THINK. Then stop FEELING and just BE. Let the Magick Circle flow into and through you. And then leave in the normal way. The last to leave is the PRIEST/ESS.

At sunset on the first day the whole group should be called to the highest place accessible by a new MODERATOR sounding a long deep note on the Conch Horn. Four new Wardens reach the MODERATOR first and stand in their relative positions around the MODERATOR. The rest of the group forms around these and a flow is set up using ATUM. When the Air Warden feels the flow is strong enough and the Sun is about to set, he says:

AIR:

All hail Ra, Lord of Being!

(All turn to face the Sun)

GROUP:

Atum

FIRE:

All Hail Ra, the Lord of Thought!

GROUP:

Atum

WATER:

All Hail Ra, the Lord of Action!

GROUP:

Atum

EARTH:

All Hail Ra, the Lord of Life!

GROUP:

Atum

PRIEST/ESS:

All Hail Atum Ra, as He sets, you share our divine Love!

All things in all times, and in all places, are One thing,

That thing is Love!

EVERYBODY:

Atum, Atum, Atum!

(Visualising Golden Aura)

The MIDNIGHT Ritual is much the same except the name RA becomes ISIS, and the word LORD becomes LADY. The PRIEST/ESSES part becomes HAIL ISIS, THE MOON AT ITS ZENITH, ETC.

This Ritual works well with a fire in the centre of the Circle and music and dancing to build the flow. Spin Clockwise to invoke, anti-clockwise to evoke; keep this up until your whole-body glows. Use cloak and arms to make a cone-shape to assist the flow of energy.

The DAWN RITUAL is the same as the Sunset Ritual except that the PRIEST/ESS says:

All Hail Khepri (Cairpra), Ra as He rises, etc.

The next Ritual is done halfway between sunrise and midday. It's the same basic form as the PAN and DIANA Ritual, except that the WATER WARDEN takes on HERMES, and the EARTH WARDEN takes on APHRODITE. Both these and the PRIEST/ESS use masks (the PRIEST/ESSES is the same as before). HERMES is called in the names of the Water Quarter. His final response is - CALL HER.

APHRODITE is then called from the Earth Quarter. Her final response is – I WILL COME.

Between this Ritual and the midday one, another **PRIEST/ESS** is chosen. Everyone else, who has reached this stage of the work, enters the Magick Circle and lies down with their feet towards the centre. Leave a path for the **PRIEST/ESS** to walk through from East to West and a small circle in the middle. Each person then takes himself or herself into a deeply relaxed, lightly hypnotic state. Close your eyes the **PRIEST/ESS** wearing the prism, carrying a copy of the Ritual and a watch to keep time, then enters the Magickal Circle. Goes around three times and then goes to the centre and says:

"You are about to go deeper into your Trance State, your body is becoming
even more and more relaxed. You will find it progressively easier to
forget your body entirely. Concentrate on your breathing.

Circulate light through the twelve meridians, up the inside of the legs, and around the
genitals, up the middle of your body. Split to go out to the nipples and down the inside of
the arms, back the outside of the arms, over the shoulders to meet between the collarbones.

Straight up and over the face up to the forehead. Circle to the right
around the head, and then continue up over and down the back of the
head. Down in between the base of the neck and the ribs.

It splits again down the back and over the outside of the leg, back under the foot. Relax very
deeply now and feel the strength of this Magickal Circle that we have built together. Think
about who you are, here at this place, and in this time. Relax your body and feel your mind
becoming more and more alert. A thing not confined to any one part of your Being. Say to
you "I am". Feel it vibrate through your form. Feel it vibrate each of your many bodies.

Feel it vibrate through your entire form, feel it vibrate each of your many bodies.
Very shortly you are going to take a journey, you are going to go to a place that
is like one that you have been to before. But it is not the same place. Very shortly
you are going on this journey. You will find yourself on a path walking in the
bush land. You will feel the Elements and the Elementals and the slight gentle
breeze, playing along beside you they will be very friendly and helpful to you.

You can treat them as friends. You will notice that the path is getting steeper and
you are beginning to descend into a deep rich valley. You will walk to the bottom
of the valley where you will see an amazing circular Temple. The Elementals beside
you will marvel at the beauty and joy that streams out of this sacred Temple.

You will gracefully enter and in the centre will be a large golden Altar, you
will go to the Altar and when you get close to it. You will see a stairway.
Leading down into the ground. You will go down these stairs. Leaving all your
companions behind you. The stairs are dark but warm and friendly. You will feel
perfectly safe and relaxed. And at last you will come out onto a beach in broad
daylight. You will look around at a strange and beautiful Magickal world.

You will hear faint but beautiful music playing somewhere up the beach. And you will feel drawn to that music. The most beautiful, warm and friendly group of gentle people is playing which you find. Wait patiently and listening.

> One of them will see you and stands up and comes over to you. This person will introduce him or herself and act as your guide. You will be taken to a special place, a place that is yours somehow. It will feel like your real home, and here you will be given back your Magickal name and image.

It is only then that you will realise that you had forgotten them temporarily. They will have grown more harmonious since you last saw them. Everything you need to work your Familiar will be found by you in this Temple of yours, and your guide will inform you how to hold the Sun in your Aura until Initiation, and anything else you need to know to prepare for your Initiation, your rebirth.

Very shortly you are going to make that journey, you will have ten minutes of clock time. But that will be ample for you to have whole weeks, months, even lifetimes of experiences, as there is no real time in the space. You will begin your journey NOW".

The MODERATOR then allows the appropriate time to pass, then says:

> "It is almost time for you to come back from this strange and wonderful land. You will remember the things that happened, the skills that they have learnt, and the advice of your guide.

> The talents you unlocked and everything else. You will soon become slowly aware of your body, your beautiful physical body. You will feel your Zen enter every part of it. Your body will feel more alive and beautiful than it ever has, and you will slowly wake up.

You will then slowly rise and go around and thank each of the Watchtowers and leave. It will take you three minutes of clock time to get back to your body and this will be ample time for you to experience all that you need to. You will begin saying Merry Part to your guide, now".

The PRIEST/ESS then leaves.

The last of the Rituals within this invocation is a second Feast of the Sun. It begins just before NOON. A new PRIEST/ESS enters the Magick Circle and does a full invocation asking each entity as it is invoked to: BRING THE SUN – OF LIFE – AND LOVE. Then as each of the Wardens enter carrying their offering the PRIEST/ESS says to them:

"I welcome you my sister/brother,
come in Peace and Love and share in my feast.
Come by the Divine Names Atum, Amon Ra!"

They then take their offering to him and go to their appropriate Quarter. The rest of the group is greeted in the same manner as they enter. When they are all in place, the PRIEST/ESS picks up the AIR gift, offers it to the Sun and says:

"We are first blessed with the Food of Thought!"

This is put down and the FIRE offering picked up and offered to the Sun saying:

"We are then blessed with the Flame of Spirit!"

This is returned to the ground and the WATER gift offered to the Sun saying:

"We are next blessed with the Water of Life!"

This is put down and the EARTH gift offered to the Sun saying:

"We are most blessed by your Gift of Love!"

The TIPHARETH MARRIAGES - the formulation of links from the centres of harmony – are now done.

This Ritual is used to Earth these links between people who love each other and wish to strengthen and deepen their communication. Whole families have done this Ritual; it doesn't HAVE to be between two people. The participants should find time before the weekend to make Talismans – a gold ring and a work of art – to be given to their partner/s during the linking. They can wear some simple costume (no black) or use body paint to symbolise their intention. Use the hour before the Feast to prepare. After the Magick Circle has been set and the gifts accepted the PRIEST/ESS invokes TIPHARETH (use the Mudra and the God-name) to the four Quarters.

A flow is started by the rest of the group and kept up during the feasting into the dancing and music. As the music builds, the PRIEST/ESS takes the white wine and unleavened bread (which has been taken into the Magick Circle earlier) from the centre and moves to the EARTH Quarter where he calls the people being married to him. He does the TIPHARETH Mudra with each person and as they receive the Sun, they place on the middle column of four fingers. The PRIEST/ESS then turns and gives this ring to the person waiting to receive it. This is repeated until everyone has given and received rings. He then flows Light into the bread and wine, and after partaking of it he shares it with those being linked. The works of art are exchanged, and everybody returns to the dancing and music. The PRIEST/ESS spreads her arms, facing East and says:

"We came, worked and played in Love.

GROUP:

Atum

HP or HPs:

In Love we thank all who helped.

GROUP:

Atum

HP or HPs:

By the Divine names Atum Amon Ra.

We leave this Magick Circle in Peace and harmony!

GROUP:

Atum

The PRIEST/ESS does a banishing Pentagram in the WEST:

In all times, and in all places, is one thing,

That thing is Divine Love!

GROUP: then vibrates in unison:

"Yehovah Elohim Gibor".

As the PRIEST/ESS pushes Prana through the Pentagram, a Kabbalistic Cross is then done in unison by everybody and this causes the Magick Circle to be BANISHED. The Chant to fix the energy is repeated 108 times. You must clean up the whole area including the campsite; leave the land with only good memories of you.

The energy of the work just done,
Aids the development of Love and Understanding in all things.

XVIII
THE MOON

XVIII The Moon
The Goddess Luna

Magickal Living-Key to the Goddess and the Lunar Mysteries

I generate Love and Understanding for all others and myself.

We have been working, through the experiences of Magick, towards a new type of community, where human and Nature will be able to live in harmony. A "city" without locks or laws, where each person has developed Auric sensitivity so that to lie to yourself or others becomes impossible and unnecessary, because everyone will have worked with and realised their own value and their right to exist. Every person in this city will be a Wicce.

This city can then be developed into a tribal system of life where nothing, (not even children or parents) is needed to be owned. Wicces are usually reasonably nomadic, so small communities will be scattered all over, but we do need reasonably permanent centres that work with the energy and intelligence of the living Earth itself. We can do this through structures and gardens, temples, etc.

This may sound as if it will be restrictive, but this is not so. Provisions (like this and other books) have been made so that anyone, regardless of race, age, sex, etc. can become an Initiated Wicce. To build a city where we can live fully and openly, we must start with the individuals. By the time you can understand enough about yourself to make Initiation work, you will also begin to realise that you need an environment where you can allow your sensitivity to develop. A modern city such as Sydney is a difficult environment to work in Magickly, because as your sensitivity increases you 'pick up' the vibe that is most predominant. This is usually hostile and on the verge of freaking. What should be a wonderful experience of unfolding can become a terrifying experience of other people's fears and hates. This is the reason you needed to build a Temple, a protected Sanctuary, a place in harmony with the living Earth. The next step is to develop your idea of a Temple into something that can be shared with everyone, a "living" Temple, a Temple to live in.

The Temple you have already built is the Fire Temple, its function is to generate and "store" the necessary "penetrative" force your work requires. You can also build Air, Water and Earth Temples.

The Air Temple's shape is spherical; this shape acts in much the same way as the cards you've worked. Its colours are blue and white. You don't use the four quarters in this temple, it is for meditation and emptying out, and it symbolises the undifferentiated Air element. The Water Temple is the balance of the phallic Fire Temple. Its shape is symbolic of the feminine genitals. The main colour is black and/or green. The Earth Temple is a golden square pyramid. All the Temples are aligned to the poles.

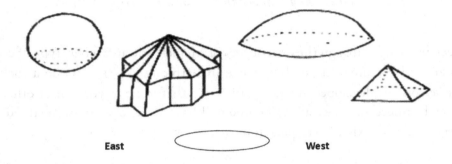

East   **West**

The Water Temple has two centres therefore this shape can be used to unite or direct the forces generated by the Fire Temple. This shape is the best shape to do your Initiation in. Initiation is the fixing and directing of the work you've done so far.

The Earth Temple is used to "charge" your auric strength, just as you've used this shape to charge talismans. In all the Temples, you can use lights and sound to assist with invoking energies. Because of the fixing property of the pyramid, it is not advisable to stay inside for too long a period, not over 30 minutes, unless you are doing specific work with an Initiate who can see what's going on.

All these Temples must be kept for your internal group work. They must be entered naked or in a specially made and Consecrated robe. The Akashic or Wood Temple is a different matter. This is your "point of interaction" with society, it can be used as a theatre, studio, dance hall, lecture room, training hall, work room, bazaar etc. It can also be used for large groups or even inter-group rituals.

Its shape fits easily into a large rectangular room.

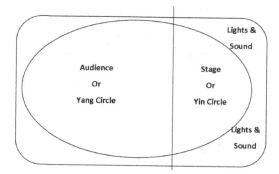

Doors and windows must be rounded, and care must be taken that there are no corners or edges on the inside shell. If you make it out of some fireproof fabric, you could "back film" onto the whole area, even the back, to create a total environment of colour, sound or even moving pictures. Performing in a theatre such as this will enable you to have a maximum amount of harmonious, flowing auric contact. You will find it easy to develop atmosphere and expression by working in this shape. Each group of people who uses this Temple could make their own "ground sheet" which could be an invoked talisman that suits their purpose. These could be used to "set" the Temple. One of the major advantages of this shape is that many different things can be done in it simultaneously and the shape "shares" the various sorts of energy that are generated.

This getting away from fixed square living shapes and habits will be an essential part of your work as an Initiated Wicce. You can modify the rooms you live in by simply hanging some material down in each corner even this little bit helps.

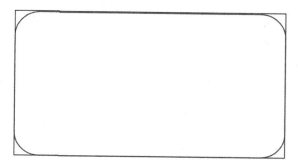

The healthiest shapes to live in are domes or cones, native American Indians knew this and built their cones as Tepee's. They don't have to be those shapes but be aware of the power the shapes you live in have over your development. Food is your next biggest hassle. As you develop your Natural sensitivities, you will find that chemically processed food becomes more and more difficult to eat. Try to get organically grown food, but in the end the only answer is for your group to grow your own.

This can be an easy and enjoyable thing for a Wicce to do. You can *"work"* with the land to heal it and make friends with the Elementals of the crops you grow. The Elementals respond amazingly well to contact with a Wicce, it's so rare for them to meet a human sensitive enough to be anything but a threat. They can teach you which food does what and the best way to grow it. They will inform you of what the land needs and they even protect and help the growth of the plants for you. You must remember to meet all Elementals as equals, they make better friends than pets, or masters and people have used them for both.

Part of our purpose, or the reason we (the Earth) have evolved the way we have, is to provide links from the more advanced levels of development, e.g. animals to the less completely brought through levels of consciousness such as plants. We do this through the Alchemical exchanges that take place when we eat whole living food in a conscious way. Take the time to radiate light to the food you are about to eat and contemplate its path from seed, growth to you. We should be aware that we are raising the vibrations of the Elementals awareness. It should be done gently and with Love. This is why prayer or saying grace over food is a Magickal ongoing strength.

"The Magickal City" is an extension of this, a retreat where we can live and grow without having to fit into other people's restrictions, or the destruction they cause to themselves and their environment. The Akashic Temple that is kept in society's city will stop us from becoming too cut off and at the same time, give us a point of distribution for the products, arts, herbs, etc., that we can put back into the society we come from. This city will be laid out so that it works with the lines of force that are like the land's acupuncture meridians. The Magick Circle you found for the Tiphareth Weekend is probably on one of these "Dragon lines" (as the Chinese and Ancients call them) but many call them Leylines. The food will be grown with the help of Elementals and will practically tend itself. Elementals can also show us the best way to use the land so that IT benefits them as well as us. Our living, learning and playing structures will be based upon curves, instead of straight lines.

The Temples will generate the energy needed and give us access to different levels of interaction. Such things as weather control and waste control are possible, even easy for such a community. Most of the difficulties modern cities face are due to the insensitive, conquering attitude the people who built them had towards Nature. You will see how many fall away once you learn to live with, instead of on the land. In the month between the Tiphareth Weekend and your Initiation, go back through your black book and see how you've changed.

Look at the other people in your group and see how they have changed as well. Think back over the inevitable personality clashes that characterise this sort of work and how you had to learn to overcome them. Look at how the group has provided you with an external vision of your own internal struggle to realise (make real) your own awareness. Reaffirm the fact that you and they are ordinary people, no different from any other person. Your progress is natural to everybody and as you were taught, you are now teaching. If each person teaches someone else the part that they have just learnt, then no one will get "stuck" in the role of teacher and each stage of your work will be Crystallised by having to convey your experiences to another person. Once you reach the PRIEST/ESS level of awareness, you no longer need the set role of either teacher or pupil, you realise you were always both.

"The energy of the work just done
Aid in the development of Love and Understanding in all things and in myself".

XIX
THE SUN

XIX The Sun
Solar Goddess Sol

Key to God and Men's Mysteries of Sol

This Chapter is sets of references or values associated with the Tree of Life, the four Quarters and the Five Elements. They are not complete but will serve as a guide to your present work.

KETHER - THE CROWN

PLANET	-	Uranus
NUMBER	-	1 – One
POSITION	-	Head of the central column
GOD NAME	-	**EH-HEH-YEH** I shall be (forever)
COLOUR	-	Brilliance – all colours
QUALITY	-	Unity – primal glory
PERFUME	-	Ambergris
GEM	-	Zircon
WEAPON	-	Lamp
METAL	-	Uranium

SHINING ONE	-	**METATRON**, Angel of presence
GODS	-	Atum – Ra, Osiris, Chronos, Zeus
INTELLIGENCE	-	Admirable
FUNCTION	-	The basic unity, beginnings
ORGAN	-	The whole nervous system
HERBS	-	Vervain
POSITION ON BODY	-	6" above the head
USE ON PHYSICAL LEVEL	-	Basic inventions, electronics, radar, new ideas, new conceptions, far future ideas
SYMBOLS	-	Point, crown, swastika
VISUALISATION	-	An ancient bearded king in profile
TAROT CARD	-	The Fool – The Universe

HOKMAH – WISDOM

PLANET	-	Neptune
NUMBER	-	2 – Two
POSITION	-	Head of right column
GOD NAME	-	**YEH** – God in all
COLOUR	-	White
QUALITY	-	Action – Time
PERFUME	-	Musk
GEM	-	White Jade
WEAPON	-	Phallus
METAL	-	Radium

SHINING ONE	-	**RATZIEL**, the herald of deities.
GODS	-	Zeus, Odin
INTELLIGENCE	-	Illuminating
FUNCTION	-	The animus, basic masculine mind
ORGAN	-	Left hemisphere of the brain, therefore the right side of the body
HERBS	-	Skullcap
POSITION ON BODY	-	Above the right shoulder, level with the eyes, outside the physical form
USE ON PHYSICAL LEVEL	-	Radio, TV, ESP, drugs, magnetism, and electronics
SYMBOLS	-	Straight line, male genitals, the Tower

BINAH - UNDERSTANDING

PLANET	-	Pluto
NUMBER	-	3 – Three
POSITION	-	Head of left column
GOD NAME	-	**YEHOVAH EL-OH-EEM** – God in all
COLOUR	-	Black
QUALITY	-	Silence
PERFUME	-	Myrrh, Civet, Musk
GEM	-	Black Jade, Nephrite
WEAPON	-	Yoni
METAL	-	Plutonium
SHINING ONE	-	**TZAPHKIEL**, contemplation of God

GODS	-	Demeter, Isis, Juno
INTELLIGENCE	-	Consenting and approving
FUNCTION	-	The anima, basic feminine mind
ORGAN	-	Right hemisphere of the brain, therefore the left side of the body
HERBS	-	Loosestrife
POSITION ON BODY	-	Above the left shoulder, level with the eyes
USE ON PHYSICAL LEVEL	-	Old people, agriculture, real estate, deaths, wills, and stonework
SYMBOLS	-	Female genitals, the cup, the outer robe of concealment
VISUALISATION	-	A mature woman
TAROT CARDS	-	The High Priestess – The Sun

DAAT - KNOWLEDGE

PLANET	-	Saturn (or Asteroid Belt)
NUMBER	-	11 – eleven
POSITION	-	Second sphere in the middle pillar - the abyss
GOD NAME	-	**YEHOVAH ELOH** - combination
COLOUR	-	Violet
QUALITY	-	Knowledge
PERFUME	-	Lavender
GEM	-	Diamond
PLANT	-	Lavender
WEAPON	-	Scroll, prism

METAL	-	Forged Steel
SHINING ONE	-	The Shining Ones of the quarters RAPHAEL, MICHAEL, GABRIEL, AURIEL
GODS	-	Janus
INTELLIGENCE	-	Knowing
FUNCTION	-	The bridge between metal (the head) and physical (the body)
ORGAN	-	Throat and neck - the base of the brain
HERB	-	Damiana
POSITION IN BODY	-	Throat
USE ON PHYSICAL LEVEL	-	Knowledge, learning
SYMBOLS	-	Empty room, hollow sphere, sacred mountain grain of corn
VISUALISATION	-	A head with two faces, one looks down, the other up
TAROT CARDS	-	The Empress - The Moon
NEGATION	-	Ignorance

CHESED - MERCY

PLANET	-	Jupiter - THURSDAY
NUMBER	-	4 – four
POSITION	-	Middle sphere on right column
GOD NAME	-	**EL** - God (the creator)
COLOUR	-	Blue

QUALITY	-	Mercy, obedience to macrocosmic flow
PERFUME	-	Cedar
GEM	-	Aquamarine
PLANT	-	live, Shamrock, Poplar, Oak
WEAPON	-	Crook
METAL	-	Tin
SHINING ONE	-	**TZADKIEL**, the justice of god
GODS	-	Wotan, Poseidon, Brahma, Kwan Yin, Diana
INTELLIGENCE	-	Radical, Compassionate
FUNCTION	-	Cleaning and interrogating the flow between macrocosm and microcosm. Development
ORGAN	-	Liver
HERB	-	Dandelion, agrimony, asparagus, dock, chicory
POSITION IN BODY	-	Right shoulder
USE ON PHYSICAL LEVEL	-	Speculation, gambling, divination, leadership, Gaining personal favors, money, and expansion
SYMBOLS	-	The solid figure, tetrahedron, orb, wand
VISUALISATION	-	A mighty throned and crowned king
TAROT CARDS	-	The Emperor - The Star
NEGATION	-	bigotry, hypocrisy, tyranny

GEBURAH - SEVERITY AND POWER

PLANET	-	Mars - TUESDAY
NUMBER	-	5 – five

POSITION	-	Middle of the left column
GOD NAME	-	Almighty God - **ELOHEEM - GIBOR**
COLOUR	-	Red
QUALITY	-	Strength, justice
PERFUME	-	Tobacco, Benzoin
GEM	-	Ruby
PLANT	-	Oak-nettle, Hickory, Absinth
WEAPON	-	Spear
METAL	-	Iron
SHINING ONE	-	**KHAMAEL**, the severity of god
GODS	-	Thor, Mars, Ares, Horus, Pan
INTELLIGENCE	-	Measuring
FUNCTION	-	Penetration of levels. Clarity, animation and involvement as well as memory. Use the clarity of this sphere to work on the negative aspects of war, police and other power freaks
ORGAN	-	Heart
HERB	-	All-heal, basil, red clover, gentian, garlic, rue, nettle
POSITION IN BODY	-	Left shoulder
USE ON PHYSICAL LEVEL	-	Clairvoyance, war, police, and armed forces memory
SYMBOLS	-	Chain, pentagon, five petaled rose
VISUALISATION	-	A mighty warrior in a chariot
TAROT CARDS	-	The Hierophant - The Tower of Destruction.
NEGATION	-	Cruelty, destruction

TIPHARETH - BEAUTY AND HARMONY

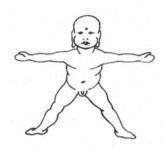

PLANET	-	The Sun - SUNDAY
NUMBER	-	6 – six
POSITION	-	Middle of middle pillar
GOD NAME	-	**YEHOVAH ELOH VED-AT** - god knowledge - god the strong
COLOUR	-	Yellow/gold
QUALITY	-	Harmony, balance, love
PERFUME	-	Olibanum, Aloes wood, Saffron, Cloves
GEM	-	Citrine Quartz Crystal
PLANT	-	Bay, Acacia, Laurel, Vine
WEAPON	-	Rosy Cross
METAL	-	Gold
SHINING ONE	-	RAPHAEL, divine physician
GODS	-	RA, Apollo, Gilgamesh
INTELLIGENCE	-	Mediating
FUNCTION	-	Harmonizing the various functions of body/mind
ORGAN	-	The solar plexus, the lymph system
HERB	-	St John's Wort, chamomile, angelica, sundew, Sunflower (and for the lymph, phytolacca)
POSITION IN BODY	-	Solar plexus
USE ON PHYSICAL LEVEL	-	Health, superiors, officials, power and success, Imagination, artistic vision
SYMBOLS	-	Truncated pyramid, cavery cross
VISUALISATION	-	A king, child sacrificed god

| TAROT CARDS | - | The Lovers - The Devil |
| NEGATION | - | Pride, insecurity |

HOD - SPLENDOUR THE GLORY

PLANET	-	Mercury - WEDNESDAY
NUMBER	-	7 – seven
POSITION	-	Bottom of right column
GOD NAME	-	ELOHEEM TSA VAOT - Lord of hosts
COLOUR	-	Orange
QUALITY	-	Intellect
PERFUME	-	Storax
GEM	-	Opal
PLANT	-	Holly, Palm, Vervain
WEAPON	-	Apron
METAL	-	Mercury
SHINING ONE	-	**MICHAEL**, like unto god
GODS	-	Hermes, Anubis, Ganesh
INTELLIGENCE	-	Absolute (perfect)
FUNCTION	-	The pushing power of body and mind. Intellect, Filtering and Transport
ORGAN	-	Kidneys

HERB	-	Juniper, Horse's Tail, Wild Carrot, Broom, Dill, Buchu.
POSITION IN BODY	-	Right Hip
USE ON PHYSICAL LEVEL	-	Business matters, intellect judgment, short Travel, information, universities, telegraph lines, communication
SYMBOLS	-	Names, hands, twin snakes, desert
VISUALISATION	-	A hermaphrodite
TAROT CARDS	-	The Chariot - Art
NEGATION	-	Falsehood, dishonesty, stupidity

NETZACH — VICTORY

PLANET	-	Venus - FRIDAY
NUMBER	-	8 – eight
POSITION	-	Bottom of left column
GOD NAME	-	**YEHOVAH TSAVAOT** - God of Hosts
COLOUR	-	Green
QUALITY	-	Sensuality, unselfishness
PERFUME	-	Red sandalwood and rose
GEM	-	Emerald
PLANT	-	Red rose
WEAPON	-	Lamp and chord around the waist
METAL	-	Copper
SHINING ONE	-	**HANIEL**, grace of god
GODS	-	Hathor, Aphrodite's, Venus, Gilgal

INTELLIGENCE	-	Hidden (instinctive)
FUNCTION	-	Perception and sensuality, Emotions, Ingestion of Prana.
ORGAN	-	Lungs
HERB	-	Coltsfoot, marshmallow, Vervain, yarrow, nettle
POSITION IN BODY	-	Left Hip
USE ON PHYSICAL LEVEL	-	All arts and artists, music, all beauty, pleasure, youth, luxury, perfumes and objects of love
SYMBOLS	-	Rose, Lush growth
VISUALISATION	-	A beautiful naked woman
TAROT CARDS	-	Adjustment - Death
NEGATION	-	Apathy, coldness, jealousy

YESOD - THE FOUNDATION

PLANET	-	The Moon - MONDAY
NUMBER	-	9 – nine
POSITION	-	Fourth from top on the middle pillar
GOD NAME	-	**SHA-DYE EL CHOI** - almighty loving god
COLOUR	-	Violet with blue marbling
QUALITY	-	Independence, communication
PERFUME	-	Jasmine, Ginseng
GEM	-	Moonstone

PLANT	-	Mandrake, Bayan
WEAPON	-	Perfumes, sandals
METAL	-	Silver
SHINING ONE	-	GABRIEL, man/god
GODS	-	Diana
INTELLIGENCE	-	Clear and pure
FUNCTION	-	The personality. The aura. The genitals - sexuality.
ORGAN	-	The genitals
HERB	-	Stillingia, adder's tongue, chickweed, cleavers
POSITION IN BODY	-	Genitals
USE ON PHYSICAL LEVEL	-	The aura, the home, short journeys, cooking, communication
SYMBOLS	-	Perfumes, sandals, the crescent
VISUALISATION	-	A very strong beautiful naked man
TAROT CARDS	-	The Hermit - The Hanged Man
NEGATION	-	Confusion, lack of sensitivity

MALKUTH - LIFE

PLANET	-	The Earth or Saturn - SATURDAY
NUMBER	-	10 – ten
POSITION	-	Lowest sphere on middle pillar
GOD NAME	-	AH-DON-NAI HA-AH-RETZ - Lord of the Earth
COLOUR	-	Living Black, olive, russet, yellow clay

QUALITY	-	Four basic drives
PERFUME	-	Dittany of Crete, Sandalwood
GEM	-	The four colored Garnets-yellow, red, green, brown.
PLANT	-	Willow, Lily, Ivy.
WEAPON	-	Magick Circle and the Triangle of the Art.
METAL	-	Lead
SHINING ONE	-	Sandalphion - the Messiah's
GODS	-	Ceres and Seb.
INTELLIGENCE	-	Resplendent
FUNCTION	-	The nourishment and protection of the body/mind.
ORGAN	-	The Spleen
HERB	-	Fennel, Holly, Mullein, Comfrey, Sarsaparilla, Phytolacca.
POSITION IN BODY	-	below and between the ankles
USE ON PHYSICAL LEVEL	-	Balancing the four drives
SYMBOLS	-	Altar of double cube, the Tau, Earth.
VISUALISATION	-	A young crowned and throned woman.
TAROT CARDS	-	The Wheel of Fortune - Lust
NEGATION	-	Paranoia - Neurosis

EASTERN QUARTER

GOD NAME - Yehovah
SHINING ONE - Raphael
ELEMENT - Air
ELEMENTAL - Sylphides
ACTION - Prime Movement - Originative
COLOUR - Blue - White
ALCHEMIC PRINCIPLE - Pure Essence - unity (The Sun)
MIND LEVEL - Collective Unconscious
KABBALA - Kether
LEVEL OF ATTAINMENT - Master - God
FEELING - Expectant
WIND - EURAS - cool soft breeze
WEAPON - Wand, Thurible and Incense
WORLD - Atziluth
LAW – Man Know Thyself
TIME OF DAY - DAWN – To Know
SEASON - Spring
QUALITY – Hot and Wet
PERFUME – Galbanum

SOUTHERN QUARTER

GOD NAME - Adonai
SHINING ONE - Michael
ELEMENT - Fire
ELEMENTAL - Salamanders
ACTION - EXPANSION - Creative
COLOUR - Red
ALCHEMIC PRINCIPLE - MERCURY – Spirit Free
MIND LEVEL - Anima and Animus
KABBALA - Chokmah and Binah
LEVEL OF ATTAINMENT - Mage
FEELING - Intimate
WIND - NOTAS – Warm soft Breeze
WEAPON - Athame, Sword, Candle, Fire.
WORLD - Briah
LAW - BE IN ALL THINGS – To Will
TIME OF DAY - Noon
SEASON - Summer
QUALITY – Hot and Dry
PERFUME - Olibanum

WESTERN QUARTER

GOD NAME - Yehovah
SHINING ONE - Gabriel
ELEMENT - Water
ELEMENTAL - Undines
ACTION - Prime Movement - Originative
COLOUR - Blue - White
ALCHEMIC PRINCIPLE - Pure Essence - unity (The Sun)
MIND LEVEL - Collective Unconscious
KABALA - Kether
LEVEL OF ATTAINMENT - Master - God
FEELING - Expectant
WIND - EURAS - cool soft breeze
WEAPON - Chalice, Cauldron and Water
WORLD - Atziluth
LAW - MAN KNOW THYSELF – To Dare
TIME OF DAY - Dawn
SEASON - Autumn
QUALITY – Wet and Cool
PERFUME – Frankincense or Myrrh

NORTHERN QUARTER

GOD NAME - Agla
SHINING ONE - Uriel
ELEMENT - Earth
ELEMENTAL - Gnomes
ACTION - SOLIDARITY - Expressive
COLOUR - BROWN - Yellow
ALCHEMIC PRINCIPLE - Salt, Seed
MIND LEVEL - Conscious
KABALA - Malkuth
LEVEL OF ATTAINMENT - Neophyte, Cowen
FEELING - Fulfilment
WIND - BOREAUS - SOFT STRONG COOL-Warm Wind
WEAPON - Shield, Pentacle.
WORLD - Assiah
LAW - LOVE UNDER WILL – To Keep Silent
TIME OF DAY - Midnight
SEASON - Winter
QUALITY – Cold and Dry
PERFUME - Storax and Sandalwood

	WOOD	FIRE	EARTH	AIR	WATER
YIN	LIVER	HEART	SPLEEN	LUNGS	KIDNEYS
YANG	Gall Bladder	Small Intestine	Stomach	large Intestine	Bladder
	yes	Tongue	Lips	Nose	Ear
	Muscles	Vessel	Flesh	Skin	Bone
	Nails	Body Hair	Breast	Throat	Head Hair
SEASON	Spring	Summer	Late Summer	Autumn	Winter
GROWTH PATTERN	Birth	Growth	Bearing fruit	Harvest	Storage
DIRECTION	Centre	South	North	East	West
COLOUR	Green	Red	Yellow	White	Black
SMELL	Oily, rancid. Roasted Baking			Raw fish/meatdecay	
TASTE	Sour	Bitter	Sweet	Spicy	Salt
PERVERSE CONDITION	Wind	Hot	Wet	Dry	Cold
NEGATIVE MENTAL EXPRESSION	Anxiety Tension negativity	Excessive Laughing	Indecision Obsessions	Worry Melancholy	Depression Fear
POSITIVE EMOTIONS	Love sharing clarity	Joy, warmth, centered hope,	Satisfaction positivity	Expectancy gentleness	Excitement
BODY FLUID *Saliva/Urine		Watery Eyes	*Sweat	Drool Eyes/run nose	

* Sweat-when the heart is bad, capillaries are expanded, and you sweat.

* Saliva-when you see a person spitting on the street, you know the kidneys are bad.

| MOTION *Stuttering | Clench fists | Anxiety | Hiccup | Coughing | Trembling |

* When Spleen (also Pancreas) and stomach are bad, the person's expression is not smooth.

| VOICE | Shouting | Talkative | Singing songs | Cry & Complain | Groaning |

GRAINS	Wheat, Barley, Rye.	Corn	Millet	*Rice	Beans

These are grains, which nourish the various organs

* Rice-when you start eating rice, your intestines work well.

ANIMAL FOOD	Chicken	Lamb	Beef	*Horse	Pork

(These are of course not advisable)

*Horsemeat is eaten for medicinal purposes in Oriental countries.

VEGETABLES Squash	Chives, Shallots Salad	Scallions	Pumpkin Chard, Kale, Leeks Cauliflower		Broccoli,

SPIRITUAL PROBLEM	Soul	High Spirit	Will, Insight	Astral	Dream

NOTE:

If Heart is not strong, you cannot act as God/dess or Spirit

If Liver is not strong, you cannot have a strong spiritual centre

If Lungs are not strong, you cannot cope with ghosts.

If Kidneys are not strong, you cannot accomplish your dreams.

If Spleen/Pancreas is not strong, you don't have will and you don't have insight.

"The energy of the work just done,
Aids in the development of love and Understanding in all things".

XX
JUDGEMENT

XX Judgment — Chicomecoatl
Aeon-Key to Trance and High Magick

The Appendixes

I GENERATE LOVE AND UNDERSTANDING
FOR MYSELF AND ALL OTHERS

Relaxation and Hypnosis
Alchemy
Scrying and Clairvoyance
Tarot and Meditation
Tarot and Ritual
Astrology
Geomancy
Making and Caring of your Magickal Tools and Weapons
Creating the Magickal Black Mirror
Relaxation

The art of relaxation is one of the most important things to learn at the beginning of all your Magickal work. To master it is essential not only for ritual work, but everyday living as well.

Relaxation is a calming, or quietening, of your meta-identity (ego), and body, so that you are free of all distractions, tensions, worries, etc. When these distractions have gone, you are then free to direct all your concentration and Auric energy, into whatever you wish. The ability to relax causes an ever-increasing enjoyment of whatever you may be doing.

A 'relaxation ritual' is any exercise of your imagination, designed to produce a relaxed state in your mind and body. These exercises are limited only by your imagination and that can be anything you like so long as you keep in mind that the intention is to relax. Always remember to lie, or sit, in a comfortable position before you start any exercise.

A very simple, but effective, exercise (once you are comfortable) is to take control, first of your breathing - breathe deeply, evenly and slowly from your stomach and not your chest, always in through your nostrils and out through your mouth. As your breathing slows, start to imagine all your tensions and worries flowing out of your body, as you breathe out. When you breathe in, your body is filled with a soft warm feeling which spreads throughout and slowly relaxes every part of your body. These rituals can be far more detailed. For example: using your imagination starts from your toes and move slowly up the body, exploring every part of it. As you explore each part, it relaxes, or, you could imagine you were in the country under a shady tree feeling the sun on your body, the gentle breeze in the air, the soft warm sounds of birds and streams. Likewise, you could be beside the surf, lying in the warm sun, etc. The main thing to remember is to try and imagine with as many senses as you can: see, feel, hear, smell and taste the whole scene that you create, keeping the theme of relaxation, feeling more and more relaxed, feeling each sense become more and more relaxed and open.

HYPNOSIS

Whereas relaxation comes from a quieting of the meta-identity (ego), hypnosis comes from and even deeper level of calmness. The meta-identity (Yesod) is relaxed or quietened; to such a degree that your true self (Malkuth) can come through to consciousness. (For more information concerning how Malkuth and Yesod relate to one another reference to the main text of this book.)

Your true self (Malkuth) is the centre of your four basic drives (i.e. survival sexual/social, self-esteem, and self-knowledge), it is only interested in fulfilling them, and your meta-identity is how society has told you to fulfill them. If you can reach your true self and suggest to it a more suitable way to fulfill its needs, then it will proceed to make appropriate changes in your meta-identity, or personality.

These suggestions may be anything you desire; e.g., more relaxed healthier, happier personality, etc. Either yourself, or whoever is helping you into a hypnotic state can make these suggestions. The exercises for self-hypnosis use the same principle as the relaxation exercises, except that the theme is one of sinking deeper and deeper into your mind.

Lie down and make yourself comfortable and relaxed. Now in your mind, state your intention (direction) 'I am now going to put myself into a hypnotic state, I will remain conscious during the whole of the exercise' (this prevents you from falling asleep).

Take five slow deep breaths and say, "relax now" when you say this you will be in a light hypnotic state. In your imagination feel yourself sinking slowly, this can be done in any way you choose. For example, you could be floating on a warm soft white cloud that is sinking gently to the ground - see the blue sky, the warm sun, smell the fresh air, feel the soft warm breeze, and feel yourself sinking very slowly into the ground; or you could be in a lift, on the 10th floor of a building - press the ground floor button, see and hear the doors close, feel and hear the lift start to sink, watch the floor numbers' lights as they change very slowly, 9 - 8 - 7 etc., until you reach the ground floor; or, you could be walking down stairs, or, drifting down a tunnel of colours. These exercises are, again, limited only by your imagination. Remember, too, that when you visualise, use **ALL** your senses.

ALCHEMY

Alchemy is the art of perfection, the taking of something that is raw or unbalanced and changing it into a more perfected state. The work you'll do as a Wicce is what is called Personal Alchemy. What you are doing is changing your state of being to a more balanced or perfect state. We call it an ART, because it involves the use of emotion and intellect (balancing of your actions and reactions). What I am going to talk about is Alchemy as an art of perfecting herbs and metals etc.

Unfortunately, this form of Alchemy has suffered in many ways because most people have refused to treat it as an Art. For many years western society has tried to find its truth through science; and science, as WE KNOW IT, is not Art, it is basically an intellectual function.

As we have said before, Alchemy or Art needs BOTH intellect and emotion. We use intellect so that we can be analytical and predict the outcome of any of our operations; and emotion so that we can feel or be sensitive enough to be able to assess what is happening (from an infinite number of possibilities) at any given time. To give an example of this, if we were treating an herb Alchemically, what we are trying to do is change the herb both physically and Aurically; we are trying to perfect the action this herb has. Intellectually we assess the possibilities of the herb; we predict the outcome of the operation, and act on bringing about the desired result. (Remember intellect is Hod, which is action.) Emotion is happening during the operation both Aurically and physically, and to assess what is happening at any time so that the herb is treated as an INDIVIDUAL THING each time.

This, together with you, makes Alchemy an Art (it is creative). YOU are acting on the herb and reacting to it. It is acting upon you and reacting to you. You have made that herb alive. It is by this process that we find the soul of the herb. We break down its Yin and Yang actions and rebuild it into a more balanced or perfected state (we balance its action and reaction).

Because in Alchemy you are acting on and being acted upon by whatever you are treating Alchemically, whatever you do in Alchemy has a direct effect upon you. You are Aurically linked to the herbs and the process, so in perfecting anything with Alchemy you are perfecting yourself. This makes doing Alchemy an extremely effective Tool to use in your own work as a Wicce, in finding your "soul".

To begin your work in Alchemy all you really need is a simple distillation apparatus and a quiet place to work. Sometime later you might decide to expand this into a full working laboratory, but not until after Initiation.

The process of finding the elixir is a relatively easy physical process (as shown following), but the difficulty you find will be auric control. To help with this, it is necessary to use whatever Tools are available to you. These Tools are only limited by your ability to understand them. The Tools you use could include: Astrology, Tarot, I Ching, Talismans, Tattwa's, Incense, Oils etc.

There is an unlimited number of Tools that can be used. Some you may find better suited or more effective than others, depending upon what you want to do, e.g. if we want to treat an herb with Netzach properties we start by beginning our experiment on the day of Venus (Friday) and then using any other Netzach attributes we could.

I will give you a BRIEF description of the simpler form of Alchemy, which you should put into practice during your Neophyte/Cowen stage: Treatment of the herb involves seven basic stages of distillation and coagulation. The first thing to be done is to distill a fair amount of water. To this we add our dried herb and soak for a period of about twenty-four hours (or at least overnight). After this we can begin our distillations.

In all the distillations you do, you must remember that we are trying to work with Nature, we are trying to help Nature perfect; so, we must work as Nature works, slowly and gently. All your distillations should take about half an hour to bring to the boil, and roughly and hour to distil after boiling.

First Distillation - This first distillation is basic and simple. The herb is boiled and distilled, the first distillation having no POSTHEAT.

Postheat: Is heat applied once all watery fluids have left the still?

Second Distillation - For the second distillation we join the residue (what is left in the still) with the distillate. Then, again, we distil gently (as with the First), only this time we POSTHEAT for 5 minutes.

Third Distillation - Same as with the second distillation, only we POSTHEAT for 5-10 minutes. During the POSTHEAT you may find that a white cloud forms in the flask (still); this is oil rising from the herb that can be collected off the distillate once the distillation is completed. The oil can be removed by using the tip of a piece of wire to pick it off the top of the distillate. The oil is then put aside and saved.

Fourth - Fifth - and Sixth Distillations - Same as with third distillation, only POSTHEAT for 15-20 minutes. (It is important to not burn the herb, when this starts to happen, stop the POSTHEAT) During these distillations you will find it helpful to crush the residue with a pestle (before rejoining residue and distillate) and calcifying it. Save the oils.

Seventh Distillation - Same as with previous distillations, only after calcifying, the calcified herb should become a redbrick colour. Once this is achieved, add a few drops of oil and distillate to residue; this should produce a yellow colour - if you have this, you have the ELIXIR.

CRYSTAL GAZING AND CLAIRVOYANCE

CLAIRVOYANCE = CLEAR SIGHT; the development of the intuition to a level of practical usage. On the Kabbalistic Tree of Life, it is the ability to perceive Hod from Netzach, and Netzach from Hod, to see them as action and reaction respectively.

The use of clairvoyant Tools such as the Crystal Ball will aid in the development of the intuition. The Crystal is a focus point for you to use your imagination in a positive visual way by a concentrated effort of Yesod's artistic energies.

Once you have acquired the Crystal Ball it is necessary to free it of any Auric influences that may be attached to it (because of previous ownership or handling, etc.). This is achieved by a Banishing Ritual performed in a salt and water Magickal Circle, followed immediately by covering the crystal with black silk, which will keep it protected until you begin work with it yourself.

The Crystal is used on a special Scrying table, which is ideally constructed of ebony with writings of gold, if ebony is unavailable, any heavy grained wood, painted matt black, would substitute. The table after completion would also need to be covered with black silk (to contain no Aura but your own). A small holder for the Crystal is required; this too should be your own construction, painted matt black and kept covered with black silk.

It is necessary for the preparation of this Magickal equipment to take place during the moons increase, i.e. going toward the Full Moon. This is most important to your success; the moons magnetic and perspective aura benefits the crystal.

Further to your success, all crystal gazing, preferably, done in a controlled environment. This is best achieved by the construction of a salt and water Magick Circle, in which you have done a full banishing and invocation ritual. The circle should be set in a clean, darkened room where you will be undisturbed. Take care that it is free of any objects that may reflect in the crystal, and thus disturb your attention. The room should not be dark, but rather, shadowed with dull light, somewhat like a moonlit room. It is necessary to time you're sitting, so set a clock where, though the face is visible, the ticking is inaudible.

Before commencing your crystal work, attention to self-preparation is of prime importance. Fasting for at least four (4) hours before your ritual is most beneficial, in contributing to a relaxed state of body and mind, enabling easy chi production. Before you start, meditate on full relaxation followed by a tree ritual. After this, you may go about constructing your circle, or if using a temple, you may enter now.

The art of Crystal vision may be classified as follows:

1. Images of your thoughts, opinion;

2. Images of ideas unconsciously acquired from other by telepathy etc.;

3. Images, pictures bringing information as to something past, present or future, which the gazer has no way of knowing;

4. The ability to see accurately, the qualities, quantities and distribution of the Elements of any given '*field*'.

Under this fourth (4th) heading, comes true crystal vision.

Do not be disappointed if, when and even after you have completed the preliminary exercises set forth here, you do not apparently perceive an answer to what you are seeking: after the first or even following attempts. On the other hand, if you have a particularly GIFTED POTENTIAL to be a Seer, you may begin perceiving on your very first sitting; you are advised to disregard it, as, continuous success will only come as a growth development and these exercises will secure it.

Commence the first week of your work on a Monday, during the waxing cycle of the Moon. Monday being significant because it is the day of the Moon. Your Magick Circle set, you re-enter with your Crystal, table and holder. Place them, after removing their covering, in the centre of your Circle, facing East. You would then sit comfortably, opposite in lotus position, facing the Crystal with your back to the West. Fix your eyes on the ball itself, not a pierce - stare out with a steady calm gaze. Concentrate on your breathing (inhale for 9, hold for 2, exhale for 9, will allow an easy even flow). Start projection through the eyes of your hands and set up a flow with the Crystal.

This is all you do for the first week, but do not underestimate the importance of this exercise, as the result and sole aim of this is to establish an auric link with your Crystal before which no SUCCESSFUL work can be attempted. This exercise should be carried out at a regular time, daily, and should not exceed more than 30 minutes.

The same piece should be used in the second week, and by this time it should be noticed that a rising cloud forms the base of the crystal. The crystal seeming to alternately appear and disappear, as in a mist. This is your signal that you are not linked with it. Go ahead, to use your ability to visualise by allowing images to form in the ball. These images should not be forced, just allow your mind to wander; letting each thought form a picture. Do not try to interpret these images, this is merely an exercise in control, the benefit of which will begin to acquire a feel for CLEAR SIGHT - the difference between what is or was and what may be merely a projection of your own opinion. (1-2 classifications).

Once you have completed these exercises for a full week, you may commence using your crystal for divination. Using the same routine as before, concentrate on what you wish to enquire about. Don't force your query, just softly hold it in mind, by using your imagination in a positive visual way, play with your query, make images while holding your steady gaze on the ball. When you see that the crystal is beginning to become dull and the cloud on clouds begin to rise, this is your signal that you are about to see what you seek, for suddenly the crystal will clear to all else but a bluish flame, against which, as if it were a background, the vision will be apparent.

Practice will develop an automatic ability to obtain results in the exploration of any given field.

Doing Oracles for people is a good start, allowing immediate reference points, depending, of course, on what they wish to enquire. When doing this the person should keep silent and remain seated at a distance opposite you, all questions asked should be in a slow and low tone.

Although the Moon is in harmony with the crystal, the days and times you do your work will depend on the nature of your enquiry. For example, if you are enquiring of a past life, then Tuesday would be used being the day of Mars; Mars is the planet assigned to the Sephiroth Geburah, the sphere of memory. A ritual for this purpose done on a Tuesday in the hour of Mars, coupled with an invocation of Geburah would be most successful. Alternately, to enquire knowledge of something more present, this life, the Thursday, being the day of Jupiter, which is the planet of plenty, growth, abundance and gain and assigned to Chesed, would be more suitable.

As you develop, your work will lead you to a kind of astral workshop. This will be your own creation and an art form of the four quarters, in action allowing you to see and use Tetragrammaton in your everyday life.

TAROT

The Tarot Cards are the Book of Universal symbolism compiled by the great God Tehuti-Thoth who gave it to his Isarum (Initiates) of Saiss as the key to the Magickal constitution of people. The word Tarot is self-explanatory; TAR - meaning ROAD, and ROT - meaning ROYAL; i.e. Road of Royal Wisdom and Divine Enlightenment.

The true pack was modified by the Hebrews to fit into the Kabbalistic system of Philosophy, which evolved from the Egyptians. The Persians and Assyrians also got access to the Cards, and the Crusaders were the first to be credited in taking the Cards into Europe when returning from the Crusades. The Gypsies (derived from Egypt-as people of Egypt) are the people mostly associated with the Cards, using them for Divination purposes. The pack most commonly used was the Marseilles Pack. And presently today the most popular is the Rider-Waite deck.

There are now numerous packs in circulation with a lot of variations in design and some variations in numerical order or attributions. The bulk of the cards are now based on Kabbalistic concepts. For example, a pack published by the Brotherhood of Light called the "Sacred Tarot" is designed to be an intellectual pack with a variety of correspondences in symbology and interpretation e.g. the concept of card one; the Magus, is described and interpretations are given in numerology, astrology, Alchemy, Bible, Masonry, Magick, and Wiccecraft etc.!

In the Rider-Waite pack descriptions and divinatory significances are given. Waite, being a Magician has designed his pack as a Tool, which can be used in Kabbalistic Magickal work. The pack designed by Aleister Crowley is an excellent pack as a work of art, as symbology and art are useful as meditation and ritual tools. They are also easy to relate to for divination purposes, but better used in Ceremony and Ritual.

MEDITATION

The Major Arcana may be used as a meditation Tool, (a map of development of the Kabbalistic Tree). It starts with the Godhead working down. Naturally the process is subject to Tetragrammaton.

Zero represents Kether, infinite being, with no experience thus labeled the Fool. This card represents the Matrix. Kether projects at right angles to itself thus causing polarity, manifesting Chokmah and Binah. Chokmah being the polarity, of will or the Thinker, is represented by the High Priestess, veiled; the second Arcanum. The result of this action brings the effect down through Daat, knowledge being represented by the card of the Empress, or Isis Unveiled. Arcanum three. The effect working down to realisation in abundance to Chesed represented by the Emperor, this state is the first manifestation of matter, Arcanum four. Proceeding to Geburah it is modified by Universal Law, regulation of infinite manifestation of being; the unity of substance represented by Arcanum five, the Hierophant, the Giver of Law. Working down this produces the manifestation of the Emperor and the Hierophant in balance, love and harmony

Tiphareth, represented by Arcanum six, the Lovers. Working down it is modified by intellect and reason, speed and action. Represented by the Chariot, Arcanum seven in Hod. Directed to Netzach it is modified by emotions indicated by Arcanum eight, Adjure. Then works down to the foundations of form and substance manifesting in self-esteem and self-knowledge, prudence represented by the Hermit or the Sage in Arcanum nine for Yesod. Then it is manifested as the physical body, survival, social, sexual, self-esteem, self-knowledge; the four basic drives. The necessity to balance these in a cycle is shown by the tenth Arcanum, the Wheel of Fortune, which is Malkuth. The eleventh card to the twenty-first represents the Magician working up to infinite consciousness and attainment of the Universe.

The eleventh Arcanum shows the Lust of Life, the Lust for development and Strength, this is the potential of Malkuth. Arcanum twelve is the Hanged Man representing the control of the Magician over his personality, which he develops to the Death in Arcanum thirteen.

Netzach, Death indicating change and a chance to develop himself through Art, represented by Arcanum fourteen in Hod. Then he appears as The Devil because he becomes a rebel and apparently a threat to society represented by Arcanum fifteen in Tiphareth. From this point he develops to face himself and judge himself by the highest form of finite and semi-infinite law in the Judgment represented in Arcanum sixteen, in Geburah. From here he develops to the Star Arcanum seventeen, free from worldly influences and reaching advanced adept hood subject to infinite law only in Chesed. He prepares to cross the Abyss represented by Arcanum eighteen, the Moon showing a path between Two Towers; pyramids, or mountains, a point of mastering infinite balance and completion of karma entering total infinite functioning and reach Binah, the eternal Mother Isis. The zodiac represented in Arcanum nineteen receiving and giving all. From here development is to the Aeon, Arcanum twenty becoming the active Thinker of Chokmah and developing into the Universe of total infinity.

ASTROLOGY

Astrology is the study of Natural cycles, the art and science of all beginnings. It is a KEY to man's understanding of himself and of others; thus, of the relationship between himself and the Universe the Macrocosm.

Astrology can be considered to take two main directions. Event Oriented and Person-Centred. The former deals with events, which occur in the material world. From the empiricism of the Cosmo biologists, through Mundane Astrology, to the prediction of events in an individual's life. This then becomes the realm of fortune telling, even in its tartest form as carried by newspapers and periodicals.

As a contrast, Person-centred or Humanistic Astrology is concerned primarily with the problems rooted in personal experience and in changes in consciousness. It endeavors to give MEANING to experience. The same event will have different meanings to different individuals. To some, an event could be chaotic and destructive, while to another it could be a crisis point from which personal growth can take place. The latter is more likely to be the instance if we comprehend the meaning of the situation in which we are involved.

The main Tools of Astrology are the ZODIAC, the LIGHTS, the PLANETS, the SHINING ONES and the HOUSES. These are the Air, Fire, Water and Earth Principles respectively.

The **ZODIAC** is simply the product of realisation by people that experience is a cyclic process. Each cosmic impulse manifests itself as a phase of human experience, or as a psychological type.

The **LIGHTS** and the **PLANETS** represent focal points of unconscious energies, associated with basic life principles. They may also be understood as Archetypal impulses. Thus, they correspond closely to the Sephiroth of the Tree of Life. In fact, they are another viewpoint of the "Tree" and what it symbolises.

Every **ASTROLOGICAL HOUSE** symbolises a basic type of human experience. The zodiacal sign at the cusp of the house and whatever planet may be found in this house, indicate the way each of the thirteen basic types of experience SHOULD be met - and indeed, WOULD be met, if there were no interference, no KARMIC pressure to disorient, confuse and alter the experiencing process.

The Birth Chart is merely a map of the heavens at the first moment of independent existence, that is, when the child takes his/her first breath. At this moment, the Cosmos impresses the being, setting the pattern for this lifetime. However, this "blueprint", this "signature" of the new being, defines only her/his POTENTIAL. An Acorn carries the "pattern", the genetic information for growth, into an Oak Tree, but there is no guarantee that the tree will come into maturity, that the 'Temple' of the "perfect person" will ever be completed. At every stage of our life journey we have choice, and responsibility for this choice.

The "progression" of the birth chart, along with the planetary transits, will tell us how the 'seed' is unfolding. The exercise is in becoming more conscious in the here and now. In comprehending the meaning of our life experiences, the Nature of our KARMA - and our DHARMA. It is in seeing who we really are, as unique individuals, and in fulfilling the destiny that brought us into a culture, at a place, and at a particular time.

Astrology has the power to reveal the 'eternal' at the core of the 'sacred' under the fleeting shapes of the profane.

GEOMANCY

Geomancy means literally 'divination by Earth' and is a form of divination, which operates through links with Earth Elementals.

A question is asked, and by the chance throwing of pebbles or random drawing of lines in Earth, an odd or an even number is obtained. This procedure is repeated sixteen times and the results are arranged into groups of four lines, one under the other in their original order. The four lined figures thus obtained are interpreted to provide an answer to the question.

Geomancy figures are not unlike I Ching hexagrams, except they have only four lines. For example, a figure consisting of two odd followed by two even lines would be recorded. There are only sixteen possible combinations, but as four such figures must be obtained initially to answer any question, the combinations number more than 65,000.

Traditional names, qualities and planetary attributions are ascribed to these sixteen figures and when used in the format given later you can expect to obtain a full and qualitative answer to any question you may ask. However, your success with Geomancy will depend on your ability to take an apparently mechanical and inanimate process and make it into a delicate and sentient Magickal operation.

Although it may appear complex and confusing at first, the basic form of Geomancy is simple and concise. The major obstacle to using this and indeed any form of divination is attaining the state of mind necessary for perceiving the simplicity. The following section describes an approach, which in time will allow this simplicity to show itself.

There are four Elements to be considered in the process. They are firstly, the person conducting the divination, the Tools used e.g. Tarot Pack, I Ching sticks, the entities or level of consciousness you aim to communicate with and, fourthly, the mechanical process itself.

To carry out successful divination these Four Elements must be made to function as a unity. They must be set up so that the interaction between them is a smooth flow of perfect communication.

In preparing yourself and your Tools you must aim to reach a level where intuition takes the place of will and reason. However, intuition is a quality of Netzach and will not be recognisable immediately, so you must use the Tools you have in Yesod. These are intellect, emotion and art used on the framework of your imagination. If you approach divination in this way, intuition will just happen by itself.

There are no rules to follow, but you must find out your own balance as you go. You could start by studying the system as it is explained later. See how it fits together intellectually and then let you feel it. Contemplate the Geomantic figures, play with them in your mind and get a feeling for them. Expand their meanings by relating them to your own experience.

The next question that arises is the choice of a method for obtaining your primary figures. Traditionally this is done by tracing random lines in soft Earth with a stick, counting the number of separate fragments in each line and thus obtaining an odd or an even number (you would have to draw sixteen broken lines).

The operation should be completely random and uninfluenced by conscious mental process. This can be difficult as the speed at which lines can be drawn in Earth often allows your mind time to count the dashes you are making - and the more you try not to, the more aware you become. If you choose this method, you could compose a suitable Chant to recite and hopefully keep your conscious mind occupied.

Any method of drawing random numbers could be valid and perhaps it may help you to personalise the system by coming up with one never used before.

It must be kept in mind, however, that the process you choose and the Tools with which you carry it out, contribute to the link you aim to form with the Earth Elementals through which Geomancy operates - the more you become involved with this, the more of an art you make it, the stronger and more functional will be those links. The Tools you use - for example a wooden marker for drawing lines in the sand - should be selected and fashioned as a Magickal Tool, with its purpose held in mind always.

Another method, which I have found quite satisfactory consists of drawing numbers of pebbles or balls out of a bowl designed for the purpose and counting the number, either odd or even. A design for a painted bowl is given here. If you decide to use this method, you should make the bowl yourself. Design it, shape it and colour it as you would when making a Magickal Wiccetool. Be careful not to let anyone touch your work or help you with it. The links you require will be formed initially as you make your Tools - any extraneous links will be difficult to sever without destroying your own.

All forms of divination have a negative or qliphotic function, which must be bound. With the I Ching this is accomplished by having a negative bundle of sticks. In Geomancy, the method of binding the negative will vary according to the method employed. With the bowl method, the snake eating its tail around the base of the bowl, binds negative. This is not the only possible way, but it is quite effective.

Once you have your Tools prepared, to perform a Geomancy reading is basically simple. It is best if you make a ritual of it, the main requirement being a Banished Circle.

First you must formulate the question you want answered, make it precise and free of ambiguities: You will obtain an answer to the question asked, not necessarily the question you think you are asking. You should write this down on top of a piece of paper, on which you will also record the Geomantic Figures you obtain.

Then proceed to derive the four primary figures of your reading, by whatever means you have decided upon. These four figures, traditionally known as the "mothers", give an absolute answer to your question. Considered Tetragrammically, they are the intrinsic, the positive, the negative and the neutral - in that order. In terms of the Elements they are Air, Fire, Water and Earth.

This absolute answer may suffice for your question. However, two other sets of four figures can be derived from the Mothers, which as a quality comment on the first four.

If you take the first (top) lines of the Mothers and arrange them in the order of the Mothers from top to bottom, you will derive a fifth figure. Repeating this process using the second, third and fourth lines of the Mothers, you will have another set of four figures. These are called the Daughters and represent the Yang or positive aspects of the Mothers in the order, Air, Fire, Water and Earth.

The Yin or negative aspects, called the Nephews, are obtained by adding together in pairs the eight figures you have already. The first two Mothers added together give the first Nephew; the second Mothers added yield to the second Nephew. Similarly, the first and second pair of daughters give in addition the third and fourth Nephews respectively.

Addition of Geomantic figures is not difficult. The first lines of the two figures when added together yield an odd or an even, which becomes the first line of the derived figure. An odd plus an odd or an even plus an even yields an even; an even plus and odd yields an odd. This process is repeated using the pairs of second, third, and fourth lines to produce the respective lines of the derived figure, e.g.

The four Nephews are the Yin aspects of Fire, Water, Earth and Air, or the second, third, fourth and first Mothers, in that order.

At this stage of the reading you should have twelve Geomantic figures looking rather confusing in columns on a sheet of paper.

CAPUT DRACONIS - literally means "The upper threshold, entrance", "The Head of the Dragon".

Elemental Ruler:	Hismael	and Kedemet
Planetary Ruler:	Venus	and Jupiter
Zodiac Sign:	Caput Draconis	
Element:	Air of Air.	

Comment: This figure and that of *Cauda Draconis* are the most Yang's of the sixteen Geomantic figures. This quality, along with the ruler ship of Venus and Jupiter suggest expansion. It is an action, a beginning or an end, depending on how you look at it.

ALBUS - Literally "White head".

Elemental Ruler:	Taphthartharath
Planetary Ruler:	Mercury
Zodiac Sign:	Gemini
Element:	Fire of Air

Comment: The Latin name suggests the wisdom of age. The Mercurial influence is communication and learning. Fire of Air is the action of Air Which is an active interweaving of macrocosmic and microcosmic forces leading to wisdom.

TRISTITIA - Literally "Sadness, grief".

Elemental Ruler:	Zazael
Planetary Ruler:	Saturn
Zodiac Sign:	Aquarius
Element:	Water of Air.

Comment: Saturn indicates contraction but can also be knowledge. Sadness is a subjective reaction to loss, and true sadness is an expression of love. This figure refers also to the separateness of individuals. The context in which the figure occurs will indicate how it is to be interpreted.

PUELLA - Literally means "a girl" or a "pretty face".

Elemental Ruler:	Kedemet
Planetary Ruler:	Venus
Zodiac Sign:	Libra
Element:	Water of Air

Comment: Venus signifies beauty, emotion rather than intellect; also pleasure or fostering. A "pretty face" can be the vision that inspires an artist or the beautiful façade that's seen from within a prison.

AEQUISITIO - Literally means "Obtaining".

Elemental Ruler:	Hismael
Planetary Ruler:	Jupiter
Zodiac Sign:	Sagittarius
Element:	Air of Fire.

Comment: Jupiter is associated with expansion and gain. This figure is traditionally taken to mean good fortune. However, he terms expansion and gain has no inherent direction, and as with all the Geomantic figures, the idea of good fortune is not a quality that can be assigned. The direction that the 'gain' indicated by this figure is to take will be indicated by the context in which it occurs.

FORTUNA MAJOR - Literally "the great fortune".

Elemental Ruler:	Sorath
Planetary Ruler:	Sol
Zodiac Sign:	Leo
Element:	Fire of Fire.

Comment: The Sun here indicates balance. In one respect it is he externalisation of what is internal.

VIA - Literally a 'street, way, journey'.

Elemental Ruler:	Chasmodai
Planetary Ruler:	Luna
Zodiac Sign:	Cancer
Element:	Water of Fire

Comment: The figure of Via and that of Fortuna Minor are the two most Yin of the sixteen Geomantic figures. As a street or a journey, it is an action; but an action of opening and allowing things to enter, rather than to attempt to change what is without!

PUER - Literally 'a boy', 'yellow, beardless'.

Elemental Ruler:	Bartzabel
Planetary Ruler:	Mars
Zodiac Sign:	Aries
Element:	Earth of Fire.

Comment: Mars has attributions of discord and war but is also a symbol for strength. The image aroused by the name Puer suggests the strivings of youth or perhaps youthful folly.

RUBEUS - Literally means 'red' or 'red headed'.

Elemental Ruler:	Bartzabel
Planetary Ruler:	Mars
Zodiac Sign:	Scorpio
Element:	Air of Water

Comment: Activity, a concentration of forces, to strive for freedom, or build a prison.

FORTUNA MINOR - Literally the 'lesser fortune'.

Elemental Ruler	Sorath
Planetary Ruler:	Sol
Zodiac Sign:	Cancer
Element:	Water of Fire

Comment: COMMENT: Along with Via this is the most Yin of the Geomantic figures. It is the action of Water. The interpretation of what is external.

POPULUS - Literally 'people, crowd, congregation'.

Elemental Ruler:	Chasmodai
Planetary Ruler:	Luna
Zodiac Sign:	Cancer
Element:	Water of Water

Comment: COMMENT: This is the effect of Water. Water is contraction; it is the most complex of the Elements. Like a crowd of people, it may represent richness or confusion in its diversity. If considered with the figure Via, Populous can be the effect of the action of Via.

LAETITIA - Literally 'joy, laughter'.

Elemental Ruler:	Hismael
Planetary Ruler:	Mars
Zodiac Sign:	Pisces
Element:	Earth of Water

Comment: COMMENT: Joy is a reaction to temporal gain, given here with the energy of Mars. As with the figure Aequisitio; the outcome of this gain carries no connotations for good or evil.

CAREER - Literally 'prison bound'.

Elemental Ruler:	Zazel
Planetary Ruler:	Saturn
Zodiac Sign:	Capricorn
Element:	Air of Earth

Comment: This appears an animus figure, Saturn being cold and contracting. Yet a prison when it applies an external condition, allows the possibility of internal freedom. Saturn is also a sign for knowledge and knowledge is gained by struggling with problems and restrictions.

AMISSIO – literally 'loss'.

Elemental Ruler:	Kedemet
Planetary Ruler:	Venus
Zodiac Sign:	Taurus
Element:	Fire of Earth

Comment: Earth is solidification, and in the context of Venus *'loss'* is an appropriate name for this action. However, the loss could also be a loss of confusion.

CONJUNCTIO - Literally 'coming together'.

Elemental Ruler:	Taphthartharath
Planetary Ruler:	Mercury
Zodiac Sign:	Virgo
Element:	Water of Earth

Comment: Mercury is communication and learning. In this present context it could refer to a coming together of formerly unrelated things that result in communication and learning, or results in a closing off channels that inhibits further development.

THE ISARUM TOOLS

The Making and Caring of Magickal Isarum Tools

All materials used in Magickal Tools or Wiccetool's should be virgin and clean. As far as possible you should make all your Wiccetool's unassisted (except to others who will be using them). Only you should see and touch the Wiccetool's from the moment you begin to work on them; again, except for other Wicces who will be using the Tools in your Coven work. This will ensure that there are no unwanted or uncontrolled links connecting your Wiccetool's aurically with any minds apart from the minds using them. To maintain the auric purity of your Wiccetool's they must be kept clean and in good repair. Also, they should be wrapped in black silk when not actually used, cleaned or repaired. As the colour black absorbs heat and light, so black, and especially black silk, tends to absorb "auric pollution" to protect your Tools from contamination. Store them in a safe place where they are unlikely to be seen or arouse curiosity.

The Magickal Wiccetool's are the Tools with which the Wicce works. Four traditional Wiccetool's - the Wand (or Rod); The Sword/Athame (ritual dagger); The Chalice (Cup), or Crucible or Cauldron; and the Pentacle (or Shield, Disc, or Seal) - are the Wiccetool's used for the Elements of Air, Fire, Water and Earth. Usually these are referred to as the Wiccetool's of the Wicce/Priest/ess; however, do not imagine that only these four are legitimate Tools for practical Magick. Mandala's, incenses, colour, oils, music, the Tarot, Mantras, Mudras, Tattwa's, Talismans, Yarrow Sticks, Herbs, Divination, Meditation, Visualisation, Trance State, these and innumerable others are the Wicces Tools or Spiritual/ Magickal Weapons. In fact, everything you can apply to help with your practical work in Magick is a true Magickal Wiccetool.

Four Elements - four Traditional Weapons - four parts of the Magick Circle you can use in Magick via the Wand, Athame/Sword, Chalice, and Pentacle. How do these Weapons fit into Tetragrammaton (Ceremonial Magick)? Eventually you, the Wicce must discover this from your own experiences but until then I recommend (from my experiences) this arrangement.

ה ו ה י

EARTH	WATER	FIRE	AIR
HE (final)	VAU	HE (primal)	YOD
PENTACLE	CHALICE	ATHAME	WAND
NORTH	WEST	SOUTH	EAST
NEUTRAL	NEGATIVE	POSITIVE	INTRINSIC

CONSECRATION OF TOOLS AND WEAPONS

As a Talisman needs to be "Charged" in order to be truly effective, so Magickal Wiccetool's must be Consecrated before their full scope can be utilised. Consecration is the linking of a physical Wiccetool through Ritual, to the source of the energy, which that Wiccetool directs on the Etheric and Astral Planes.

To Consecrate a Wiccetool, set up an Auric flow with the rest of your group while sitting in a Magick Circle. If you are Consecrating a Wiccetool for personal use only, by yourself, then sit in a semi-lotus position facing in the direction of the Element used (e.g. for the Athame/ Sword, face South). You might like to use incense appropriate to the Element of the Wiccetool (Galbanum for the Wand; Olibanum for the Athame; Jasmine or Onucha for the Chalice, and Storax or Sandalwood for the Pentacle).

Visualise the colour of the Element, its appearance, texture, sound, and taste. When you "feel" the Element, pass a flow from your hands through the Wiccetool. Thus, the Wiccetool is linked to you Aurically. In a group ritual, pass the Wiccetool around to each person to see and handle and then place the Wiccetool in the centre of the Circle. Then everyone in the Magick Circle visualises the Element as mentioned above and directs a flow through the Wiccetool.

Remember to begin and end with your rituals with an Isian or Kabbalistic Cross.

In dealing with the Mysteries of Wiccecraft, it is said that no secrets can be ever given away, secrets do not belong to anyone, and knowledge over the years has been lost due to secrecy and superstition. Here is a single main definition of the objects of all Magick Ritual; it is the uniting of the microcosm and the macrocosm. In examining the Working Tools, you will notice I have grouped the Tools corresponding them to the three Degrees of the Craft, as part of a complete formula. I will concentrate a good deal on their esoteric uses rather than the more Elemental associations, although I will make references to these as well.

1st Degree:	Wicce	Temple of Luna	The Moon	The Goddess:

Thurible - Purification; Athame - Illumination; The Pentacle - Perfection; The Altar - Faith; The White Robe - Freedom; White Singulum (Magick Cord) - Umbilicus and Ladder to the Goddess. Bolline – Herbal Herbcraft.

Other Wiccetool's not mentioned are the Pen of the Art, Black Squid Ink, Blank book for your Book of Shadows, and a Pentacle or Pentagram to be worn.

2nd Degree:	Priest/ess	Temple of Sol	The Sun	Horned God:

Wand - Will power; Chalice - Fertility; Tabard - Shield of Faith; Cloak - Invisibility.

3rd Degree:	High Priest/ess	Temple of Astrum	The Stars	Unity:

Magick Cords - Sacred Space; Scourge - Time; Sword - Infinity; Bell - Harmony; Sistrum - Wisdom; Besom - Power of the Crone; Cauldron - Inspiration/Truth; Sceptre – Magickal Control.

THE CEREMONIAL WAND

Traditionally is Magick there are several types of Wands, as each tradition or system of belief differs in their analogies. You have the Ceremonial Wand, the Ritual Wand, the Wicces Wand, the Magick Wand, the Elemental Wand, the Magicians Wand, the Celestial Wand and the Healing Wand. Every single one of them is used for different reasons and purposes. But Traditionally the Wand is the Tool of Air, the intrinsic Element in which Fire, Water and Earth interact.

CEREMONIAL or MAGICIANS WAND: Alchemists call the Air Principle "Prime Movement" and Alchemists Gold' representing the beginning and end of the Great Work - which is the same point. As the Serpent eats his own tail, the tail and the head become the same point, like the point at which a Circle "begins" and "ends". The Circle is thus an Air symbol, as also is the number ONE, the first number; so too is YOD, the seed-shaped letter.

A most useful macrocosmic Wand is the Lotus Wand. The Lotus Flower is the Yoni, while the stem is the umbilical cord connecting all things to the Source of Life with a vital cord. Three whorls of petals, the calyx and centre, make up the Lotus flower. An outer ring of eight petals represents Earth, and Water, in each of the four worlds; similarly, eight petals in the next ring (going towards the centre) are for Fire and Air. Ten petals of the inner ring answer to the Sephiroth of the Kabbalistic Tree of Life and calyx has four sepals for the four Elementals. Air is the centre.

The petals are made from a thin sheet of silver that is thick enough to hold the petals 'shape' but sufficiently thin enough to produce a "rustling" sound when the Wand moves. Either the petals can be cut individually, or they can be cut in rings (of 8, 8 and 10 or perhaps 4, 4, 4, 4, 5, and 5). The two sets of 8 petals are painted olive green outside with five veins on each leaf (for the four Elements plus Akasha, the fifth Element or Spirit). The inner surface of these petals is left bare silver or painted very bright gloss white. The ring of ten petals is silver or gloss white on both sides while the calyx is vivid orange inside and out. The centre is gold, conveniently a gold-plated screw perhaps, to fix the lotus flower to its stem. In accordance with its numerical attribution, ONE, the overall length of the Lotus Wand is one unit (one yard or meter is best).

TWO RINGS OF 8 PETALS

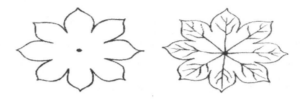

White inside and olive green outside - 5 veins on each petal.

INNER RING OF 10 PETALS

White on both sides

CALYX OF 4 ORANGE SEPALS

Centre of God

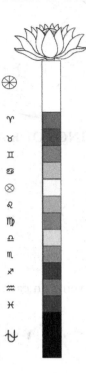

The Lotus stem is a wooden rod painted in colored bands, that is hollow and has a central core of Mercury, with copper around the outside and a silver disc on the bottom. At the top of the stem is the widest band, white in colour and painted with the symbol (spirit). Slightly narrower, the black band is at the bottom and bears the symbol (Earth). Stretching between are even narrower bands, twelve in number, bearing the zodiacal spectrum of colours and symbols. Note: the order in which the four Elements appear in the colour of the Lotus stem.

In use, the appropriate colored band is held to correspond to the nature of your work. This makes the Lotus Wand a very finely tuned, versatile Weapon. When working with the four Elements blue, red, green or yellow is used. For Spiritual work, white is appropriate or for more physical work - black. Zodiacal attributions and Imagination will also help you to choose the most effective band for your work. Try to keep the Lotus flower above the level of the stem when using the Wand since inverting the Wand tends to reverse the affects you seek.

THE RITUAL WAND: A Wand for microcosmic use can be made from a hollow rod of wood bamboo which is convenient - one foot long (including tips). At each end are metal tips and a piece of wire (gold ideally, but copper will serve) connects them, which is wound around the Wand clockwise, (I use copper wire as it is readily available and easy to work with and not so expensive.) The base of the Wand has a hole drilled into the end and your blood on a cotton wool bud placed inside then sealed with beeswax. There should be metal-to-metal contact from end to end. Making caps for the top and bottom of the Wand is easy, just cut two circles of copper plate to fit and then mould and bend to fit securely over the tips. The back end of the wand should be flat where the tip of the Wand is rounded.

The tips should be roughly spherical and either gold, gold plated or copper. As copper is also a conductor for energy especially as an electro-magnetic polarised energy that can attract or repel. Round brass curtain ends with thin gold plating are quite effective as well. After plating one tip should be painted black and one white to induce polarity. The shaft is sky blue and could be painted with sigils or talismans for Air.

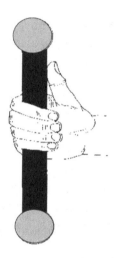

THE CELESTIAL WAND: Has many uses as well but is mainly used for connecting with celestial Beings especially the Shining Ones, the Angels that connect with us and teach and guides us in our spiritual endeavours along the path to finding our Divine Truth.

The perfect timber for this is a long piece of Bamboo as it is hollow, it must be from the crook of your elbow to the tip of your middle finger. Again, a swab of blood in the back end of the Wand and a Celestial Crystal or better still a piece of Meteorite to be placed at the tip of the Wand. The Wand should be dipped in silver or chrome. After it has dried and hardened you then add the crystal to the tip, making sure that it is secure.

When using the Celestial Wand, you should be in a hallowed placed such as your Magick Circle. We never demand or summon them, we must always be polite and ask for their company and assistance. Make sure that what you ask is not of greed or of something that time can take care of itself. When thanking them and making an offer it must be of your time and service and not an object, it must be of self-sacrifice in the giving, as this is the only thing they accept.

A HEALING WAND: Is traditionally by individual choice, your Wand must represent you and your Truth as a soul spiritual Wicce. You must take an object of the Earth that has been absorbed and created by Mother Nature as a gift to you. It must have electro-magnetic qualities. But the most important part of this Healing Wand, is you! You must be TRUE to yourself and your abilities as a Wicce, and know that you are only the object of Healing, and it is the Universal Divine Light Force of Goddess/God and All That Is that is the Power behind your Wand.

We cannot truly heal if we need Healing, we must first heal our own wounds physically, mentally, astrally, psychically and spiritually before we can become a true instrument of the Divine Spirit and assist in Healing of another.

Healing is about connecting, absorbing and working with the Magick of the Universe to either remove, or heal what needs to be corrected by working with Nature, and changing it through one's Will-power.

THE ELEMENTAL WANDS: Elemental Wands are created by their own Element, infused by all the other Elements to a lesser degree. Such as the **Earth Element** should be of the Earth such as a Crystal that has certain properties that has been formed and created over a long period of time by Nature's own Magick. The **Air Wand** should be of a branch that has never touched the living Earth, it must be high about the ground as though reaching for the stars. Different tree's give off different Magickal powers such as the Willow for healing sadness, Oak for healing strength, Ash for new directions, Rowan for changes, Rosewood for divine love, Apple for fertility, Birch for courage, Eucalyptus for healing etc.

The **Fire Wand** should have been forged by Natures power and fire such as the Obsidian Crystal, forged by the volcanic flow of lava sealing the essence of the earth by water and cooled by air. A **Water Wand** should be of the sea such as a Cornet Shell which has a long spiral pattern that is either Deosil for directing healing powers, or Widdershins for removing sickness and ill health.

WICCES/PHALLIC WAND: The Phallic wand is primarily for invoking the Goddess and or God, traditionally ours was a normal length of Oak with an Acorn fixed to the tip. This was called the Phallic Wand. Some other Traditional Covens had similar, but it was a pine rod and a small pine cone fixed to the tip as their Phallic Wand for Invoking deity.

Only the Ordained Priesthood use the Phallic Wand as it is used on special occasions such as Full Moons for Invoking the Goddess and or God, for Major Festivals such as Beltane, Lughnasadh, Samhain, and Imbolg. We also use the Phallic Wand for impregnating fertility into plants, fields, orchards and crops to give more life to the plants, that they be healthy.

All Wands are Magick Wands, but they each have a specific reason and should never be used for anything else, as this would cause adverse effects and may create a negative result instead of the intended desire of the Wicce. Your Wand should be cut between the season of Spring and Summer when the sacred mana of the tree is flowing faster. I love working with the Rowan or Oak tree. If the branch is long enough it is advisable to also cut a length for your Besom, which is to be used by the Female Elder of your Magick Circle to cleanse and purify the Temple space. When using a Wand or making a Wand make sure you impregnate the intention of its uses, a Magickal Tool is like a child and needs to be always considered, nurtured, fed with emotional support and love, and taught of its reason for being as a positive amplification of your Divineness. A Wand can be as elaborate or as simple as you desire, but make sure it is NATURAL with no chemical added gums or glues.

THE ATHAME — RITUAL
DAGGER - MASCULINE

Where the Thurible is the Element of Air and represents Purification, the Athame is fiery and represents Illumination or Enlightenment, the Wicce learns that there is much to 'cut and free themselves from', and that there is much to unlearn. Superstition and ignorance cloud the Wicces consciousness. It is the Will of the Higher Self, which is eventually to be awakened. We then set to work developing clarity of Will in the consciousness through the practices of concentration. This step is for the developing Wicce, is a formidable one. It is not merely that attainment of powers of concentration, but mastery of emotional power over the self. The formula for this is expressed in the Universal Wiccan Rede "AN IT HARM NONE, DO WHAT YOU WILL". Or phrased in modern idiom, "LOVE AND DO YOUR WILL". Or more simply, "LOVE UNDER WILL".

So, the Athame is to become a key to the expression of the Wicces Will, but it depends on her Magickal maturity. In any Magickal Ritual you cannot act on your authority alone. You must awaken within the consciousness a Will of Deity. Invoking Deity does this, and so uplifts your consciousness into the Akashic Plane of Spirit, thus being the Goddess and God. The importance of the Thurible is used to raise the vibrations of the Magick Circle and is paramount if the Will is to change on all Planes. The Athame is therefore an implement that no Wicce is without, well, from a ceremonial and Magickal point of view anyway. From a practical point of view, one does not venture forward in Magickal operations without a 'Willed Intention', which should come from the Will of the Higher Self and not the mundane mortal self. It is very important that the Athame, as a symbol of Will, be well planted in your consciousness, the faculties and corresponding powers symbolised by the Wiccetool.

Thereby you have complete control to Banish that, which has been invoked or evoked. Remember the plight of the Sorcerer's Apprentice, who upon splitting the broomstick he had brought to life, found he had two problems to tend with, and so on, ad infinitum. Such is the fate of the BADLY DEVELOPED WILL.

The Lesser Wiccetools of the Fire Element are the Four Akashic Flames/Candles. The Altar represents the microcosmic Fire Element (the invisible within the visible), the Wicce calls forth from within the Magick Circle. This she uses within the Magick Circle demonstrating the Hermetic Principle: "AS ABOVE, SO BELOW, AS WITHIN, SO WITHOUT". Flanking the four Cardinal Points of the Magick Circle are the Four Akashic Flames of the Four Elements, the macrocosmic forces of Earth, Air, Fire and Water, expressive also of the Four Planes; Material, Astral, Mental and Spiritual. This is always a reminder to the Wicce, that the work is always effective on all Planes, so always be cautious. In my Covens we perform the preliminary ritual, which is called the "Warming and Awakening of the Temple". Our Man in Black, who is the Principal Ritualist under the High Priest/ess, usually carries out this ceremony. He is also a character called "Lucifuge", and carries The Flame/Light "Spirit", into the Magick Circle and onto the Altar. From this Sacred Flame all lights within the Magick Circle are ignited. The Circle is opened in the names of the Goddess and God, demonstrating that Deity is the source of all Light/Knowledge/Power.

So, we have a Wiccetool called an Athame but what is it and where did it come from. The Truth is that during the period known as "The Burning Times" where an estimated 9 million men, women and children were taken, imprisoned and tortured. The Athame had a more horrific purpose, but as horrific as it seemed, it was a necessity in the saving of many lives. The Inquisition proclaimed that anyone with any protuberances or external markings such as moles, tumors, warts, or any unusual markings or even scars, especially birth marks, were called the marks of the devil. The Inquisitors believed that these markings were signs of the devil and were used to suckle the Wicces Familiars known as Incubi and Succubi.

So Wicces in defense, when hearing that they may be taken and questioned by the local Inquisitors, would take their dagger (Athame) and cut the markings from their bodies preferring the slow bleeding, and sometimes blood clotting and eventual death than that of the Inquisitors slow torture and eventual death, usually by starvation. We today reclaim the Athame as a symbol of all those that perished and died, and as a symbol that we are free to sever the bonds of slavery and all IGNORANCE, past, present and hopefully future. It has now through the ages been used as a Tool of great significance and power that no Wicce is without.

The Traditional Athame is black hilted or an antler handle with a double-edged blade. The handle is preferably made from wood (Ebony or dark wood) or antler, or even stained bone. It should not be a sharp dagger, as it will never actually cut anything physically, it is an Astral Tool only. Its blade length should be from the tip of your middle finger to the end of your palm. It should be as plain as it can be, with no markings whatsoever on them prior to the Initiation Ceremony (which are done in squid ink). It should be clean and virgin. After Initiation the sigils are painted on it in black ink, then you do them yourself once the Athame is Consecrated and charged. It is used to direct and to absorb the electro-magnetic energies within the Universe. After the Rite of Initiation, when the new Wicce is presented with their Dagger, which is readied to become their Athame, after it is etched with the Magickal sigils of the Craft, it is then Consecrated.

After the end of the evening, the Wicce then takes it to their own personal Magick Circle and plunges it deep into the centre of their Circle up to the hilt. The Athame is left they're until the next Full Moon where it is drawn out and cleansed with spring water, but never scrubbed or sanded clean as it must keep its patina, as this is the blessing of Mother Nature. So, you have blessed it, your Coveners have blessed it, the Full Moon has blessed it and Mother Nature has blessed it, now it is time to use your sacred Wiccetool to cast and mark up your Magick Circle and work with the sacred Pentagrams of the Mysteries.

It is the same with all Tools of the Craft. They are all specially prepared and Consecrated within the Magick Circle. They are awakened to the connectedness of the Inner Wicce. It takes a long time in being Properly Prepared to hold such a sacred object. It is not a toy, but a sacred Tool/Weapon that helps us to remember the pain and suffering of our ancestors during the last Millennia, and as we reclaim our heritage and the Athame, and especially the title of Wicce. We will respect both, and thus the powers of the Wicce will unfold. When the time is right, the Athame will seek you out and find you! Also know that an Athame is different from a Ceremonial or Ritual Dagger of a Magician.

The Athame originally was carved from pure Oak and is one of Five, which are all cast and made the same way over 100 years ago by my mentor and spiritual grandmother Lady Margaret, She was of the Hartsburg Wicces and of the Black Forest Coven known as the Dragons Lair. She was such a grand lady that she even upon meeting Sibil Leek presented to her one of the five Athame's as a gift to teach the younger generation that of the old Tradition of Wiccecraft in the US. Sibil did do this upon her arrival back in the United States but many things were changed in her teachings and by her adding her original patriarchal views from the Golden Dawn that she was a member of and due to Gardner's teachings.

THE BOLINE — WORKING DAGGER — FEMININE

The Bolline is the counterpart of the Athame, but where the Athame is never used to touch or cut anything, the Bolline is used within the Magick Circle and without for the preparation of Magickal items such as the cutting of herbs, candles, engraving or etching, and the infusing of feminine energy into an object.

The Bolline has a white handle, usually made of white wood or a sun-bleached antler is perfect. The blade should be very sharp and is best formed into the shape of a crescent like a scythe. All Magickal Wiccetool's have sigils of the Art placed on them but not etched or engraved but with pure ink so it can be washed off afterwards. These means that the Sigils are infused in to the object with the mind forcing the ink to penetrate astrally then the physical is removed.

When Consecrating the Bolline you use the tip of your Athame (blade facing east) touching the tip of the Bolline (blade facing west), so it absorbs certain Magickal energies, they then have a sort of marriage which makes them a working pair on all levels, where the Athame works in the astral and Magickal planes the Bolline works on the physical and mental planes. Infused together they become the perfect working pair of Magickal Tools. This Wiccetool is a 2nd degree tool, but it should be worked with as a 1st degree Wicce, as this training helps you in reaching your Magickal maturity into the Priesthood where you will be taught the greater meanings and uses of the Bolline. Usage for the Priesthood of the Bolline are for Psychic Surgery.

THE CEREMONIAL MAGICIANS MAGICK SWORD

The Sword is the active Weapon of Fire and hence its action is hot and energetic – "The Phallus of Living Flame". Three is the Sword's number because activity requires three Elements – the actor, the action and the object acted upon.

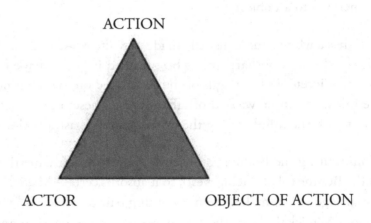

ACTION

ACTOR   OBJECT OF ACTION

Thus, the Red Triangle – Tejas – is Fire.

The blade of the Sword is Iron or Steel, the martial metal. One side of the blade bears the inscription:

SHALOM – (Peace) painted as –
in black on a white background
and framed with gold. The other
side is inscribed in white.

CO-ACH – (Force) painted as
on black and framed with gold.

The inscriptions are close to the hilt leaving the rest of the blade a bare polished metal colour. For coagulating, the SHALOM side is used and for dissolving the CO-ACH side.

The quillions, or crosspiece, of the Magickal Sword is made from two crescents of Silver, the watery aspect of the Sword to contain and direct the fiery energy. Double Crescents also emphasize the duality of the Sword's potential actions. On the crescents are inscribed the names of the Sephiroth of RUACH as shown in the diagram.

The grip is a seven-coiled serpent of copper. Seven is the number of Earth; hence this is an Earth Serpent. With its head resting on the quillions on the SHALOM side, the serpent winds Deosil into head and tail on the SHALOM side, however, on the other side just the seven coils are visible.

The pommel of the Sword is a hollow silver ball containing Mercury which screws onto the tang to hold the Sword together (SEE DIAGRAM). Two more silver balls containing Mercury are attached between the Crescents. These three balls represent Air, being three in number since this is the numerical attribution of the Sword.

For this reason, also, the Sword is three feet in length from end to end.

The Sword is a macrocosmic Weapon, but for microcosmic work an Athame similar in design can be made. A good overall length for the Athame was explained before, but usually 30 centimeters.

HEBREW NAMES FOR THE SWORD AND CHALICE:

נֶצַח	Netzach
הוֹד	Hod
תפ**א**רת	Tiphareth
גְּבוּרָה	Geburah
חֶסֶד	Chesed
רְפָאֵל	Raphael
מִיכָאֵל	Michael
גַּבְרִיאֵל	Gabriel
אוּרִיאֵל	Auriel

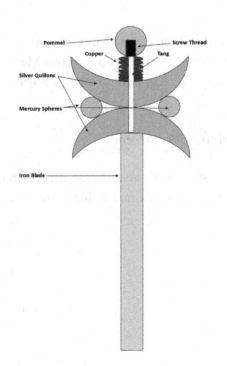

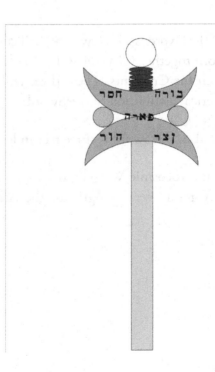

THE MAGICK SWORD OF THE
HIGH PRIEST AND HIGH PRIESTESS

The Magick Sword is only handled by the High Priestess, High Priest or the Maiden and Man in Black, and they must all be of sufficient levels in the Priesthood. When I see Covens of untrained knowledge into the Sword, I get annoyed. In ancient times it was forbidden for most people to possess a Sword, so they were in short supply, usually just one to a Coven, and usually held by the leader and at times wielded by the Man in Black, the Guardian of the Coven, or as I affectionately call them "The Coven Cop".

I had my traditional sword made by an armourist, a professional who could make medieval armour and weaponry. I gave him the design and he made it perfectly. The length of the Sword should be from the ground to your waste.

The hilt design is of "The Breasts of the Goddess" or better known as the "Triple Moon" which is two crescent moons back to back with a solid disk in the centre. These represent the New Moon, Full Moon and Dark Moon. Or specifically the Maiden, Mother and Crone. We made these out of solid brass with a bound leather studded handle with the Coven Pentacle and Seal of my Family at the end of the hilt.

It must be kept away and wrapped in pure silk, I had always had ours placed back into a special handmade wooden case that I used for when I travelled so as to take it with me.

8. E Solidification
□

7. A Prime Movement
●

6. W Contraction
☾

5. F Expansion
▲

4. A Prime Movement
●

3. W Contraction
☾

2. F Expansion
▲

1. E Solidification
□

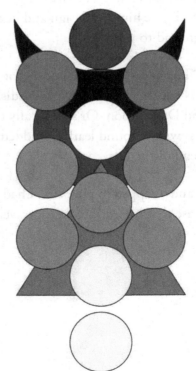

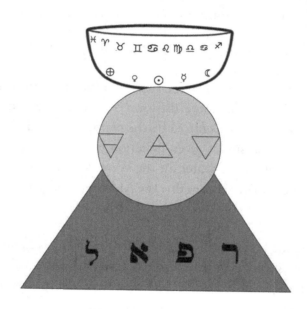

THE CEREMONIAL CHALICE

The Chalice is the passive Water Weapon, the receptive Yoni. The letter VAU means, "CUP" so the Tetragrammaton correspondence is evident. The Chalice contains things which would otherwise flow away and disperse. As the polarity of Fire, the Chalice contracts as Fire expands. Water contracts, contains, directs the undisciplined energetic Fire to harness its energy for use.

Five is the number of the Chalice being the four Elements plus Akasha.

The Chalice is the Alchemists crucible in which solid realities are refined Initially, Fire expands solidarity, so it becomes larger and more diffuse (1) and (2) - less defined. This action is represented in the Cup of Stolist (or Solstices) by the copper tetrahedron (triangular pyramid), which forms its base. The expansion is given direction by the contracting, defining influence of Water (3) as it rises to the world of Water. At the Water level the tetrahedron disappears into the centre of a gold sphere (Air) that contains the Mercury, and gives meaning, a new Prime Movement (4), to the work.

As the gold sphere enters the Fire level (5) of reality this meaning is expanded and as the sphere merges into the silver crescent-bowl (6), Water defines it anew. Air reality provides Prime Movement (7) for the newly defined work creating a new reality - an infinite reality. This is the Alchemists GOLD, the product refined to pure essence from waste (8).

Hence the Chalice is a guide how you, the Wicce, can refine yourself to the pure essence of your being by dissolving and coagulating yourself. The Chalice uses the reality that is stated by the Pentacle to create Perfection. The Pentacle states the Wicces reality, the Chalice uses it, the Sword gives it energy and the Wand is the result (*hence the ideal*).

When making the Chalice of Solstices ensure that the overall height is five or ten units (*e.g. inches*). The apex of the pyramid sits into a hole in the sphere so that it coincides with the centre of the sphere. The following symbols are painted or inlaid on the Chalice using gold for the bowl and pyramid, and silver on the sphere:

Around the rim of the bowl are the zodiac signs. Place the Chalice so that only one face of the tetrahedron is visible to you. Imagine a straight line running vertically up the centre of the Chalice. Pisces is on your left of Aquarius and then the signs continue in order Deosil round the bowl to finish at Capricorn on the right of Aquarius.

Further down on the bowl close to where it joins the sphere are the four Alchemical principles - Salt   Mercury   Sulphur   and Gold.

The symbol for gold is directly below Aquarius on the centre line.

On the sphere around its "Equator" line are the Elemental symbols for

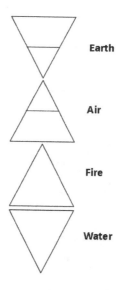

Earth

Air

Fire

Water

The Air symbol is vertically aligned with the Aquarius and Gold. Near where the sphere joins the pyramid, the serpent eating its tail encircles the sphere. The serpent's head is below Air, Gold and Aquarius and its body runs Deosil (towards Pisces) around the sphere.

On the face of the pyramid, which is below; Aquarius is the name Raphael. On the next face moving Deosil round the Chalice is Michael and on the third face Gabriel. (You will find Gemini is directly above Michael and Libra above Gabriel). Auriel is on the bottom surface of the pyramid as this is closest to the Earth. These Shining Ones names may be written in their original Hebrew if you prefer. For microcosmic work you can design your own Chalice. Any metal Goblet or Cup will serve if it is new and clean. If you like you and buy a cup and paint or engrave appropriate symbols on it. The Chalice does not have to be metal either - it can be glass, clay, plaster or whatever material, although I do not recommend plastics for Magickal work.

I have acquired several Chalices over my years and my first was a large Sea Snail Shell that I used as my first Chalice, then I found at an antique store on my travels a rare 17th century silver embossed Roman Catholic Church Chalice with etchings on it and gems and used this thereafter as my wine Chalice. I then had a special Shell Chalice made in Bali etched in pure silver and covered in gemstones, it was a copy of an early 16th century Chalice found and now in the Vatican museum. I also have a very large Museum piece Festival Chalice that holds about 3 bottles of wine etched with the story of King Arthur and the Holy Grail. All these pieces will be donated to the Buckland Museum of Witchcraft and Magick when I am not using them anymore.

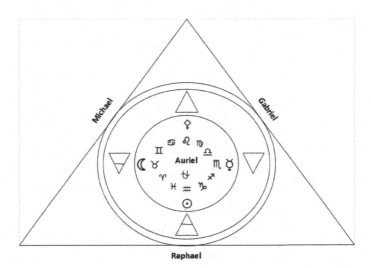

THE SACRED PENTACLE – HIGHER PENTACLE OF THE PRIESTHOOD

The Pentacle is flat and round, as the Earth itself was once believed to be. Earth is solid and acts as a foundation, a basis from which to start. As such the Pentacle is a basic statement of the Wicces reality. This Pentacle unlike the Magick Circle Pentacle as shown in my second book "The Complete Teachings of Wicca Book Two-The Witch". This one is for working on the Higher Planes of existence as a High Priesthood.

You will already be familiar with four of them; - Earth, Air, Fire and Water. When you begin to work on the Astral Plane you will encounter the three AKASHIC ELEMENTS, or Elements of Life. The best we can do with words is to call them the consciousness (or Mind), Interaction and Death (meaning simply non-existence).

One face of the Pentacle shows how the Pentagram in a Circle expresses this seven-fold reality in the Microcosm. The pinnacle of the Pentagram is AKASHA, also the Kabbalists Ain Soph Aur; the other four points are the four ELEMENTS. The Circle itself is Ain, and the space inside it is Ain Soph. Inside the five points are the letter of Tetragrammaton plus

Tau - "The Path". In the centre of the Pentagram is ADAM - "MAN".

The opposite face of the Pentacle illustrates macrocosmic reality with the Hexagram. The Alchemists use the Hexagram to represent the Hermetic Law - "AS ABOVE, SO BELOW". In the centre of the Hexagram at the seventh point' is the looped Tau Cross of Ankh, the symbol of Life, surrounded by three Yod's for the three AKASHIC ELEMENTS.

The Pentacle is seven inches in diameter, being made of Lead or Copper, the gross metal of Earth. The characters on the Pentacle are traced in gold (gold paint is sufficient. A Space containing an amalgam of the 7 metals and reflecting the overall shape is in the centre.

In use the Pentacle is held with the Pentagram facing you, the microcosm, and the Hexagram faces outwards to reflect the Macrocosm. It is because of the Pentacle's quality of reflecting the Microcosm inwards and the Macrocosm outwards that it is also called the Shield. Hence it is also the point where the Microcosm and the Macrocosm meet, which makes the three AKASHIC ELEMENTS so significant here. When holding the Pentacle, it is essential to ensure that the pinnacle of the Pentagram is always at the top. Inverting the Pentagram changes the symbolism from "Perfect Man" to "Man at the lowest point of which he is capable".

The new Pentacle of the Wiccans is very different and draws from the Elements at a more involved level, ruling the Higher Mind over the lower Elements of our being of human nature. It still signifies the Awakening of the Cosmic Consciousness, and the beginnings of human consciousness, manipulating its environment beyond the realms of the physical form and perceptions limited into 5 senses. Today this High Magickal Tool is to be used as a Paten, for the ritual Consecration of salt and water in preliminary work within the Magick Circle. It is represented as a SYMBOL OF AUTHORITY to the Guardians of Wicca and the Magick Circle. All other Tools may be charged on this High Tool of the Earth for Coven or Solitary alike.

The symbols, which are placed upon the Pentacle of Wicca, are placed in a set position to represent an ancient KEY to unlock the EPAGOMENES (The Secrets and knowledge of the Craft) when used correctly.

CREATING THE MAGICK BLACK MIRROR

"You sit, silent, bare
awareness towards soulless
blackened lens, empty space empty
mind, empty colour sister of the mirror, becoming
substance of Light, melting to form the mirror within a
mirror, slow swirling converse carrying consciousness
gently, tunnels of time, tunnels of space, tunnels
of energy. We enter the blackness of
nothingness to become something
That is far reaching the depths
Of our
inner mind
and soul."

YOU FEEL - sensations of the corners of time.
YOU THINK - your thoughts, orange, expand to the laws of the Universe.
YOU LOVE - the Sunshine's on the reaches of space, sunbeams melt becoming Stars.
YOU SMILE - infinitely.

"Deep in the mountains, a long time ago a Wicces settlement lay in the middle
of a lost and forgotten valley To the East of the valley the mountain Air
enriched in colour by its own thinness, harbored textures and shades of blue
very rarely seen on Earth To the South, a volcano infrequently threw small
embers of Fire into the Air. To the West, a huge waterfall fed the river, which
ran by the settlement. And to the North, the mountains rose ever steeper.

The fog was just starting to lift off the valley and the sunlight barely filtering
through, when a door in a building opened and a boy walked out into the gardens.
He passed flowerbeds, ponds and rockeries and finally, came to a small clearing

where he sat cross legged facing an old tree. The tree was tall and thick giving the appearance that it had grown there for thousands of years. The tree was huge and solid giving the appearance that its roots held the world together. Beneath the tree was another figure even more solid and aged. An old woman sat unmoving, a monolith of rock, hewn and etched by the process of time. A face bleak and barren.

The boy having sat still for a few minutes considered the woman's face "Old One, I had a dream last night. I was sitting alone in a darkened room the only light present was coming from me ... In front of me was a black box enclosing an even blacker mirror it seemed to reflect the light back towards me. It made me feel very old and I could remember things I'd never known before". A slow smile came to the woman and she turned to watch the Moon hanging over the valley in the bright daylight ... Words of stone "Before the floods in the great Mother country the Black Mirror was used as a lens to focus and direct Auric energy. The Lemurians centered it mainly on living matter whereas, after the floods the people of Egypt were using it more for non-living things. It was one of the machines used in the construction of the Pyramids" She looked away from the Moon. "The younger members of Magickal communities found enjoyment in using it for time travel and other spectacular but rather meaningless exercises". A small child stumbled into the clearing and headed towards the old woman who immediately became engrossed in laughing and playing with the child.

It was a month later when the boy thought of the Black Mirror again. He had searched all day and finally found the old woman sitting next to the waterfall at the end of the valley. The scene surprised him. The spray from the waterfall was being caught by the Sun and produced myriads of rainbows that seemed to play down into the woman's hair. He sat himself in front of her, a look of contemplation on his face and spoke.

"Old One I dreamed again of the mirror last night" Silence - he tried to recall the details more clearly. 'I think I learned how the Mirror was made I was searching for a watch glass I finally found one about twenty centimeters across, it had no scratches or defects. I then found some camphor wood and made a box and lid to enclose the glass I remember I lined the inside of the box and lid with black felt and painted the outside the same colour with a dull paint I think I remember taking the rest of the black felt and sewing a bag to keep the box in I then had to make a Talisman using the four Shining Ones and a Goddess or a God.' He watched the rainbows, "I think that choosing the Goddess or God was the most interesting part of the dream' He laughed.

The rainbows that had been playing with the woman's hair now seemed to float down into her face it was as though each section of her face took on a colour giving life and beauty to the form.

"The dream then changed I was sitting in my Temple I had just sterilised the glass and had fixed the windows and doors so that no light could enter. It was totally dark, and I was sitting in the middle of the Magick Circle the four Shining Ones standing around me smiling. I seemed to have a macrocosmic Middle Pillar flowing around me and at that moment I was invoking the God in the Talisman to come and help me. I then put a flow through the Talisman and asked the Shining Ones and God to help me build and use the Mirror I placed my Talisman in the bottom of the box and lit a beeswax candle this was the only source of light in the Temple. I then took the watch glass and passed it slowly over the flame so that the soot from the flame formed a layer of blackness on the outside curve of the glass. It took many layers of soot to form a film so strong that no light could pass through.

I then gently lay the glass down in the box with the Talisman resting underneath it. I had to be careful not to smudge the black upper surface of the dome with my fingers. I thanked the Shining Ones for their help in ritual and them in turn spoke to me of its use. For one month, I was to take it out in the dark room every night I was to look at it, think about it, and imagine being it …

Her eyes peering gently through the rainbows the colours now melting down over her body so that her dull gray robe became a garment of serene greens and gold's, every part of the cloth ever changing hue.

"After I had used it for a month in that manner I was to try and see images and scenes from that day's events in the mirror. Once accomplished, I was to try to see events a few days previous then slowly work back further into the past. After having spoken thus the Shining One left amidst glorious sounds and fires and I slowly awakened.

The rainbows were becoming richer and vibrating the Sunlight as they seemed to engulf her leaving only a vague outline of the woman. A stone sitting in a mist of rainbows and sparkling water drops. Strangely, her whisper seemed to transcend the roar of the waterfall.

"My young friend, it appears as though you are to make a Black Mirror". She chuckled, then more seriously. 'Camphor wood has properties that make it a very dense Astral material. It is this denseness enclosing the glass that protects it Aurically. The black felt stops light from entering the box and destroying the Mirror. The Mirror is very sensitive to light and exposure will harm its properties. Felt also carries an electrical charge very similar to the Mirror. The Black paint helps to absorb any light present. The glass must be exceptionally clean for the final step, so sterilising it was a good idea ... The soot from the beeswax sets up a layer of district nine over the outer surface of the Mirror the thicker the better as it is this layer of the chemical that sets up the Auric Mirror. The Shining Ones are invoked in the Talisman to control and regulate any adverse effects. At first you must choose the areas of Magick you wish to use the Mirror in, be it healing, communication, Scrying, time travel, introspection, or whatever, and invoke the appropriate God-form into the Talisman. The God will then guide and teach you in these Areas. For example, if you wanted communication with nature you could invoke Pan to help you. If you choose healing, then you could call on one of the Goddesses like Kwan Yin to guide you.

The ritual for the final stage of physical construction consists of firstly a microcosmic banishing of your Magick Circle, then a Banishing of your implements in the Magick Circle. Invoke the Shining Ones, to follow that with an invocation of a macrocosmic Middle Pillar, then sit down in front of your Talisman and call the Appropriate God. When you feel its presence, pass a flow through the Talisman then put it in the box after you have lit the Candle and completely blackened the Mirror, thank the Shining Ones and God then finish the ritual in the usual manner. Do not, after this stage, ever let the mirror meet light. The four-week contemplation and observation of the Mirror will produce an Auric link which will be your means of entering it."

The boy looked up and noticed the rainbows were now engulfing the space between him and the woman, seeming to link the two of them in colour and sound.

'After this stage is finished you will find there are many uses for the Mirror. You must experiment carefully, searching for as many effects as necessary. Find out more about the mechanics of the Wiccetool, become fully competent in the understanding of its workings. You will find, after the first months' work, the mirror will seem to form a whitish dome facing the opposite direction underneath the black dome. This will happen as the Auric link solidifies. Once there, try letting yourself drift through it. Instead of seeing the scene in the mirror, as at first, you will be there in the scene. This whitish anti-mirror is the heart of the machine. She looked through the rainbows at the boy, she smiled - infinitely. Words of stone, laughter of rainbows. She moved the rainbows ever closer around him.

"The mechanics of the Mirror are simple. The Auric energy you give is taken, refined and very finely focused by the machine. It is then sent back into your tree. Example - the time travel, is a refined reflection of the Geburatic memory. As you become more competent with it, my young friend, always remember to use it to help others as much as it has helped you. There are some Wicces who have fallen from great heights by negligent use of the Mirror and Magick.

Hearing this, the boy looked at her. All he could see were rainbows and sparkling water drops in the air before him. Beautiful golden flowers grew out of the rainbows and sang windy songs. The scene then floated upon the ground and became a flowerbed, one of the many lying beside the waterfall. The young boy smiled, said "Thank you", and walked away.

The car pulled up to the curb, a young lady slid out, locked the door and trotted up into the building. She got out of the lift and walked over to the open door. An old man was sitting on the sofa. She smiled and said "Teacher, a friend of mine had a dream last night in which he saw me sitting before a Black Mirror". The old man returned the smile and glanced through the window at the Moon.

"The energy of the work just done
Aids the development of Love and Understanding in all things".

RITUAL OF LOVE

XXI The Universe —
The Universal Mother Nammu
Journey to Everything-the Key to Light

"I generate Love and Understanding
For all others and I".

This ritual is done for the first time at least one full Luna cycle after the TIPHARETH WEEKEND and at least one full week after you banish your personal Watcher. After that, do the Initiation as often as you feel the need to. For example, it's good to do Initiations for each season.

One of the functions of Initiation is to "crystallise" a working tree in your Aura. This will mean that you will then be able to build and store specific types of energies, which you will then be able to call on at any time. The tree enables you to call on the positive side of any planetary force, even when it isn't above the horizon and this allows you more control over your "internal" cycles and rhythms.

You choose the "strongest" Magick Circle available to you - your Temple. Your list of requirements is;

1. Your Robe and Cloak

2. Your Seal and Banishment Stars.

3. Elemental Cards and 4 beeswax candles and matches.

4. Distilled water or spring water for the Circle, Altars and drinking), salt, for the Circle.

5. Black "sealed folder containing your "Black Book" and white drawing paper.

6. Writing and drawing implements.

7. Silent watch to tell time.

8. Unleven bread.

9. Frankincense and Myrrh, Oil of Roses, Salt Water, Lush Earth.

10. Black 'sealed' bag to carry all this in.

11. Fast for as long as you feel appropriate and **FROM** what you consider being a source of strength for you. The ritual begins at 3 pm.

If the four Temples are available to you, the rest of your work group "works" the Fire Temple, while you use the Air Temple to clean and empty your Aura so that you have no distracting "links" to drain off your concentration during the coming night.

When you feel that the strength coming from the Fire Temple are enough (about half an hour usually) you come silently from the Air Temple into the Fire Temple. As you enter the others close their eyes. You circle the Temple three times then go from the North to the Centre. Here you visualise your Aura filling with the power of the invoked field. When you feel it is at the level you want, intone the God name of the sphere that is appropriate for that day and leave to go to the Water Temple. The rest of your Coven continues for twenty minutes after you leave then they silently leave. One of them should be appointed to come around half an hour before dawn to stand beside the Temple and call out "WAKE UP" you answer "THANKYOU", and nothing else. The other person then leaves.

PART ONE - THE MICROCOSM:

Shower; anoint your four Auric Eyes with Eucalyptus Oil, or the oil used in the Ra Rituals. Invoke the Kabbalistic Cross as you enter the Temple. Place your "offerings" and light one candle at each Quarter, then leave.

Start the main body of the ritual wearing your cloak and carrying all you need. Go through the Middle Pillar and before you enter contemplate the first law "MAN KNOW THYSELF", as you step over the threshold think about the second Law "BE IN ALL THINGS".

- BANISH - then do the "Generation Mantra" 108 times, use MALA beads (Buddhist prayer beads).

- Make a Salt Water Circle (use your Cord if you have one) using the mantra AUM.

- Invoke the GODS of the Quarters.

- Lie with your head to the East and do a FULL TREE ritual as in Chapter XI.

- Set up your cards in their bags around your Circle. Take out the Air card and work it for 15 minutes.

- Rest.

- INVOKE the SHINING ONES.

- Heads to the South - FULL TREE.

- Take out and work the FIRE CARD for 15 minutes.

- Rest.

- INVOKE the WINDS.

- Head to the West - FULL TREE.

- Take out and work the WATER CARD for 15 minutes.

- Rest.

- INVOKE the ELEMENTALS.

- Heads to the North - FULL TREE.

- Take out and work the EARTH CARD for 15 minutes.

- Rest.

- Take out the Bread and Water, set up a flow of your Prana through it and say;

> "I am Thoth, your Prophet, one of the Shining Ones,
> the one to whom you gave your Mysteries,
> the Ceremonies of Egypt.
> You produced the moist and the dry, and that which
> Nourishes all created life, hear me!
> For I am the Shining One Paphro-Ororronophris,
> This is your True Nature.
> Handed down to the Prophets of Egypt".

Then eat some of the bread and then hold up the Water with the fingers of your left hand and visualise sprinkling pure PRANA into the Water from the tips of your right-hand fingers, which you gently shake over the top of the Water, as you breathe out. Then drink it.

- Blow out the candles and lie with your head towards the Southeast.

- Go up the Lightning Flash from MALKUTH to KETHER, allowing a couple of minutes for each sphere.

- Come back DOWN the Lightning Flash at the same speed.

- Light the candles and write about your experiences. Put out candles.

- Rest, sleep with your head towards the South-East (East if you're in the Water Temple) cross your arms on your chest and your legs at your ankles - alternate them occasionally. Contemplate your whole body. Beginning with your toes, follow the flow of Chi as if you were circulating the Yin and Yang meridians but feel deep inside, take your time, try to feel the balance of the Elements in each organ and part. This is called naming your body. Then visualise your legs flying off to infinity, then your head, and your arms and finally visualise your whole body breaking up and flying off in all directions. All your internal organs falling off into deep space. You are dissolving your old self. Never will you be the same again. This is called dissolution or giving away. Contemplate the idea that you share yourself with the Universe and vice versa, then sleep nameless and bodiless.

PART TWO THE MACROCOSM:

- Wake up half an hour before Dawn.

- Stretch your body, exercise for 5-10 minutes.

- Check the offerings on the Altars, replenish each one.

- Write down any dreams etc.

- DAWN RITUAL - face East in the pain control position and say.

> "Hail to you, who is Ra as you rise, even to you who is Ra,
> The strength that travels over the sky in your ship with the Rising Sun.
> Tehuti stands in His splendor at the prow and Ra-Hoor stands at the Helm.
> Hail to you all from the Houses of the Night".

- "Call down" the Sun.

- Breakfast - repeat 19.

- Finish writing up dreams or anything else you feel.

- **MACROCOSMIC INVOCATION RITUAL:**

Use both hands as Wands and take the right hand to the top point that is level with the Air *"eye"* in the forehead. The left hand goes to the bottom point level with the genitals. The right hand is taken down visualising a line of *"Blue Flame"* to a point level with the EARTH "eye" below the navel and about 10 cm out from the right side. Then take the line straight across to a corresponding point on the left side, then bring the visualised line back up to complete the top Triangle filling with red penetrating energy (the lines are drawn on the **out** breath, the **in** breaths fix each point.)

You then hold that Triangle with your right-hand Wand while you construct the lower Triangle with your left. You take a line of force from the point in front of the genitals up to a point level with the left shoulder about 5 cm to the side. Then take the line across to the right shoulder. You visualise the Triangle filling with blue Prana as you complete the lower Triangle. Make sure you do draw a six-pointed star and not two independent Triangles. The colours should mix in the middle to form purple. You then take both hands back to the prayer position and you "vitalise" each of the macrocosmic invocation Hexagrams with the God name of the Quarter and the SUN MUDRA (chapter XVII).

Call the God/dess, Shining One, Wind, and Elemental of each of the Quarters and introduce yourself by your Magickal Name and tell them that you will work WITH them in peace and love.

- Complete the Circle then go to the Centre and stand in the pain control position facing East. Evoke and Invoke the Shining Ones and the Pentagram and Hexagram. With full visualisation!

- Concentrate on **RAPHAEL** and say: -

"Salve Raphael cuius Spiritus Est Aur Mortibus ET Aurata cus Solis Lumen".

(Greetings RAPHAEL whose spirit is the dawn from the mountains thus the first Light radiates from your Sun).

(The action of Air is the beginning of other actions)

Then turn to MICHAEL and say:

"Salve Michael Quanta Splendidora Quam Ignes Sempiterni Est Tue Majestos".
(Greetings **MICHAEL** more splendid than the everlasting fires in your Majesty)
(The Fire of Fire is the Fire within all others.)

Then turn to **GABRIEL** and say: -

"Salve Gabriel Cuius Nomine Trement Nymphal Subter Undus Ludentes".
(Greetings GABRIEL, at whose name the nymphs tremble under conquering waves.)
(The Fire of Water is sensuality itself.)

Then turn to AURIEL and say: -

"Salve Auriel Nam tellus Et Omina Viva Regno Tuo Per Quadent".
(Greetings AURIEL, for the Earth and all living things are guided by your reign.)
(The Fire of Earth is the guiding and fixing force of all life.)

- Light the Candles.

- Stand facing North and say:

> "I invoke you, the One who was never born,
> You who created the Earth and the Heavens.
> You who created the Night and the Day,
> You who created the darkness and the Light.
> You are Osorronophris, who nobody has ever seen at any time,
> You are Alpha, you are Omega.
> You have distinguished the Just and the Unjust,
> You have made the female and the Male.
> You produced the Seed and the fruit.
> You formed people to Love one another".

- Face the East and Invoke DIANA.

- Face the South and Invoke PAN.

- Face the West and Invoke RA-APOLLO.

- Face the North and "take on" the form of the Pregnant ISIS.

- Complete the Circle then go to the centre and say;

"Excubitores In Nomine Gabrieli, fas Mithi, Tangere, Illa".

- Kabbalistic Cross - fixing Mantra 108 times.

- Thank all the entities you've met and used as you Circle the Temple three times and then as you are leaving (don't look back) contemplate the third Law "DO WHAT THOU WILT".

- After leaving the Temple (if you have access to the Earth Temple go to it for about 20 minutes) contemplate the fourth Law "LOVE UNDER WILL".

If you find it necessary to leave the Temple at any time you must Circle the Temple three times, do a Kabbalistic Cross then leave. Shower before you return, anoint your "Eyes", then do a "Middle Pillar" and a Kabbalistic Cross as you re-enter.

"The energy of the work just done aid
in the development of Love and Understanding in all things".

THE ROAD BEGINS

This may all sound a little confusing but in time and with the assistance of the Shining Ones you will begin to sense and feel the Universe and all around you. You will find that we are not separate from anything on this planet, and that we are all an incredible part of everything. In scientific circles I heard many years ago an incredible phrase which was *"ONTOGONY RECAPITULATES PHYLOGYNY"*, which basically means that within the human living womb the life of the embryo goes through every evolutionary stage of growth from fish - scales, to amphibian, to bird, to animal - thus ending up human. So, within the human womb is the essence of **ALL** CREATION/ Like unto God.

In understanding the life of a Wicce, you must firstly understand the life of a female through all her cycles and growth patterns and changes. The fundamental basis of our Old Religion is in honouring everything that is feminine and in equilibrium. Once this is understood and accepted as a fact of human evolutionary life, then we can understand that which is outside ourselves. We must know who and what we are before even trying to understand what the rest of the Universe is.

It is our basic requirements and essence of who and what we believe, even though we are a eclectic bunch of Pagans, we still maintain the basic ideas of our ancients, and this MUST NEVER, AND CAN NEVER be changed. It can be added onto or increased through inner awareness must never be changed to suit your own ideals.

These and much more are in my first two books "Complete Teachings of Wicca-Book One-The Seeker" and "Complete Teachings of Wicca-Book Two-The Witch". Which gives a deeper insight into the Wiccan Mysteries and requirements of becoming a true servant of the Goddess and God. I would like to tell you a little about my training experiences and myself.

I was firstly initiated into a Satanic Coven when I was only 13, this was what I thought Wiccecraft was all about, until I found out that they were not of the Craft. I was then introduced to a man who called himself David the Fifth, and he was a Traditional Wicce who ran a Coven in the foothills of Perth called the Coven of Draconis. I studied and remained after Initiation with this Coven until I was 18 years of age when he died, and the Coven disbanded. During this time, I also attended (on and off) The Centre for Christ in Victoria Park which was an Order of the Melchizedekian Priesthood run by an occultist named Mario Schoenmaker, which was very interesting. I attended here for about 18 months.

I was then in a documentary called "Supernatural Influences", where I was introduced to a High Priest named Simon Goodman, who was an Alexandrian Wicce. I joined his Coven, as my original Coven of David had closed due to his passing and along with me came Astra, Margaret, Layla and Dorrie Flatman, but Astra did not remain as she did not like Simon. Eventually I was Initiated into his Circle, the Coven of the Acorn, and copied out his Alexandrian Book of Shadows which was presented to him from Alex Sanders and Maxine and studied with his tradition until I was 21. During being with my Traditional Coven of Dragons Lair, I had met up with Hereditary Wicces Lady Margaret (mother) and Layla (daughter) Quain, and they took me into their fold and taught me many things of the old Craft. There was no Initiation as such with Hereditary Wiccecraft but a rebirthing ceremony of bringing me into her family, where they adopted me. So, we had a special ceremony where I was adopted by Margaret (Ma as we called her but Magickally known as Arwen, my GM). I eventually broke away from Simon's Coven because of Politics and decided to start my own Coven.

But I was also introduced to Green Village Wiccecraft from a lady named Rhiannon Ryall, who was a follower of the Old Ways of England and a great author, she Initiated me to the higher level which was different and exciting. Her Craft was like Margaret and Layla's Craft as they told me it came from the Black Forest Coven and the Hartsburg line of Wicces.

When I started my own Coven, my High Priest was a lovely English gentleman named Geoff Camm (Imhotep) who was Initiated 2nd and 3rd by Alex and Maxine Sanders. He along with Olwen took me 2nd and 3rd degree, whereas I became his High Priestess for many years. We had a large Coven and members were plentiful with Olwen as our Elder, Layla as Maiden, my boyfriend at the time was Man in Black. Since then I have been a Wiccan and Traditional Wicce Teacher and Mentor to many hundreds of Seekers who have sought me out. I also formed and Founded The Church of Wicca in Australia as Australia's First Legal Neo-Pagan Church in 1989, eventually with many Covens/Churches across Australia and hundreds of Initiates. I eventually resigned due again to politics and personal attacks on myself and handed the reins over to the new High Priestess, Lady Amaris.

I still teach to those who ask and shall always remain a teacher until I can learn no more! If you wish an autographed copy of any of my books, please email me direct to my website on www. witchofoz.com and https://tamaravonforslun.com

Wicces Calendar

Isarum Wicces Calendar

JANUARY:

World Peace Day	1 January
Sir James Fraser, author of "The Golden Bough".	
Fiesta of the Black Nazarene (the Philippines).	1-9 January
Nativity of The Goddess Inanna, Sumerian Goddess of Heaven and Earth	2 January
Advent of Isis from Phoenicia	
Earth is at Perihelion to the Sun, closest to the Sun than any other time of the year.	
Women's Fertility Festival, Pueblo Deer Dancers	3 January
Aquarian Tabernacle Church Australia by Lady Tamara Von Forslun	4 January 1994
Day of the Goddess Isis and Hathor	
Doreen Valiente	4 January 1922 - 1 September 1999 *
Sir Isaac Newton	4 January 1643 - 31 March 1727
Eve of the Epiphany of Kore and Paeon.	5 January
Ritual to the Goddess Venus	
Feast of the God Poseidon	
Night of La Bafana who brings gifts to children, lump of coal if they have been bad	
Day of the Sacred Triune, Maiden, Mother and Crone	6 January
The Beatific Vision of the Goddess 6 January	
Arrival of the magi to Christs Manger in Bethlehem	
Joan of Arc	7 January 1412 -
Decrees of the God Sokhit and the Goddess Sekhmet (Justice and Law)	
Magical Day of the Seven Herbs	
Magical Day for healing with Herbs	
Old Druids New Year's Eve	8 January
Samuel Macgregor Mathers	8 January 1952 - 19 November 1918

Day of the Goddess Justicia, bringing justice to the world	
Day to Honour all Midwives	
Day of Antu - Isis searches for Osiris	9 January
Day to gather Yarrow to dry for insect sachets for dog's collars	
Dirge to the Goddess Isis and Nephthys	
Plough Day - until 1980 it was illegal to plough the fields before this day	10 January
Securitas - Invoke when threatened	
The Juturnalia	11 January
Day of the Goddess Carmenta - Goddess of childbirth	
Day of the African Mother Goddess Oddvdva	12 January
Basant Panchami Day - Day of Wisdom and Art	
Day of the Goddess Sarasvati	
Final Witchcraft Law Repealed in Austria in 1787	13 January
Festival of the God Faunus (St. Valentine's Day)	
Day to bathe for purification in the Ganges River	13 January
Blessing of the Vines dedication to the Gods of Wine	14 January
Official Confession of error, made in 1606 by the Jurors of Salem Witch Trials	14 January
Hindu Festival - Makar Sankranti	14 January
World Religions Day	15 January
Day of the Goddess Vesta	
Feast of the Ass	
Day of the Goddess Concordia	16 January
Honour the Gods of the Eight Winds	
Day of the Queen of the Universe in France	16 January
Day of Rest and Peace - dedicated to the Goddess Felicitas	17 January
Women's Festival Honouring the Goddess Hera	18 January
Dorothy Clutterbuck	19 January 1880 - 12 January 1951
Day of Honouring the Goddess Minerva	19 January
Blessing of the Waters	

Dorothy Clutterbuck who Initiated Gerald Gardner

Blessing of the Waters and all Water Goddesses

Grandmothers Day   20 January

Festival of Peace and Harmony

Feast of the Goddess Hecate   21 January

Day of St. Agnus

Day of the Goddess Yngona (Denmark)

Day of Visions

Sir Francis Bacon - Philosopher

Rasputin's Birth

The Herb Mullein to be infused in olive oil for ear drops   22 January

Day dedicated to the Goddess Mawu

Beginning of Aquarius

Marija Gimbutas   23 January 1921 - 1994

Day to honour the Goddess Hathor by having a milk bath   23 January

Day of the Goddess Venus

Sementivae Honour the Earth Goddess Terra   24 January

Blessing of the Candle of the Happy Women

Tu Bi-Shivat - Hebrew holiday showing respect for trees   25 January
and growing things

The Shekinah - Sarah and Esther   25 January

Celebration of the Triple Moon   26 January

Day of the Goddess Cerridwen and Copper Women

Day of the God Alacita, god of Abundance

Dedicated to the Goddesses of the Grain and Harvest

Gamelion Noumenia honouring all Deity   28 January

Up Kelly Aa (Scotland) Norse derived fire Festival to
sacrifice to the Sun

Peace Festival   29 January

Day of the Goddess Hecate

Feast of the Goddess Charites   30 January

Dedication of the Altar of peace and Harmony

Purification ceremony dedicated to the Goddess Yemaya

Zsusanna Budapest Witch and author	30 January 1940 - 14 March 2008
Dr Frian - Alleged HP of North Berwick Witches, executed in Scotland in 1591	31 January
Feast of the Goddess Aphrodite	31 January
Candlemas Festival	
Festival of the Goddess Brigid	
Day of the Goddess Hecate	

FEBRUARY:

Festival of Lughnasadh Southern Hemisphere	1 February
Festival of Imbolg Northern Hemisphere	
Festival of the God Dionysus	
Festival of the Goddess Februa	
Ethnic Equality Month	2 February
Original Ground Hog Day	
Day of the Goddess Ceres and Proserpine	
Day Dedicated to the Horned Gods	
Lesser Eleusian Mysteries	3 February
Day dedicated to the Goddess Demeter and Persephone	
Halfway point of Summer in the Southern Hemisphere	
Lantern Lighting Ceremony Festival	4 February
Day of the Goddess Maat	5 February
Day to Honour Air Spirits	
H. R. Giger	5 February 1940 - 13 May 2014
Feast of St. Agatha - Patroness of Fire Fighters	
Day of the Goddess Maat - Goddess of Wisdom and Truth	
Festival of the Goddess Aphrodite	6 February
Day of the Goddess Artemis	
Day of the Goddess Selene	7 February

Stuart Farrar passed into the Summerland's 2000

Death of Thomas Aquinas 1274 - whose writings refuted the Canon Episcopi

Day to honour all Moon Goddesses

Chinese New Year   8 February

Eliphas Levi   8 February 1810 - 31 May 1875

Celebration of the Goddess Kwan Yin   9 February

Day of the Goddess Athena   10 February

Festival of Toutates

Feast of Our lady of Lourdes - visitation of   11 February
the Goddess

Day of the Goddess Persephone

Day of St. Gobnat

Day of the Goddess Diana   12 February

Day dedicated to the Ancestors   13 February

Day of the Goddess Vesta

Betrothal Day (later adopted by Christians   14 February
and changed to St. Valentine's Day)

Women's plea to the Goddess Diana for
children are granted this day

Heinrich Cornelius Agrippa   14 February 1486 - 18 February 1535

Day of the Goddess Rhiannon   15 February

Pope Leo X issued the Bull Tonsured - that
secular courts would carry out executions of
Witches condemned by the Inquisition in 1521.

Day dedicated to the Goddess Juno Februata

Day of Lupa - The She-wolf

Day of Honouring Light   16 February

Christ accepted as the God Quetzalcoatl in   17 February
South America

Festival of Women - dedicated to the Goddess   18 February
Spandermat

Birthday of Ramakrishna - Hindu Mystic

Day of the Wicces Sacred Tree - The Ash

Day of the Goddess Minerus   19 February

Birthday of Copernicus - Astronomer

Day of the Silent Goddess Tacita - averter of   20 February
harmful gossip

Healing Day of the Goddess Kwan Yin   21 February

The Sun enters into Pisces

Holiday of St. Lucia - Goddess of Light   22 February

Sybil Leek   22 February 1917 - 26 October 1982

Day of Blessing Land Boundaries   23 February

The Regigugium -   24 February

Flight of Kings, when the Year King is sacrificed,
and successor crowned by the Goddess

Day of the Goddess Nut   26 February

Shrove Tuesday - the first day of Lent

Day of the Goddess the Morrigan   27 February

Time of the Old Woman

Anthesterion Noumenia honouring all Deity

The Great Wicces Night   28 February

Sabbatu - cakes and wine offered to the
Goddess for Prosperity and Luck

Leap Year - when women rule the Earth and   29 February
can ask men for marriage

Day of the Goddess St. Brigid

MARCH:

The Golden Dawn Founded   1 March 1888

The Covenant of the Goddess Wiccan Church was
formed in 1975

Day of the Goddess Hestia

First Day of autumn

Bale Fires are lit to bring back the Sun

Festival of the Goddess Rhiannon .... 2 March

Day of the Goddess Spider Woman

Women do not work on this day or the Goddess
will send storms to destroy

Doll Festival for young girls .... 3 March

Founding of the Church of All Worlds First Wiccan ..... 4 March 1968
church to Incorporate in USA

Festival of the Goddesses Artemis and Diana

Feast of Flowers dedicated to the Goddess Flora
and Hecate

All Souls day – Greece

Navigum Isidis of the Goddess Isis who opens the .... 5 March
seas to navigation

Laurie Cabot Official Witch of Salem .... 6 March 1933 *

Junoalia — Celebration of matrons and young girls

David J Conway author .... 6 March 1939

Day of the Goddess Ishtar .... 7 March

Ceremony of Peace

Day of the Goddess Juno

Birthday Celebration of Mother Earth .... 8 March

Day of the Goddess Ilmatar

International Women's Day

Mothering day - original Mother's Day .... 9 March

Feast of the Year Goddess - Anna Perenna .... 10 March

Day of Our lady of Lourdes - appearance of the .... 11 March
Goddess Persephone

Festival of the God Marduk .... 12 March

Day of the Goddess Demeter

Discovery of the Planet Uranus - 1781 .... 13 March

Bale Fires are lit to call in the Rain

Birthday of Ronald Hubbard - Creator of Scientology

Jacques de Molay - Head of the Knights Templar .... 14 March

Festival of the Goddess Ostara .... 15 March

Pete Pathfinder becomes the first Wiccan Priest elected as President of the Interfaith Council, 1995.

Day of the Goddess Levannah	16 March
Day of the Goddess Morrigan	17 March

Feast of Liberalia - Women's Festival of the God Bacchus and the Maenads

Festival of the God the Greenman

Sheelah's Day - The Goddess Sheelah-na-gig of Sexuality	18 March

Birthday of Edgar Cayce

Manley Palmer Hall	18 March 1901 - 29 September 1990 *

Marriage of the Goddess Kore to the God Dionysus

Quinquatrus Festival of the Goddess Minerva`	19 March

Lesser Panathenacea - dedicated to the Goddess Athena

Criminal Witchcraft Stature enacted under Queen Elizabeth - 1563

Day of the God Aries	20 March

Day of the Goddess the Morrigan

World Forest Day	21 March

Day of the Goddess Athena

Day of the Autumnal Equinox Southern Hemisphere

Mandate of Henry VIII against Witchcraft enacted in 1542, repealed in 1547

Birthday of the Goddess Athena	22 March
Rev. Pete Pathfinder Founder of the Aquarian Tabernacle Church	22 March 1937 - 2 November 2014
Day of Fasting	23 March

Day of the Goddess Ishtar

Day of the Goddess Bellona - Witches Power day	24 March
Lady Day - Feast Annunciation of Mary	25 March

Pope Innocent III Issues the Bull establishing the Inquisition in 1199

Day of the Goddess Ceres (named for cereals)	26 March
Feast of Esus the Hunter	
Day of the Goddess Ceres, who lends her name to breakfast cereals	
Day of the Goddess Hecate	27 March
Birthday of Rudolph Steiner	
Elaphabolion Noumenia honouring all deity	28 March
Death of Scott Cunningham in 1993	
Birthday of Kwan Yin Goddess of Mercy - Healing Day	
The Delphinia - dedicated to the Goddess Artemis	29 March
Festival of the Goddess Athena	30 March
Anita Festival	
Festival of the Goddess Aphrodite and the God Hermes	31 March
Last Witch trial in Ireland in 1711	
Day of the Goddess Hilaria	
Day of the Goddess Rhaeda	

APRIL:

Veneralia Festival of Peace	1 April
Day of the Goddess Hathor	
April Fool's Day	
Feast of Ama - Goddess and Patroness of Fishermen	2 April
Birthday of Hans Christian Anderson	
Descent of the Goddess Persephone into Annwyn	3 April
Day of Ceralia - Seed Day	
Day of the Goddess Ceres	
Descent of the Goddess Persephone into Annwyn	
Honouring of Aesculapius, The Great Healer	4 April
Day of Megalesia of the Goddess Cybele	
Day of Fortune	5 April

Birthday of Kwan Yin

Birthday of Harry Houdini the Magician   6 April

Stanislas de Guaita Occultist and author   6 April 1861 - 19 December 1897

World Health Day   7 April

Church of All Worlds Founded in 1962 in the USA

Day of Mooncakes   8 April

Day of the Goddess Ata Bey's

Empowering of Women day   9 April

Day of the Amazon Goddess of Women

Day of the Goddess Bau - Mother of Ea (The Earth)   10 April

Day of Kista - Spiritual Knowing   11 April

Day of the Goddess Ceres

Day of the Goddess Anahit - Armenian Goddess of
Love and the Moon

Anton La Vey Founder of the Church of Satan USA   11 April 1930 - 20 October 1997 *

Day of the Goddess Chy-Si-Niv Niv   12 April

Festival of Change

First Confession of Witchcraft by Isobel Gowdie in 1662   13 April

Blessing of the Sea

Festival Honouring all Nordic Deity   14 April

Adoption of Principles of Wiccan belief at the 1974
Gnostica Witch Meet

Day of the Goddess Venus

Birthday of Elizabeth Montgomery (Bewitched)   15 April

Bernadette sees the Goddess at Lourdes

Day of the Goddess Luna, Tellas and Venus

Day of the Goddess Luna   16 April

Margot Adler Author and HPs of Wicca   16 April 1946 - 28 July 2014

Day of the Goddess Isis (Aset)   17 April

The Chariot Festival

The Rain Festival

Day of Honouring the Air Element   18 April

Day of Temple Offerings to the Goddess in Bali   19 April

Day of the Goddess Hathor, Isis and all Horned Goddesses	20 April
Astrological Beginning of Taurus	
Feast of the Goddess Pales	21 April
Roma Dea Roma	
Day of the pastoral Goddess the Perilya	
Earth Day	22 April
The Rlenteria	
The First day of winter	
Clothes Washing Day	
Festival of the God the Greenman	23 April
Pyre Festival of the Goddess Astarte, Tanith, Venus and Erycina	
Birthday of actress Shirley MacLaine	24 April
Children's Day	
First Seasonal Wine Festival of Venus and Jupiter	
Day of The Goddess Robigalia of Corn and harvest	25 April
Passover originally dedicated to the God Baal	
Day of the Goddess Yemaya	26 April
Birthday of William Shakespeare	
Mounikhion Noumenia Honouring of all Deity	
Feast of St. George originally derived from the God Apollo, the twin of Diana	27 April
Festival of the Goddess Florala (Flora)	28 April
The Ploughing Ceremony	29 April
Women's Day in Nigeria	
Walpurgis Nacht (The Wicces Night)	30 April
Samhain (Halloween) Southern hemisphere	
Beltane (Northern Hemisphere)	
Remembrance Day	

MAY:

May is dedicated to and named after the Goddess Maia.   1 May

May Day and Samhain day dancing with the Maypole for fertility to the Earth

Day of the Goddess Maat The Goddess of Truth

Day of Moon Goddesses Asherah, Damia, Latona, Bona Dea and Dea Día

Day of Ysahodhara the Wife of Buddha   2 May

Festival of the Goddess Bona Dea for public welfare   3 May

Chloris Tarentia

National Day of Prayer   4 May

Festival of the Goddess Cerridwen

Veneration of the Sacred Thorn (Moon Tree)

The beginning of Hawthorn Moon

Rain Ceremony   5 May

Day of the Goddess Maat of Truth

Birthday of Sigmund Freud   6 May

The Goddess visits Mut, Mother of Gods and Goddesses

Festival of the Earth Spirits   7 May

Hathor Visits Anukis the Goddess of the Nile

Festival of the God Apollo

Furry Day   8 May

Morris dancing for Maid Marion originally the Goddess Flora

Day of Honouring the Great White Mother   9 May

Joan of Arc canonised 1920

Day of Ascension

Day of Tin Hau the North Star   10 May

Celebration of the Goddess Anahit

World Nations Reduce Greenhouse Emissions

Day of Russali, the Triple Goddess - Ana, Badb and Macha   11 May

Shashti - The day of the sacred Forest   12 May

Founding of the Church of Wicca in Australia by Lady Tamara Von Forslun	13 May 1989
Procession of our lady of Fatima	
The Goddess as a Young Maiden (Persephone, Athena, Artemis and Diana)	
Time of the Midnight Sun	14 May
The Panegyric of Isis - Her finding Osiris	
Honouring the Great Stag	15 may
Honouring the Queen of Heaven	16 May
Festival of the Goddess Hathor	17 May
Goddess with Child	
Festival of the Horned God	18 May
Feast of the Horned God Cernunnos	
Day of Nurturance	
Day dedicated to the Goddess Pallas Athena	
Festival of the God Pan	19 May
The Goddess Hathor arrives at Edfu in Neb	
Festival of Springs and Wells	
Beginning of Gemini	
Day dedicated to Night and Day being Equal	20 may
Birthday of the Bard Gwydion Penderwen	21 May
Biological Diversity Day	22 May
Adoption of the Earth religion Anti-Abuse Act 1988	
Day of the Rose	23 May
Celebration of the Birthday of the Goddess Artemis	24 May
Festival of the Triple Goddess	25 May
Sacred Day of St. Sarah for Gypsies	
Thargelion Noumenia honouring all deity	26 May
Day of the Warrior	
Morning Glory Zell HPs and author of Wicca	27 May
Night Time Healing Ceremony	
Scourge of Pythia - Seer at Delphi, the Delphic Oracle of the Goddess	28 May

Feast of the Oak Apple	29 May
Family Day	
Blessing of the Fields	30 May
Death of Joan of Arc 1431	
Thargelia Honouring the Goddess Artemis and the God Apollo	31 May
Honouring of Joan of Arc in Commemoration 1412 –1431 (19yrs of age)	
Pucelle of the Goddess	

JUNE:

June named after the Goddess Juno.	**1 June**
Festival of Opet in Egypt	
Feast of the oak Nymph	
Day of Epipi the Goddess of darkness and Mysteries	
Festival of the Goddess Ishtar	2 June
Birthday of Alessandro of Cagliostro Alchemist and Heretic	
Marion Zimmer Bradley author Mists of Avalon	3 June
Buddhist Blessing for young girls	
Free Women's Festival Skyclad (nudity)	5 June
Alex Sanders King of the Witches	6 June 1926 - 30 April 1988 *
Leave Cakes at Crossroads for the Goddess Artemis for luck	
Vestalia Festival of the Goddess Vesta	7 June
World Oceans Day	8 June
Day of the Goddess Rhea	
Mater Matuta Festival honouring all Mothers	9 June
Day of the Goddess Venus	10 June
Lady Luck Day	11 June
Dolores Ashcroft-Nowicki HPs and author	11 June 1929
Grain Festival to the Goddess Ashtoreth	12 June

Gerald B. Gardner Founder of Gardnerian Witchcraft 13	June 1884 - 12 February 1964
William Butler Yeats author	13 June 1865 - 28 January 1939
Day of the Goddess Epona The Horse Goddess	
Day of the Muses	
Starhawk HPs and author	14 June 1951
Lesser Quinquatrus of the Goddess Minerva	
Day of Our Lady of Mount Carmel	15 June
Feast of the Water of the Nile	16 June
Night of the Goddess Hathor	
Day of the Goddess Eurydice the Goddess of the Underworld	17 June
Day of the Goddess Danu	18 June
Birthday of King James 1st of England	19 June
Day of all Hera's Wise women dedicated to the Goddess within	
First day of Cancer	20 June
Midwinter Solstice (Southern Hemisphere)	21 June
Midsummer Solstice (northern hemisphere)	
Festival of the God Herne the Hunter	22 June
Final law Against Witchcraft Repealed in England in 1951	
Day of the Faerie Goddess Aine	23 June
Day of the Burning Lams at Sais for the Goddess Isis and Neith	24 June
Janet Farrar Alexandrian HPs and author	24 June *
Day of Praises to the Goddess Parvati	25 June
Skirophorion Noumenia honouring all Deity	26 June
Stuart Farrar Alexandrian HP and author	26 June 1916 - 7 February 2000 *
Day of honouring all Corn Mothers	27 June
Scott Cunningham HP and author	27 June 1956 - 28 March 1993
Birthday of the Goddess Hemera the Daughter of Ayx	28 June
Day of the Sun God Ra	29 June
Day of Aestas the Goddess of Corn	30 June

JULY:

Named after Julius Caesar.	**1 July**
International Save the Species protection day	
Day to Honour all Grandmothers	
Day of the Goddess Selene	
The Coldest Day of the Year	2 July
Day of the Witch Gaeta	
Day of the God and Dogstar Planet Sirius	3 July
Ceremony of the Mountain Spirits	4 July
Earth is at the Perihelion to the Sun-the Furthest between the Earth and the Sun	5 July
Day of the Goddess Hera	6 July
Running of the Bulls in Spain	
Day of the Goddess Hera	
Day of the Goddess Hel Goddess of the Underworld	10 July
Let Fete de la Magdalene (Mary Magdalene) the Sacred harlot	11 July
Day of Justice	
Honouring of all Children	
Day of Forgiveness	
Dr. Margaret Murray HPs and author	13 July 1863 - 13 November 1963
All Souls day honouring the Spirits of Ancestors	14 July
Festival of the Sacred Rowan Tree	15 July
Day of the Goddess Carmen Healer and Midwife	16 July
Day of the Goddess Freya	17 July
Birthday of the Goddess Nephthys Goddess of Death	18 July
Lady Sheba HPs and author	18 July 1920 - 2 March 2002
The Opet Festival of Egypt the marriage of Isis and Osiris	19 July
Day of the Dragon	20 July
Pope Adrian VI issues the Bull	
Day For Binding the Wreaths for Lovers	
Mayan New Year	
	21 July

Feast of the Forest Spirits	
Beginning of Leo	22 July
Day of the Goddess Amaterasu	
Max Heindal Author and leader of the Rosicrucians	23 July 1865 - 6 January 1919
Day of Salacia The Goddess of Oceans	23 July
Hekatombaion Noumenia honouring all deities	
Day and the Games of the God Lugh	24 July
Day of the Serpent Goddess	25 July
Birthday of Omar Kha	
Death of Pope Innocent VIII	25 July
Feast of St. Anne	26 July
Sacred day to all Buffalo Gods and Goddesses	
Dr Carl Jung Occult psychiatrist	26 July 1875 - 6 June 1961
Day of the Goddess Hatshepsut Healer Queen and Architect	27 July
Procession of Witches in Belgium	
Day of the God Thor	28 July
Voudoun Sacred Day for Ceremonies	29 July
Day of the God Jupiter	30 July
Eve of Imbolg the Festival	31 July

AUGUST:

Named after the Emperor Augustus.

Imbolg Festival (southern hemisphere)	1 August
Lughnasadh Festival (northern hemisphere)	
Day of the Goddess Taitu	
Fiesta of Our Lady of Angels	2 August
Day of Saoka	
Day of the Dryads dedicated to Maiden Spirits of the Woods and Water	3 August
Day of the Goddess Hathor	4 August

Day of the Lady of Snow

Day of the Goddess Mara   5 August

Day of the Benediction of the Sea

Day of the Cherokee Corn Dancers   6 August

Gaia Consciousness Day   7 August

Breaking of the Nile

Day of the Goddess Nut

Birthday of the Virgin Mary   8 August

Festival of the Goddess Venus   9 August

Festival of the Spirits

Day to Honour the Star Goddesses   10 August

Holy day of St. Claire   11 August

Lychnapsia the Festival of Lights for the Goddess Isis   12 August

Helena Blavatsky occultists and author   12 August 1831 - 8 May 1947

Birthday of the Goddess Aradia Queen of the Witches   13 August
Born in Volterra in 1313

Celebration of the Goddess Diana and Hecate of the Moon

Day dedicated to the Goddess Selene   14 August

Day of the Goddess Tiamat   15 August

Birthday of Charles Godfrey Leland

Celebration of the Goddess Dea Syria

Day of Giving   16 August

Feast of the Goddess Diana   17 August

Day of Healing the Past   18 August

Vinalia Thanksgiving   19 August

Day of Vinalia Rustica Venus of the Grape Vine

Birthday of HP Lovecraft   20 August

Sacred Marriage of Heaven and Earth

Harvest festival   21 August

Metagetnion Noumenia Day to honour all Deities   22 August

Beginning of Virgo

Festival of the Furies   23 August

Festival of the Goddess of Fate Nemesis

W. E. Butler author and occultist	23 August 1898 - 1 August 1978
Festival of the Opening of the Mundas Cereris the Womb of the Labyrinth to the Underworld of Demeter	24 August
Opseconsia the Harvest Festival Ritual of Thanksgiving	25 August
Feast day of the Goddess Ilmatar	26 August
Birthday of the Goddesses Isis and Nut	27 August
Opening the World Parliament of Religions	28 August
Birthday of the Goddess Athena	
Birthday of the Goddess Hathor	29 August
Egyptian New Year's Day	
Charistheria The Thanksgiving ceremony	30 August
Raymond Buckland HP and author	31st August 1934 – 27th September 2017

SEPTEMBER:

Awakening of the Women's Serpent Power Life Force	1 September
Ostara - First day of spring (southern hemisphere)	
Festival of the Vine dedicated to the Goddess Ariadne and the God Dionysus	2 September
Day of the Goddess Polias and the God Zeus	
Women's Healing Ceremony for the Four Directions	3 September
Pilgrimage to test One's Soul	4 September
Day of the Goddess Cybele	5 September
Day of the Goddess Artemis	6 September
Day of the God Bacchus	7 September
Birthday of the Goddess Yemaya	8 September
Feast of the Shepherd	
Birthday of the Goddess Yemaya	
Day of Mercy	
Te Veilat the Gathering of the Fruit	9 September
Reunion Festival	10 September
Marie Laveau Queen of the Voudoun	10 September 1801 - 16 June 1881

Day of Honouring all Queens of Egypt	11 September
Day of the God Bel	12 September
Day of the Goddess Nephthys	13 September
Ceremony for the Lighting of the Fire	
Day of Honouring the Black Madonna	14 September
Day of the Goddess Kore	15 September
The gathering of Initiates	
International Day of Democracy	
Goddesses Ascent from Annwyn	16 September
Holade Mystai the Ritual bathing in the Sea	
Day of St. Sophia	17 September
Day of Faith, Hope and Charity	
Feast of St. Hildegarde	
Stephen Skinner author	17 September 1932 - 24 September 1997
Giving of Grain and Food to the Poor	18 September
Blessing of the Rain Goddesses	19 September
Boedromion Noumenia Day to Honour all Deities	20 September
Festival of Epopteia the day of Initiation	
Spring Equinox (southern hemisphere)	21 September
Autumn Equinox (northern hemisphere)	
Feast of Honouring the triple Aspect of Maiden, Mother and Crone	
Festival of Mabon the Wicces Thanksgiving	22 September
Day of the Goddess Demeter	
Beginning of Libra	23 September
Genesia Day to make offerings to the Dead	24 September
Day of Mercy	
Birthday of the Goddess Sedna	25 September
Thoth's Festival of Akhet	
Day of Atonement	26 September
Birthday of the Goddess Athena of Knowledge	27 September
Day of Saleeb the Cresting of the Nile at its greatest height	28 September

Feast of Michaelmas (honouring archangel Michael) 29 September

Day of the Goddess Meditrinalia of Medicines 30 September
and Healing

OCTOBER:

Day to Forgive Your Enemies 1 October

Neville Drury author 1 October 1947 - 15 October 2013

Isaac Bonawitz Druid and author

Power Day for Arachnids

Day of the Goddess Rhiannon 2 October

Feast of the Guardian Spirits

Rosaleen Norton witch and author 2 October 1917 - 5 December 1979

Arthur Edward Waite witch and author 2 October 1857 - 19 May 1942

St. Dionysis Transformation of the Pagan God of Wine 3 October
into Christianity

Oddudua The Santeria Mother of the Gods and Goddesses 4 October

Fasting day for the Goddess Demeter

Byzantine day of the Holy Spirit for the Goddess Sophia 5 October

Wine festival for the God Dionysis

Day of the Goddess Artemis 6 October

Day of the God Bau 7 October

Francis Barrett occultist and author 7 October 1872 - 21 February 1941

Oschophoria The bearing of Green Branches to 8 October
commemorate Theseus Return

Day of the God Horus 9 October

The Eye of the God Festival

Day of White Buffalo calf Woman 10 October

Thesmophoria of the Goddess Demeter 11 October

Aleister Crowley occultist and author 12 October 1875 - 1 December 1947

Day of Women's Prayers

Day of the God Eros 13 October

Victory day of Good over Evil 14 October

Day of Lady Godiva	15 October
Day of the Goddess Gaia and Nymphs day	16 October
Festival of Fortune	
Day of the Goddess Isis	17 October
Day of Clean Water	18 October
St. Luke's day The Great Horn Fair Honouring Horned Gods Day	
Day of Good Luck	19 October
Pyanepsion Noumenia Day to honour all deities	20 October
Birthday of Selena Fox HPs and author	
Day of the Virgin Mary	
Kite Flying festival	
Day of the Goddess Aphrodite	22 October
Sacred day of the Willow Tree	
Timothy Leary	22 October 1920 - 31 May 1996
Day of the Goddess Aphrodite	
Beginning of Scorpio	23 October
Day of the Goddess Lilith	24 October
Feast of the Spirits of Air	
Day of the God Ge	25 October
Proerosia Festival Harvest	
Festival of the Goddess Hathor	26 October
Honouring the Womb in all Female Life	27 October
Patricia Crowther HPs and author	27 October 1927 - 5 February 2009
Day of the Goddess Isis	28 October
Feast of the Dead	29 October
Day of the God Osiris	30 October
Day to Remember the Burning Times	31 October
Beltane Festival (southern hemisphere)	
Samhain (northern hemisphere)	
Wicces Remembrance Day	

NOVEMBER:

Day of the Banshees	1 November
Rebirth of the God Osiris	3 November
World Communication Day	
Stag Dances	4 November
Birthday of the Goddess Tiamat	6 November
Day of the Goddess Leto	7 November
Sacred day of Elphane	11 November
World Tolerance Day	16 November
Day of the Goddess Ereshkigal	
Israel Regardie author and witch	17 November 1907 - 10 March 1985
Maimakterion Noumenia Day to honour all Deities	18 November
Day of the Goddess Ishtar	21 November
Thanksgiving	23 November
Elders Day of Respect	
Lady Tamara Von Forslun Elder HPs and author	23 November 1956*
Day of the Goddess Cerridwen	26 November
Day of the Goddess Sophia	27 November
Oberon Zell Witch and author	30 November *

DECEMBER:

Franz Bardon occultist and author	1 December 1909 - 10 July 1958
World Aids Day	1 December
Day of the Goddess Pallas Athena	
Day of the Goddess Arachne	2 December
Day of the Goddess Bona Dea	3 December
Day of the Goddess Bride	5 December
Dione Fortune author and occultist	6 December 1890 - 8 January 1946
Day of the Goddess Tara	9 December
Day of the Light Bringer	13 December
Day of the Goddess Sapientia	16 December
Festival of Saturnalia	17 December

Poseidon Poumenia   18 December

Day of Saturnalia

Day of the Goddess Kwan Yin

Day of Opalia   19 December

Day of the Goddess Selene and the God Janus   20 December

Festival of Evergreen Trees   21 December

Birthday of the God Mithras   22 December

Mid-Summer Solstice (southern hemisphere)

Mid-Winter Solstice (northern hemisphere)

Day of the Goddess Hathor   23 December

Festival of the Goddess Freyr and the God Freyja   25 December

Festival of the of Poseidon   25 December

Birthday of the God Horus   26 December

Birthday of Buddha

Birthday of the Goddess Freya   27 December

Day of the Goddess Artemis   29 December

Festival of Father Time   31 December

Day of the Sun God Ra

EPILOGUE

Now that you've completed this part of our (yours and the planets) Magnum Opus, you will begin to see what it is that we are engaged in. The symbol for this planet is the Spirit contained in and containing matter. The reason we seek incarnation here is to learn the lesson of making a physical form and animating it. You have also learnt that each organ has a close relationship with a planet that directs its development. When the planet Lemuria exploded, this left the pineal body and development wisdom eye without a continual rhythmic force to guide its evolution so that part of us simply stopped. Suddenly we were all blind. The work you have just done will provide you with the means of reawakening this organ.

To fully create an Etheric machine capable of assisting this, this system is worked by a group of Australian Wicces and has been for the past 50 years. We've had whole families, (children love Circles), all ages and all types; work with us during that time.

Now with hundreds of Seekers being Initiated by me and by my Priests and Priestesses. The way wasn't always smooth (still isn't) because we have 2,000 years of blind fear to overcome, but with love and patience we, with this Earth, can regain our places as Divine witnesses to creation.

My series of Books outline an ancient system that uses internal and external Alchemising to heal and cause a reawakening of the Awareness of other levels of Conscious existence. By improving our communication with our subtler levels of rhythm and change, we can move more easily and completely into the Age of Aquarius, the Matercentric period known as "The Golden Age".

The changes of the Dawning Age are inevitable, part of the macrocosmic tides, but it is up to us, as individuals and as a planet, whether these changes are forward or backward. We have made the choice to be incarnated at this time, we must now make the choice that we will decide whether we use the energy to recapture the past, by attributing all that happens to our Old external Gods and Goddesses, fix the development of the future by limited or one-sided projection, or learn at last to grow and take our place in the flow by awakening our potential sensitivities and Love.

The system outlined is functionally complete as it is, but at the same time it is an art. It can and must be developed and shaped by each situation it is used in. you will find that the results are proportional to the amount of artistic involvement you invest. Use your intellect to develop rather than inhibit your experiences.

If you are doing this work as an individual or small group (less than five) then it must be done in the country at least 55 kilometers away from any major disturbing influences.

This book uses the Major Arcana of the Tarot as doorways/portals to greater learning and knowing from all over the world. The Tarot cards are keys to different dimensions of thinking and aid in the ascension spiritually to become the Wicce you truly are.

"All ritual and ceremony are total theatre,
and even the environment becomes part of the play.
There are no spectators,
Only participants".

Tamara Von Forslun
The Witch of Oz
The Alchemist

Authors Books and Oracle Decks
Tamara Von Forslun
The Witch of Oz

Complete Teachings of Wicca Book One – The Seeker
Complete Teachings of Wicca Book Two – The Witch
Tarot Mysteries of Thoth – Initiation and Inner Alchemy
The Witches Coven - Tools and Activities

Coming Soon

Oracles of the Divine Feminine – Goddesses of the World
Tarot Magick of Thoth – Journeys of the Arcana
The Shining Ones – Angels of Heaven and Earth
The Divine Feminine – Goddess of 10,000 Names
The Divine Masculine – God of 10,000 Names
Tarot Magick of Thoth Tehuti – Tarot Book and Card Boxset